# EL MUNDO ZURDO

## SELECTED WORKS FROM THE MEETINGS OF THE SOCIETY FOR THE STUDY OF GLORIA ANZALDÚA 2007 & 2009

EDITED BY
NORMA E. CANTÚ
CHRISTINA L. GUTIÉRREZ
NORMA ALARCÓN
AND RITA E. URQUIJO-RUIZ

First Edition



Aunt Lute Books
P.O. Box 410687
San Francisco, CA 94141
www.auntlute.com

Cover design: Amy Woloszyn, amymade.com
Text design: Amy Woloszyn, amymade.com
Cover Art: Deborah Kuetzpalín Vásquez

Senior Editor: Joan Pinkvoss
Managing Editor: Shay Brawn
Production: Soma Baral, Ashley Bonifacio, Noelle de la Paz, Chenxing Han, Vanessa Nava, and Kara Owens

Funding for the production of *El Mundo Zurdo* was provided in part by support from the Vessel Foundation and Three Dog Foundation.

Library of Congress Cataloging-in-Publication Data

El mundo zurdo : selected works from the meetings of the Society for the Study of Gloria Anzaldúa, 2007 and 2009 / edited by Norma Alarcón, Norma Cantú, Christina Gutiérrez, and Rita Urquijo-Ruiz. -- 1st ed.
p. cm.
A collection of essays about the work of Gloria Anzaldúa.
ISBN 978-1-879960-83-1
1. Anzaldúa, Gloria--Criticism and interpretation. 2. Mexican Americans in literature. I. Alarcón, Norma. II. Cantú, Norma Elia, 1947- III. Gutiérrez, Christina L. IV. Urquijo-Ruiz, Rita. V. Society for the Study of Gloria Anzaldúa.
PS3551.N95Z79 2010
818'.5409--dc22
2010041258

Printed in the U.S.A. on acid-free paper

10 9 8 7 6 5 4 3 2

# CONTENTS

## PART 2 POETRY



## PART 3 CROSSING BORDERS: LEGACIES OF GLORIA ANZALDÚA

# FOREWORD

NORMA E. CANTÚ

It gladdens my heart to be writing these words as foreword to this book that gathers the work presented at the 2007 symposium Güeras y Prietas: Celebrating 20 Years of *Borderlands/La Frontera* and the 2009 Mundo Zurdo: An International Conference on the Life and Work of Gloria Anzaldúa. My aim is twofold, to introduce the Society for the Study of Gloria Anzaldúa (SSGA), its origins and goals, and to introduce this volume comprised of essays, poems and art work from the 2007 and 2009 gatherings.

## ANZALDÚA AND THE SOCIETY FOR THE STUDY OF GLORIA ANZALDÚA (SSGA)

Gloria Anzaldúa's work inspired and shaped thinking by women of color in the 1980s and 90s, and it continues to do so in the 21st century. Through her anthologies, essays, and her radical book, *Borderlands/La Frontera: The New Mestiza,* first published by Aunt Lute Books in 1987, she laid the groundwork for feminist theorizing of Border Studies. Since her passing in 2004, interest in Anzaldúa's work and her life has continued to grow. By 2007, several awards named after Anzaldúa appeared in various venues such as The University of California at Santa Cruz, the Macondo Summer Writing Workshop, and the American Studies Association. The sessions on Anzaldúa at the Modern Language Association, the National Association of Chicana and Chicano Studies, and the American Studies Association meetings drew hundreds of scholars, friends and creative writers who came together not just to honor the name but to continue the work, scholarly and academic as well as creative and spiritual. Taking the momentous 20th anniversary of the publication of *Borderlands/La Frontera*, the SSGA came into being in November 2007 as its members, mostly scholars and a few community mujeres, met at the University of Texas at San Antonio sponsored by the Women's Studies Institute, the academic home of the SSGA. The SSGA acquired affiliate status with the Society for the Study of American Women Writers, at whose meetings the SSGA sponsors two sessions on Anzaldúa scholarship.

## THE SSGA GATHERINGS

At our first meeting, a symposium held in San Antonio in November 2007, scholars from Mexico and the U.S. gathered to discuss Anzaldúa's vision, her impact and to draw a plan of action. At her urging, we took the name of a conference that Marisa Belausteguigoitia had hosted at the Program in Gender Studies at the Universidad Nacional de Mexico (UNAM), and thus established another link, a bridge with the scholars and community participants who had engaged Anzaldúan thinking in Mexico City at the UNAM. The organizers of that first gathering decided that the next meeting would commemorate the fifth anniversary of Anzaldúa's passing, and the date was set for May 2009 for the next gathering; they also chose to call these gatherings, which will occur every eighteen months, El Mundo Zurdo, signaling their desire to establish that space—metaphorical and real—that Anzaldúa wrote and spoke about, as a gathering point, an interstice, a center where varied and seemingly disparate threads could be woven into the rich cloth of her legacy. Leading the effort to keep Gloria's legacy alive and adding an essential thread to this tapestry are Noemi Martínez and Lina Suárez, the women who organized the Anzaldúa Legacy Project in South Texas, the very land where Gloria was born and lived her early life,. The Legacy Project and faculty like Emmy Pérez at the University of Texas at Pan American, Gloria's undergraduate alma mater, hosted a luncheon as part of the 2009 gathering for those participants who traveled to the cemetery at Hargill, Texas. The luncheon speaker, Norma Alarcón, and the poets and performers whose participation contributed in a very special way to the 2009 Mundo Zurdo event are not represented in the collected essays but formed an important part of the multigenre, and very Anzaldúan collage that was the 2009 Mundo Zurdo gathering. The altares set up for both gatherings honored Anzaldúa and her work. Glenda Schaffer a set up the 2007 altar; Patricia Trujillo and Deborah Vasquez set up the altar in 2009.

## A BOOK OF PROCEEDINGS: THE SSGA GATHERINGS, 2007 AND 2009

Recognizing that the SSGA and the various venues where scholars present their work—such as meetings of the MLA and ASA—only reach a few who attend such meetings and seeking to make the work accessible to a wider audience, the Adelante Project, in 2009, published *Güeras y Prietas: Celebrating 20 Years of Borderlands/La Frontera* in time to distribute it to the attendees of the 2009 Mundo Zurdo gathering. As discussion of the publication of the 2009 El Mundo Zurdo arose, the editors, members of the SSGA Publications Committee, chose to keep the original 2007 *Güeras y Prietas* collection as Book 1 and to have as Book 2 the essays, poems and artwork from the *2009 El Mundo Zurdo: An International Conference on the Life and Work of Gloria E. Anzaldúa.* Thus, this volume published by Aunt Lute Books brings together the work from both SSGA gatherings.

You will find between the covers of this book work, sometimes scholarly, other times creative, but at all times focused on Anzaldúa. The aim of the editors remains true to Anzaldúa's desire to gather the voices of scholars, activists, poets, artists, and all who are called to contribute their voice to the cacophony of voices exploring new ways of being in the world. Culled from the submitted essays and poems, the writings reflect the variety of voices, academic and not, that spoke loud and clear at the gatherings. Anzaldúa often brought disparate and seemingly divergent voices together in her anthologies, putting them in dialogue with each other.

Each Book represents the content of the gathering. For example Book One includes essays and poetry, but no art since the symposium did not have an art exhibit. Book Two, on the other hand, includes art work from the exhibit curated by Anel Flores and a cadre of dedicated and committed SSGA members.

The exhibit opened at the Esperanza Peace and Justice Center on May 16, 2009, the second day of the gathering. The cover art is the work of Deborah Vásquez, "Kuetzpalín" Chicana artist based in San Antonio, Texas.

Drawing my comments to a close, I offer a blessing to all who have worked to bring the project to fruition and to those who will read these words, I ask that this book finds its way to where it is needed and to the readers who are ready for the insights and the knowledge it brings. Gracias, Gloria for your ever present spirit; we are merely attempting to do what you urged we do, work that matters. You were right (as always), sí vale la pena.

Norma E. Cantú

San Antonio, Tejas

March 2010

**VOLUME ONE**

# GÜERAS Y PRIETAS

CELEBRATING 20 YEARS OF BORDERLANDS/LA FRONTERA

Conference Proceedings, 2007

Edited by Norma E. Cantú and Christina L. Gutiérrez

# INTRODUCTION: BECOMING MEXICANA WITH GLORIA ANZALDÚA

*NORMA ALARCÓN*

In her introduction to the second edition of Anzaldúa's *Borderlands/La Frontera: The New Mestiza* (1999), Sonia Saldívar-Hull reminds us that Anzaldúa invokes The Treaty of Guadalupe Hidalgo (2/2/1848) as a document that constituted a "new U.S. minority: American citizens of Mexican descent" (2). Saldívar-Hull adds, "Anzaldúa's testimonio-like pedagogy offers knowledge that Anglo-centric schools tend to erase, interjecting a counter-narrative that tells of the appropriation of land by Anglo-Americans who did more than take territory: the process of absorption into the U.S. included the imposition of White Supremacy aided by the overt terrorists tactics of the Texas Rangers" (2). Or, as Hernández says in this volume, Anzaldúa offers a "counter hegemonic discourse."

Indeed, by the 1940s, Enriqueta Vásquez tells us in the columns she wrote for *El Grito* (1968-73), she had learned of this conquest through the stories her mother told. Through these stories she was awakened into the realization that she was a colonized subject, dispossessed of her land. It is dispossession and colonization to which Anzaldúa alludes when she says, "This is my home/…/ This land was Mexican once,/ was Indian always/ and is./ And will be again." Further, I think, it is their "wild tongues" que dieron a luz sus proyectos descolonizadores through the practice of "testimonio-like pedagogy," as Saldívar-Hull calls Anzaldúa's textual narrative.

None of my academic training and knowledge had prepared me for the encounter with Anzaldúa's text *Borderlands*, though there was a "structure of feeling" that linked with mine. But what to do with the dissonance produced by the "conventional scholarly methods" I had learned? I decided to privilege the text and not the methods. Indeed, all the contributors privilege the text, and in some instances, decry the conventional scholarly methods, as Anzaldúa herself did, which perpetuate marginalization of the text in the academy as it simultaneously often delinks from its communities of color. In this sense *Borderlands* is a liminal text that has the capacity to deconstruct the academy on the one hand, and to forge articulations and alliances transnationally as well as locally. Though in this text, as Saldívar-Hull reminds us, Anzaldúa is a Tejana, a paisana of hers, and I dare say after three years in the borderlands region I have learned that I am not a paisana to Tejanas, not yet. Paisana invokes a sameness through which difference can be located in the non-paisana, as such one may not ever become a tejana-paisana!

All of the contributors are nepantleras in spirit, though at times the "in-betweenness" is neither invoked nor structured similarly. However, all of these nepantleras bear witness, and deploy a "testimonio-like" pedagogy from the most intimate to the most critically distant, though the former outnumber the latter. At the center of it all, however, is the enabling pedagogy that Anzaldúa wrought in relation to experience, transformation of consciousness and the production of knowledge. As Torres testifies, for example, "[Anzaldúa] validated my instinct to draw connections between explicit experiences and analytic critiques…." To which I would add, she also validated instincts to draw disconnections or distinctions between explicit experience and analytic critiques. As Anzaldúa said, "deconstruct, reconstruct," (cited in Barceló).

The facticity of the geopolitical border looms large for some contributors for whom "in-betweenness" evaporates when the demand for documents is made as the border is crossed in everyday life continuously (Tabuenca), from another vantage point (Hernández), the "in-betweeness" or third space risks marginalizing other subaltern subjects whose voice has yet to "emerge into hegemony" (Spivak's phrase). Yet as others testify (Torres, Montes, Cortina, Barceló), Anzaldúa's text serves pedagogically to bring others into voice which is a prerequisite for political activity and action. As Matt Richardson has said, one goes from silence, to speech, to action in order to effect transformations of experience and consciousness in oneself and others. One begins to move towards a self-decolonization which, I believe, as well as most in this volume, Anzaldúa intends with *Borderlands.*

Every single contributor testifies to the transformative powers of Anzaldúa's text which, given its cornucopic, heteroglossic, and palimsestic qualities, invites all readers to engage with aspects of the text which as a whole refuses politically correct engagement. Yet Hernández cautions against idealizations not only of the text's own epistemologies, but of those who see purchase in the text and are tempted to indulge "nostalgia for wholeness." Hernández insists that we note how "differences and conflict structure that history." That is, the borderlands and their facticity. That facticity challenges any unitary notion of the subject, which is Anzaldúa's purview. According to some in this volume, Anzaldúa conceptualizes a "subject-in-process" (Cortina, Tabuenca, Hernández), emphasizing the mobilities and fluidities of identity in the New Mestiza.

Though as Tabuenca points out the Mexican side of the border, in its facticity, is erased in Anzaldúa's text which leaves Tabuenca without a "map" para "el otro lado..." and Mexico becomes a symbolic invocation which in turn renders the borderlands a "mythological space." How to negotiate a text that simultaneously speaks to you and erases you? Experience functions as an interruption and disruption and cuts against the "desire for wholeness," though, as Hernández notes, Anzaldúa's text does not address the failure of experience to radicalize consciousness. In Anzaldúa's personal case it did; her work is a testimonial to that. Also, all of the contributors testify to how Anzaldúa's work radicalized and expanded their consciousness. Thus, the text itself has the capacity to radicalize consciousness, if we do not resist it.

The concept-metaphors of Borders and Borderlands, which intimate the bridging that may be necessary to traverse silences, gaps, and walls, also move from their facticity and symbolicity in the terrain of the Mexico/United States State frontiers, to other sites. As Barceló says, "borderlands present an opportunity for engagement…across the borders of race, ethnicity, class, gender, sexuality, disability, and religion." *Borderlands*, the text, is a tool for engagement with other kinds of borders than that of Mexico/U.S. which Anzaldúa herself had pointed out in the difference between actual land-based terrain and the psychic, spiritual and sexual border/lands. The categories largely constructed by the academy, an apparatus of the state, produce borders between people who may be inclined to self-aggregate into one or several or all of them. How can all of the categories be claimed by one person? Is hybrid consciousness an answer of sorts, or is it Anzaldúa's Coyolxauhqui Imperative (cited in Joysmith), which brings forth both processes of fragmentation and dismemberment, and, reconstruction and reframing? For Barceló, Anzaldúa's work in its entirety has the capacity to do bridge-work with diverse students in pursuit of equity.

Bacchetta engages in critical bridge-work between Anzaldúa's epistemologies and "lesbian of color" activists and intellectuals in France. Though the facticity and specificity of borders is quite different, there are tactics of resistance that are shared and there is articulation with Anzaldúa's texts. Among these are self-definitions, retrieval of outlawed knowledges and decolonizing practices. Bacchetta, in effect, not only summarizes some of Anzaldúa's thought, but also that of "lesbians of color" in Paris: the construction of a critical relationship to official historiography; the reconceptualization of genealogies of the present that are relevant to feminist and "lesbians of color" subjects-in-process; and the politics of self-naming. Spanning great transnational distances as well, yet closer to the Mexican/U.S. border, Belausteguigoitia elaborates a "politics of reading," and does critical bridge-work as she articulates the subjects located at the limits of the nation: Rosario Castellanos's representation of indigenous of Chiapas, and Anzaldúa's representation of the USA's border dwellers, as the subjects-in-excess of the nations in question. Two sets of border dwellers share the status of "outcasts," "foreigners" to their respective nations. If Indians become Indians through the eyes of non-Indians, then they share with Anzaldúa in that, as she says, one becomes Mexican through Anglo eyes. For both, citizenship in the nation is annulled, forgotten, and dismissed. The nation delimits equal citizenship as it constructs itself as representative of the people. What people? A subalternity is produced by the nations in question, each according to their means and irreducible to each other in their specificities.

Finally, there's also the question of the "wound" which Joysmith brings to our attention. There's no doubt that Anzaldúa privileged the wound as a source of conocimientos throughout her work and beginning with the violent construction of two nations in 1848. In what may be one of the last pieces Anzaldúa wrote for publication—cyberspace testimonio on 9/11/01—she virtually chants throughout, "let us be the healing of the wound." As Joysmith remarks, Anzaldúa is a "cultural curandera."

In that cyberspace testimonio, Anzaldúa says, "As I see it, this country's real battle is with its shadow—its racism, propensity for violence, rapacity for consuming, neglect of its responsibility to global communities and the environment, and unjust treatment of dissenters and the disenfranchised, especially people of color. As an artist I feel compelled to expose this shadow side which the mainstream media and government denies. In order to understand our complicity and responsibility we must look at the shadow" (93).

Notwithstanding our differences which must be bridged, Anzaldúa adds, "The survival of the human species depends on each one of us connecting to our vecinos whether they live across the street, across national borders, or across oceans. A calamity of the magnitude of 9/11 can compel us to think not in terms of 'my' country or 'your' nation but 'our' planet" (101).

In a contradictory vein, however, I must conclude by also citing the sign that one sees on every freeway and byway: DON'T MESS WITH TEXAS!

# PART 1

## THE U.S./MEXICO BORDER: ANZALDÚA AND BORDER STUDIES

# 1

# TWENTY YEARS OF BORDERLANDS: A READING FROM THE BORDER

*MARÍA SOCORRO TABUENCA-CÓRDOBA*

*To you whom I never chanced to meet but who inhabit borderlands similar to mine, to you for whom borderlands is unknown territory....*

—*Gloria Anzaldúa,* Borderlands/La Frontera

I first heard about Gloria Anzaldúa's work during the spring of 1992 when I began doing research for my dissertation. I don't know if Google existed back then, but if it did, I didn't know about it; therefore, I didn't use it. However, I managed to travel to several universities in California and New Mexico, UTEP and UT Austin in Texas, and my own at Stony Brook. Every time I checked the library for "borderlands," "border literature," or "U.S.-Mexico border," it didn't matter which library database I went through, the result was the same: Gloria Anzaldúa; *Borderlands/La Frontera: The New Mestiza.*

I bought *Borderlands* and read it in one day, non-stop, with a pencil and a yellow text marker in my hand. I underlined many paragraphs and made notes in others. I questioned several of the poems, marked some stanzas, tried to explain some verses, and wrote "Imp" (for the word "important") when I read something I thought I could use later in my dissertation. At that early stage of my work, I could not tell what I was going to do with the material I had just read, but I was pretty sure Anzaldúa was going to be part of it.

Having spent ten years away from academic life, I was pleasantly shocked with the way the book was elaborated. I left academic life when the importance of form and beauty (whatever that means) and "the literary" were part of the discussion, and I returned to find a book full of different approaches to a very old and much-too-new theme in itself. I also found a book that talked about something that was very close to home, yet very distant and distinct. It was a book that questioned many topics I had studied before: form, beauty, theory, the literary, the sociological, the anthropological, and the political. It also questioned issues of race, gender, religion, justice, values, and traditions. Actually, the more I reviewed my notes, the clearer I was regarding Chicano community and traditions. However, I was becoming more confused about Anzaldúa's concept of the borderlands. For me, a beginner in the studies of the border, specifically on what I was calling border literature, and being a border dweller myself, this book on the U.S.-Mexico borderlands was fascinating, provoking, puzzling, and disturbing.

I found *Borderlands* fascinating because it talked directly to me. I could relate and respond to many of Anzaldúa's thoughts regarding the geopolitical area we had in common. I could share her anger against Anglos mistreating Chicanos and Mexicanos. I was fond of the way she intertwined her personal narrative with ancient Mexican and Chicano myths and history. I admired her passion in most of her poems and her devotion when talking about family and community. It was stimulating to read such a subversive text, and to know that many people also had access to it.

But, after reading the book a couple of times, and having advanced in my dissertation research, I felt it lacked what I was looking for: a comprehensive view of the U.S.-Mexico borderlands; a definition of border literature; an inclusion of Mexican border writers and border dwellers. As I mentioned before, my reading of Gloria Anzaldúa was coming from me as an inhabitant of the borderlands, one who crosses the geopolitical border on a daily basis. I was trying to get the whole picture, but I got only a piece of it. Therefore, inasmuch as I enjoyed and admired Anzaldúa's book, I needed to point out that absence.

Anzaldúa's attempt to decolonize the border in her trace of "a longing for unity and cohesion" (229) found a new mythological space in *Borderlands/La Frontera*. For critics in the U.S. academy, she became the quintessential representative of the border, but without wanting or being aware of it; that effect allowed the erasure of the Mexican side of the border. As I have stated previously:

> In Anzaldúa's work the border functions primarily as a metaphor, in that the border space as a geopolitical region converges with discourses of ethnicity, class, gender/sex, and sexual preference converge. Nevertheless, Anzaldúa's book, despite its multiple crossings of cultural and gender borders—from ethnicity to feminisms, from the academic realm to the work of blue-collar labor—tends to essentialize relations between Mexico and the United States. Her third country between the two nations, the borderlands, is still a metaphorical country defined from a First World perspective.... [Even though her border is] anchored in real referents...these referents are defined solely in terms of an outcast's status. Anzaldúa's famous analysis does not take into cognizance the many othernesses related to a border existence; her "us" is limited to U.S. minorities [and some Mexicans]; her "them" is U.S. dominant culture. Mexican border dwellers are also "us" and "them" with respect to their Chicana/o counterparts; they can in some sense be considered the "other" of both dominant and U.S. resistance discourses. (Castillo-Tabuenca 15)

But as years passed, and since I have recently read *Borderlands/La Frontera* again, I am convinced that from the Mexican border perspective Anzaldúa's contribution to our border studies relies precisely on her silences and absences. It may sound paradoxical, but it is not.

Anzaldúa's reflections invite the readers to place themselves not only in the actual geopolitical border but to "enter uncomfortable borderlands of word and silence" (Cáliz-Montoro viii). By reading her experiences and reflections one can learn to get in touch with her silences and her language, and also with our own silences and languages. And as Anzaldúa constructs her theory through her practice, we, as readers, can also learn to theorize while recounting and retracing our own experiences.

As Cáliz-Montoro has mentioned about border writers:

> Anzaldúa's considerations place the readers in a collective reality of living in a kind of borderland space [which] is aggravated and reinforced by the natural disasters the planet is undergoing. [Her] literature [as a border dweller] responds to a moment of transition and deep changes both as an individual and at a global level. These realities are exacerbated by humanity's loss of universal values and ethics. Values that have been exhausted in the latter part of an age too focused on pure reason and logic that is a compound of arbitrariness and double standards. To counteract these tendencies [her writings brought back old and] new myths and new forms of imagination. (x)

*Borderlands/La Frontera* represents an emerging literature characterized mostly by multiple literary and linguistic border realities of what Anzaldúa calls *la new Mestiza*. Twenty years after, the reality of that new *Mestiza* (and *Mestizo*) continues to be the reality of many *Mestizas/os* that inhabit a broader borderlands. Gloria Anzaldúa initiated an important shift to the studies of the U.S.-Mexico borderlands, as well as to a wider concept of borders.

Nevertheless, for those of us who are dwellers and crossers of the actual geopolitical border, it is difficult at times to enter the wider concept of the borderlands. Sometimes the reality is so tangible (e.g., waiting in line for one to four hours to be admitted in the U.S.) that we are not able to differentiate that crossing the bridge, the gate, the line, the river, the desert, or whatever political marker you cross (documented or undocumented) is almost identical to switching from one language to the other, from one set of laws and rules to the other, from one currency to the other, from one culture to the other. The reality is that these other crossings are unconscious. In that sense, Anzaldúa's reflections place us in a path of "interconnection between internal and external landscapes. The physical dimension of [her] work finds its roots in the geographical borderlands; however it does not rest there, but moves back and forth" (Cáliz-Montoro 10). In fact, for Anzaldúa those internal and external landscapes are intimately related to the physical experience of the land and the physical body.

Anzaldúa's *Borderlands* is important to border studies because it invites the reader to cross into other realms and really look into those realms. It allows us to investigate our own identities by questioning them, and it invites us to question our national identities too. Anzaldúa dismantles both the U.S. and Mexico's national hegemonic identities and pushes us to see beyond the red-white-and-blue, the green-white-and-red, or both. By silencing the other othernesses that I mentioned before, Anzaldúa drives us to reflect on them and suddenly they begin to appear in our border geographies. We begin to see our landscapes filled with different faces, which are excluded most of the time from our discourses. We can then acknowledge the many indigenous groups belonging to this geographical area that arrived before our ancestors or we arrived. I am talking about, among others, the yaquis, mayos, seris, kickapoo, pimas, cucapacas, pueblo, cochimíes, tohono O', and odhames, as well those who have arrived—and continue arriving—with the migratory flows, and those who have settled—and continue settling—in the different communities in this territory and beyond. I am speaking of the mijes, mazahuas, mixtecos, zapotecas, huicholes, rarámuris, nahuas, tzotziles, and others, who many times are visible to our eyes but invisible to our thoughts.

Questions of identity and culture became key elements in Anzaldúa's work. Consequently, *Borderlands* allows us to discover and uncover the multiple identity spaces a subject can occupy simultaneously without rendering the identities as meant in a hierarchal model. In that sense, Norma Alarcón's words help us understand these multiple positions of *la Mestiza*: "The critical desire to undercut subject determination through structures and discourses, in my view, presupposes a subject-in-process who constructs *provisional* identities" (135). In the case of Anzaldúa, living in the borderlands "reflects the reality of a subject-in progress; one who moves and evolves regardless of fixed artificial geopolitical spaces" (Cáliz-Montoro 12). In the case of many border dwellers and many Mexican border writers, we can see numerous subjects-in-progress constructing provisional identities, as I have discussed in previous publications and lectures.

Before closing, I would like to mention that there is much more to say about Gloria Anzaldúa and her contributions to border studies and border literatures, as conveyed in her other works. I would also like to say that after revisiting *Borderlands/La Frontera* recently, I noticed that I was underlining different passages than before, concurring with some of my previous marks, disagreeing with others. I also found myself agreeing more with Anzaldúa's concepts of the borderlands, even though I still disagree with parts of the text. However, my disagreement has made me reflect on my own work and especially on my own provisional identities. By arguing and dialoguing with her text, I must say that I owe Gloria Anzaldúa many of my reflections on our own border identities, and I am sure that other scholars from the border also owe many of their reflections to her work.

I would like to conclude by sharing a fragment of a reflection that I would have enjoyed having with Gloria Anzaldúa and Victoria Novaro. I am the daughter of a Mexican mother who migrated with her family from Aldama, a small town near Chihuahua City, to Juárez in 1925. I am also the daughter of a Spanish father who migrated first to Mexico from Barcelona at the end of the Spanish Civil War, and in 1945 to Juárez. I was born in El Paso, Texas, and crossed the border to Ciudad Juárez, Chihuahua, Mexico, three days after being born. I lived in Juárez for almost 20 years and crossed the bridge to go to college and work. Now I live in El Paso and work in Juárez. I have crossed the U.S.-Mexico border on a daily basis for almost 30 years. I speak English and Spanish and understand French and some Portuguese. However, I only know a few words in Náhuatl, which is widely spoken in Mexico, and I do not know any words in Rarámuri, the language of the native peoples from Chihuahua. I am a *Chicana* or *Latina* in the U.S. and a *Mexicana* in México. I've been called *güerita* in Mexico City, Italian in Boston, Venezuelan in Spain, and Palestinian in El Paso. I have been stopped and questioned innumerable times at the U.S.-Mexico border when declaring my U.S. citizenship. After the first Gulf War, an immigration officer believed I was a Muslim at the Juárez-El Paso Bridge, and after September 11 a customs officer in Amsterdam mistook me for Turkish. A Colombian woman could not believe that I was raised in Mexico because I do not have the accent from Mexico City. Some friends from Puerto Rico have said my Spanish was "very Mexican." And a prominent Ph.D. in Spanish Linguistics and a Mexican classmate at Stony Brook have told me that for being from the border I speak Spanish "very well." I think, for Anzaldúa I have survived the Borderlands and I have learned to be a crossroads. I believe that now I've got Gloria's "whole enchilada."

**Works Cited**

Alarcón, Norma. "Conjugating Subjects: The Heteroglossia of Essence and Resistance." *An Other Tongue: Nation and Ethnicity in the Linguistic Borderlands.* Ed. Alfred Arteaga. Durham, NC: Duke UP, 1994. 132-145. Print.

Anzaldúa, Gloria. *Borderlands/La Frontera: The New Mestiza.* San Francisco: Aunt Lute Books, 1987. Print.

Cáliz-Montoro, Carmen. *Writing from the Borderlands: A Study of Chicano, Afro-Caribbean and Native Literatures in North America.* Toronto: TSAR Publications, 2000. Print.

Castillo, Debra, María Socorro, and Tabuenca Córdoba. *Border Women: Writings from la Frontera.* Minneapolis: U of Minnesota P, 2002. Print.

Romero, Rolando. "Postdeconstructive Spaces." *Siglo XX/Twentieth Century* II (1993): 225-233. Print.

# 2

# WOUNDS OF FIRE: ANZALDÚA'S CULTURAL PRODUCTION FROM PAIN TO THEORY

*EDÉN TORRES*

The first time I met Gloria was a rehearsal for how I would ultimately remember her. The details are clear because at the time I already considered her a celebrated writer. Though still largely unknown to the general public, she was important in any circle that mattered to me. It was the late 1980s and I was convinced that it was neither a coincidence nor fate that we met, but was instead a simple matter of my being in the right place without effort or intention. She had come to Minneapolis to lead a six-week writing workshop for the Loft Literary Center. I was not part of the group taking the course with her, but a mutual friend had given her some of my poems and she had agreed to meet with me to discuss them. Can you imagine? Gloria Anzaldúa reading my poems. As the oldest of twelve siblings, I was not used to thinking of myself *como una esquincla*, but at that moment I felt like a child.

Gloria was staying in a small apartment in the basement of a huge mansion in Kenwood, a section of the city built and occupied by old money. A local matron of the arts—elegantly thin and blonde—owned the house. The woman with steel blue eyes met me at the door when I rang the bell and led me down the stairs to Gloria's rooms. In some ironic aligning of the cosmos, her guidance was unnecessary for I already knew my way to that apartment. My mother had worked for this woman some thirty years earlier.

In the late fall of 1957—one of the many times my mother and father fought and she refused to go back to Texas with him—my three brothers and I moved with *Mamá* into that peaceful little apartment, originally meant for servants rather than visiting writers like Gloria. Like mice smug in a safe haven for the winter, we were almost unaware of the luxury that surrounded us. As I recall, we were supremely uncritical of the Protestants upstairs, and the only whiteness that held our attention was the snow as it piled up and covered the windows to our rooms. We thought them good people when they shared the toys their children had outgrown, and we were grateful. Even now, I wonder what it was that made them take in a brown pregnant woman and her four children. My mother cleaned and cooked for them, occasionally watched their children, washed their clothes, and talked to them about Mexican music. The husband was a collector of "race music," and they often threw parties with exotic themes where people played instruments and read poetry aloud.

Returning to the house to meet Gloria that day was like walking into a museum decorated with the memories of that strange winter of my childhood. So much had changed in the intervening decades, and I moved through the space with a political consciousness that Gloria had helped to shape. I was carrying with me the words, "This is my home. This land was Mexican once, was Indian always and is. And will be again." The woman's gracious manner and tone when she talked to Gloria was familiar, yet much more childlike than I had remembered. Though Gloria was meeting me for the first time, she told the white woman my name as if we had been old friends and she was formally introducing me. As the owner of the house shook my hand, I savored the secret bits of knowledge I had about who she was all those years before. I knew she would not remember me as the little girl whose head she had stroked, and cooing, "Such pretty hair you have. It's so dark, I didn't expect it to be so soft." Even hearing my name sparked no memory for her.

"Are you a writer too?" she asked. She wanted me to be an artist, something more than just brown. Before I could answer, Gloria said "yes" and easily dismissed her. The woman retreated up the stairs, visibly disappointed not to be asked to join our conversation. She was clearly fascinated with Gloria. "Was I any different than this white woman," I wondered, "any less intrigued and simultaneously frightened by this small yet powerful *Tejana*?"

I faced Gloria, not knowing where to begin. Alone with my legend, I was eager to set aside my natural cynicism and my insecurities to engage with this *Xicana* who had taken her own wounds and turned them into literary and philosophical fire—this Queer, female savior sacrificing her privacy to show us a new way to burn through life with the ferocious freedom of self-definition. I was created in her image and she in mine. Similar ages, from small Texas towns only twenty-five miles apart—born into Mexican families and borderland spaces. She exposed the whole hideous, yet nourishing stew of *La Familia/La Raza*. She'd given me new languages, methods, and styles with which to interrogate patriarchal power, as well as racial, sexual, and class inequalities. And, she had challenged me to eat colonialism's complex meanings, and never be afraid to throw it all up on the page for anyone to contemplate, or consume. I believed in her vision of the borderlands because I had never known a moment when I didn't feel caught in-between. She was my Joaquin come to life, my moment of having a name to claim, my mirror in which I saw reflected both the transgressive possibility *and* the concreteness of the border. *La Gloria* standing before me. I knew that one day I would write not only about this meeting, but also about the irony of meeting her in this house. While I was being reverential, however, Gloria was ever practical.

"Here," she said, handing me a basket of dirty bed linens, "take these to the machine over there and start a load for me." I was surprised but did what she told me. "Bring the ones in the dryer back and we'll talk while you fold them."

Over the rest of the afternoon, I finished her laundry, took out her recycling, and cleaned out her refrigerator while she critiqued my writing. She was neither patronizing, kind, nor easily impressed.

When I have related this story of that first meeting to others, many have misunderstood it. They are either fiendishly amused or appalled by what Gloria asked me to do. But it was nothing more or less than I have asked my younger sisters to do for me when they come to my house. Gloria was treating me like family and treating the space as if it were one in which we could both be as comfortable as at home. She would not allow me to recede into the shadow of her celebrity, had no intention of creating a sacred space where I c/would worship her. We were simply two women exchanging our labors.

Almost twenty years later, I am still using Gloria's work in my courses and insisting that doctoral students who have not yet had the privilege must read her. Quite simply, her work is relevant to any student who wants me on their committee. Even if they eventually decide that her work has little relevance or meaning to their projects, I want them to understand the foundational nature of her cultural production and the importance of lived experience, as well as the intellectual and political responsibilities they assume as they write from a named social location. I do this even as I realize that in many ways, much of the academy has moved away from identity and oppression-based models.

* * *

The department of Chicano/a Studies at the University of Minnesota sponsors and works with a cohort of students who live and take classes together their freshman year. The students self-select to join the group called CASA SOL (Community Action Student Achievement and Student Opportunity for Leadership). To some extent, these students understand and define themselves as Latinas/os. Yet like so many of the students I face in my classrooms, the vast majority of them identify with mainstream cultural norms, values, and desires without even realizing that they do. Always a feature of our oppression, a profound erasure of history has occurred in the past decade of conservatism, technological advances, and meaningless application of the most benign forms of multiculturalism. Such students have been led to believe that it is okay to be "ethnic" in a diverse nation as long as your ethnicity is not expressed in political terms. While these students seem to know that they are Latina/o, and that there are certain cultural markers they're supposed to claim, only a few seem to have any real understanding of what it means in terms of power relations and continued socio-economic inequality.

The lie of meritocracy continues to convince far too many middle class Latinas/os that the working poor are to blame for their poverty, that their inability to afford health care and being one paycheck from economic disaster are somehow entirely the product of individual choices. In short, they've lost sight of the systematic nature of oppression. Corruptly executed and rhetorically hollow nods toward diversity have convinced them that being Latina/o poses no real threat to the consumerist nirvana that they have learned to desire through ever-increasing and seductive representations of the rich at the near exclusion of representations of the poor. Moreover, with its border-crossing capabilities, that sexless, colorless, accent-less, gender-less orderly god of the modern world—technology—has only increased the cult of U.S. style celebrity and spectacle. It has produced a cacophony of isolated, individual, and apolitical "networks" of "friends."

Everyone knows how to voice their opinion, share their experience, and expose their sexuality. But few know how to construct a reasoned argument or turn experiences into theory. To be sure, technology has also expanded the reach of *Latinidad* and *Chicanisma* and put an amazing array of knowledge within easy reach. In that sense it can still make some valid claims of having the potential to create worldwide revolution. Critical interventions and resistant cultural production can be disseminated around the world instantly. Real news, history, and political arguments are available outside the barren, corporate-owned media. For these reasons, I do want to believe in what some think of as the unchecked possibility of technology. But the reality is that much of technology is still largely class-based, culturally and/or economically. It is subject to government eavesdropping, and its primary use among mainstream students seems to be for either entertainment or a shortcut to completing research assignments rather than as a tool for communal, intellectual growth.

* * *

Where is the twenty-first century Gloria Anzaldúa and how is she using technology? How will she rise among students who have no memory or knowledge of the 1968 Blowouts, the Chicano Moratorium, or *This Bridge Called My Back*? Perhaps I am too weighed down in my own time to understand or recognize the significance of blogs by women of color. Would I be able to recognize someone of Gloria's importance if she's out there? Valid questions, no doubt.

At times it feels as if there is no such thing anymore as an intergenerational orthodoxy of ethnic studies texts—something known and revered across the generations. Perhaps such a thing is too conventional and not something we should aspire to in the first place. Yet it does not seem good practice to discard ideas or theories and methods before they can be fully employed, tested, imbued with meaning and purpose, or appreciated across the many borders that continue to exist in now global societies. Technology demonstrates the old dicho that many things can be true at the same time, even as it homogenizes the world's people in many ways. What technology seems less successful at producing is a historical narrative—a map of how and why we ended up in a place where so many young Latinas/os and Chicanas/os still have no idea of their resistant, civil rights, and feminist legacies. Clearly this is reason enough to form such a thing as the Society for the Study of Gloria Anzaldúa.

Perhaps it is precisely because of the power Gloria has had as a writer that she is still regularly challenged and left to face the tyranny of critique even in death, sometimes by people who have not read her or who have a political need to dismiss her or lessen the impact of her scholarship, but more often by people who understand her importance but have a less personal investment in her theories or cultural production. Part of the beauty of the symposium and this subsequent volume is not only in remembering and revisiting Gloria's work, but also in countering the fickle rules of scholarly or institutional creation—the artificiality of dismissing that which we find in any way "problematic," of moving on to the next sexy idea, of paraphrasing or re-labeling her ideas without citing her, thereby converting her revolutionary concepts into gentrified commodities—disembodied (and thus less Queer) voices that technology easily distributes but cannot help readers process.

Maybe it's because Gloria treated me like family all those years ago, or maybe it's because every time I read and teach *Borderlands/La Frontera* (and am still impressed by its depth), that I refuse to let her go—to relegate her wholly to some dead past. I still marvel at her ability to speak to so many people across racial, class, gender, and sexuality divisions. And at the very same time, I feel that there is a piece that is just for Chicanas—you know, eye to eye, *entre la raza, entre las mujeres.* I believe that her cultural production continues to exist within me. It is eternally new each time I encounter the irony and pain that comes with living in an oppressive society, and I need to use that experience to create theory as a framework that might be useful to activist projects, even if that only means providing a concrete example of how inequality functions and is maintained.

It has to be possible for us to critique Gloria's work, of course. To acknowledge the specificity of her social location and time, or trace the evolution of meanings a text like *Borderlands* can have without giving anyone the idea that it is okay to dismiss her. Perhaps my fear is misplaced and she will never be in danger of being discarded. Many noted scholars like Norma Alarcón and Aída Hurtado continue to engage her work. For everyone who attended the symposium dedicated to her, I trust that it is not possible that she will be forgotten no matter the pressures of moving on or of the vastness of technology.

But sometimes I worry that she needs our protection and our loyalty. Every day I am reminded that sexism, racism, and homophobia sometimes come disguised in academic standards that we Chicanas too often have little power to define. These biases may hide deep within experts with big credentials who nevertheless fail to recognize not only the complexity of Gloria's intuitive representational strategies and cultural production, but also her (and our) intellectual commitment to critiquing any systematic power that desires domination, no matter how wide or "free" that borderland space may appear to be.

In the specificity of who Gloria was and what she experienced, she saw and created theory that might be used beyond the singularity of one woman, having the power to inspire a plethora of ongoing dialogues. She validated my instinct to draw connections between explicit experiences and analytical critiques of subconscious forms of racism, the way that good intentions lead to paternalism and the appropriation of culture, and the ways in which the realities of the poor remain invisible in the unconscious consumption of images and fame. It is a method to which I must return again and again. Because no matter how well trained I become in more conventional scholarly methods, I am constantly opening doors in the present that usher in the pain and humiliation of past inequalities. It is a firm base from which to produce *and read* all the theory I will ever need.

# 3

# ANDAMOS HUYENDO, GLORIA: ACADEMIA, FRONTERAS Y LA NUEVA MESTIZA

*GUADALUPE CORTINA*

En este trabajo me propongo subrayar algunas consideraciones personales en cuanto a la manera en que la obra de Anzaldúa ha impactado mi desarrollo como académica mestiza fronteriza. Mi lectura de Gloria Anzaldúa ha estado siempre influida por mi perspectiva fronteriza y feminista. *Borderlands/La Frontera: The New Mestiza* es importante y crucial en mi formación académica ya que fue el primer texto que me autorizó a utilizar mi posicionalidad de mujer de frontera para interpretar no solamente los textos culturales y políticos que se manipulan en y desde la academia, sino también para rechazarlos o negociarlos. Esta influencia no fue obviamente a nivel individual; mi grupo de compañeras latinas en el programa doctoral de la University of Arizona se vio también hondamente afectado, aunque algunas de ellas habían vivido movimientos político-sociales muy de cerca. *Borderlands/La Frontera* marcó un hito a partir de 1987 en la manera en que los sujetos de las Fronteras se identificaron, particularmente las que se extienden a través de Estados Unidos y México, sin limitarse solamente a éstas. A partir de este texto, que en realidad es varios, las identidades por y de la frontera alcanzaron visibilidad y proliferaron, particularmente desde el ámbito académico. Sin embargo, fue inevitable que trascendieran a la esfera popular ya que era desde aquí que habían sido desarrolladas. A partir de entonces ha habido múltiples estudios literarios, culturales (incluyendo educación, economía, sexualidades alternas, etc.) y políticos sobre las fronteras. También surgió una rica literatura que reclamaba identidades contestatarias en Estados Unidos: a partir de Anzaldúa estos textos contaron con una palestra posible y visible, ya que teóricamente respondían a circunstancias histórico-culturales. Aunque las luchas por los derechos civiles y políticos de las minorías en este país se iniciaron en los campos de cultivo, en las calles, en los barrios y luego en los jurados, este texto dio curso a un reclamo de validación que todavía debía ser más inclusionista porque además circunscribía habitantes y problemas de los márgenes: fronteras, mujeres, sexualidades alternas y subalternas, cultura, economía, política, educación, intelecto, religión y espiritualidad, entre muchos otros. No obstante que los análisis sobre las fronteras y la teoría, como la de Michaelsen y Johnson, parten de Anzaldúa, es inevitable que le impugnen algunos aspectos, le acepten otros, y aun haya los que se extiendan más allá de lo que tradicionalmente se estudia de *Borderlands*, pero partiendo de sus concepciones.[1] El texto de Anzaldúa vino a recoger y a asimilar los resultados de las luchas civiles de los chicanos y luego las de los latinos en Estados Unidos. Indudablemente, sin éstas no hubiera tenido la misma audibilidad. La proyección fue muy importante debido sobre todo a su intención inclusionista, todos los márgenes y centros se cruzan en sus textos, y creo que ese aspecto es que le ha dado la vigencia que aún ahora sigue teniendo. Para mí es una sorpresa y un recordatorio constante de cuánto falta por hacer en cuanto a validar identidades cada vez que estudiamos en mis cursos universitarios ya sean los ensayos de Anzaldúa sobre cultura, privilegios lingüísticos, teoría inclusionista, o los cuentos de Cisneros, poemas de Lorna Dee Cervantes, ensayos o novelas de Castillo, o autoetnobiografía de Cantú en los undergraduate o graduate courses de español. La sacudida intelectual que experimentan, especialmente mis estudiantes mujeres, es total y reveladora. A partir de su lectura, se construyen a sí mismas como chicanas mestizas, y los estudiantes masculinos reclaman una identidad válida, legalizada cultural, lingüística, sexual y políticamente. No he encontrado todavía la misma reacción a los textos de un Paredes, un Méndez o un Hinojosa. La reacción fue similar desde mi experiencia personal. A Anzaldúa la leí por primera vez cuando estudiaba el doctorado, en un curso sobre el ensayo latinoamericano, y fue como si de pronto se me cayera literalmente una venda de los ojos. Hay que subrayar el hecho de que fue otra feminista y teórica latina, Eliana Rivero, la que incluyó a Anzaldúa como parte del canon ensayístico latinoamericano.

Pudiera parecer contradictorio hablar de "limitaciones" por algunos de los críticos de Anzaldúa, y al mismo tiempo otros califiquemos su escritura de inclusionista. Estoy de acuerdo con la clasificación de inclusionista porque fue una de las primeras escritoras chicanas que reclama una identidad fronteriza en muchos aspectos, además del geográfico que parece ser el menos significativo desde su propia perspectiva. La(s) identidad(es) que su teoría o planteamiento proponen se forma en las intersecciones de las ya sancionadas, incluso entrando en el terreno de lo espiritual. Este aspecto, aunado a lo sexual, lo cultural, histórico, político-económico, además del geográfico, en proceso continuo de hacerse, en ese estado que ella propone como nepantla, no subraya las fragmentaciones, sino las formaciones, las posibilidades de alianzas eclécticas y fructíferas. Sin embargo es claro que desde el punto de vista hegemónico su discurso pueda parecer ininteligible, ya que previene y cuestiona todo tipo de autoridad e intento de homogeneizar identidades y lenguas. Cuando hablamos de hegemonía no nos referimos solamente al control del discurso de la cultura y todas sus manifestaciones incluyendo la política y el arte, sino también a quienes nos hemos infectado con él cuando no transigimos con las diferencias y nos cerramos a las interpretaciones.

En segundo lugar, es importante para mí comentar la manera en que la teoría y la crítica procesan la obra de Anzaldúa. Éste es un aspecto problemático para gran parte de estas áreas porque la propia Anzaldúa se declara en contra de las limitaciones y falsedades del discurso académico.[2] Su postura es revolucionaria, por ello la enorme influencia hasta hoy y la que continuará ejerciendo. La academia, como lo dice Alicia Partnoy,[3] necesita revolucionar y activamente buscar empoderar al subalterno, ésa debe ser su razón de ser, y ésa es la teoría que los textos de Anzaldúa quieren proponer. Evidentemente, los textos de Anzaldúa y sus congéneres no se construyeron en el vacío y se alimentaron en su momento y época de conceptos que retaban lo que los discursos hegemónicos y monolíticos representaban. Entre las influencias están la crítica marxista en lo político/económico/social, Bajtín y la polifonía y heteroglosia del texto; Lotman y el lenguaje como vehículo primordial en la construcción de identidades y la cultura como texto interpretativo; Foucault y su análisis de los aparatos reguladores de los sistemas hegemónicos y su definición del conocimiento.[4] Spivak publica su ensayo seminal "Can the Subaltern Speak?" un año después de *Borderlands*, además el feminismo de color (Marta Vidal, Ana Nieto Gómez), y lésbico radical de su momento (Monique Wittig y *Les Guérrillères*, Cherríe Moraga), entre muchos otros conceptos que fructifican en estos años. Estas ideas que permeaban el ambiente intelectual y político de las décadas de los sesenta y que finalmente se reflejaron en los ochenta, se evidencia en Anzaldúa como en otros intelectuales que también expresan preocupaciones similares en ensayos o textos de ficción, teatro, poesía, novela, cuento y cine, entre otras creaciones culturales. Su(s) texto(s) exudan teoría, ésta se encuentra embebida/imbuida en los diseños identitarios políticos, culturales y sexuales planteados a través de toda su obra, no sólo de *Borderlands/La Frontera*, sino en sus demás ensayos, en su ficción, particularmente la infantil en sus cuentos de *Prietita*. Esta colección para niños es un practicum de su teoría de la identidad cultural, la espiritualidad y la nueva economía política de sus ensayos. En cuanto a ésta última, la que ella propone deja de lado los valores tradicionales de un país/cultura, para incorporar el valor de las identidades intersticiales o limítrofes. Y aún éstas, Anzaldúa las incorpora en el proceso de crecimiento individual, psicológico y espiritual de las personas, sean éstas del país que sean (*Interviews/Entrevistas* Gloria E. Anzaldúa 10). Sin embargo, una de las posturas más radicales que ella toma es la de asalto al discurso académico y teórico. En "Haciendo Teorías" Anzaldúa propone la construcción de nuevas teorías desde el margen que tomaran en cuenta las categorías de raza, clase, género sexual y etnia como categorías de análisis, para leernos desde nuestras propias experiencias y particularidades y no continuáramos siendo interpretados por el discurso hegemónico.[5]

También es interesante explorar las maneras en las que la obra de Anzaldúa (y su generación intelectual, además de los textos precedentes al suyo)[6] influyó en ondas expansivas no sólo en el imaginario nacional de este país, sus fronteras, y su academia, sino también en el ámbito mexicano y las maneras en que sus escritoras y escritores son leídos en Norteamérica. Glantz, Poniatowska, Monsiváis, Fuentes, Boullosa, y otros que evidentemente la han leído y los ha provocado quizá a revisitar y modificar sus percepciones culturales de eventos y grupos marginales al norte del Río Bravo. Esto se manifiesta tanto en el respeto con el cual se acercan a la cultura latina de los Estados Unidos cuando son invitados a visitar este país y dar charlas en congresos e instituciones académicas, así como en la manera en que abordan temas que tienen que ver con estas culturas en Norteamérica. Fuentes publicó *La Frontera de Cristal* en 1995, Poniatowska ha traducido al español a Sandra Cisneros, Carlos Monsiváis es un crítico y escritor intrigado por el Spanglish y culturas en Estados Unidos. A Carmen Boullosa la emparentan con Anzaldúa en tesis como la de Julie Hempel, y Glantz y Anzaldúa escribieron sobre su fascinación sobre la influencia de largo alcance que ha tenido la Malinche, reivindicándola. La nueva mestiza es todavía un concepto que continuamente hay que formular y aceptar, particularmente en las áreas que ideológicamente se identifican con los centros. En la esfera académica, a pesar de que se hayan incorporado en las universidades centros, departamentos, secciones y temas que quieran reflejar las actuales tendencias hacia las identidades alternas todavía se está muy lejos de entenderlas y aceptarlas verdaderamente, con todas las implicaciones culturales e identitarias que Anzaldúa propone. Por ello, cuando me invitaron a participar en este homenaje, la relación que encontré con la vida y obra de Garro, a quien en ese momento estudiaba, particularmente *Andamos huyendo, Lola*,[7] fue evidente. Ambas obras fueron una respuesta a la nulificación y mutilación de textos/sistemas/culturas masculinistas. El otro ensayo seminal en cuanto a la identidad mexicana por mucho tiempo fue, y quizá siga siendo, *El laberinto de la soledad*, del Premio Nobel mexicano Octavio Paz. En ese ensayo Paz manifiesta que en la cultura mexicana la mujer es la negación al no ser hombre, su anatomía la condena a la nada. Anzaldúa experimentó esta realidad, por ello en *Borderlands* habla de culturas que traicionan (37-45). La identidad femenina en *El laberinto* está centrada en su anatomía, la mujer no puede ser nada, no puede reclamar nacionalidad porque su condición es la traición: "la rajada, la chingada" es femenina.[8] La ideología del traductor cultural en *El laberinto* fue la que, de acuerdo a Garro y sus críticos, intentó siempre anularla como intelectual y escritora. Por un lado, en público la estimulaba y la adulaba, comentando el gran talento de Garro, como lo atestigua Poniatowska en el prólogo a *El asesinato de Elena Garro*, de Rosas Lopátegui.[9] Sin embargo, en privado buscaba invalidarla y hacerla dudar de la calidad de su capacidad creativa, así lo representa Garro obsesivamente a través de toda su ficción, particularmente en *Andamos huyendo, Lola, Reencuentro de personajes, Testimonios sobre Mariana, Mi hermanita Magdalena, Un corazón en un bote de basura, Un traje rojo para un duelo*, entre otros más. Se afirma que Paz no la perseguía ni la coartaba, pero lo contrario es evidente en el campo intelectual mexicano: Garro pagó con creces rebelarse y enfrentarse con el status quo, su nombre y obra fueron proscritas por mucho tiempo en México y se vio obligada a exiliarse del país junto con su hija Helena Paz. A causa de la situación de sitio que experimentó, vivió innumerables privaciones en su exilio y murió casi en la indigencia al regresar a México. Aún ahora, a través de documentos dudosos y posiblemente fabricados, el gobierno y sus agentes en los círculos intelectuales todavía continúan desprestigiándola acusándola de espía. Una mujer con el extraordinario talento que poseía Garro sufrió severo castigo para doblegar su intelecto y su energía creadora. Desafortunadamente, aunque parezca ser una regla de conducta en las culturas patriarcales de anular el intelecto femenino, Anzaldúa rescata valores culturales de México en los Estados Unidos a través de un replanteamiento histórico, serpentino, de acuerdo a Saldívar-Hull, siendo éste uno de los trazos teóricos de su obra, y lo reafirma en el resto de su obra autoensayística.[10] Su intención es reinscribir el sujeto histórico femenino en las historias de las culturas al lado norte del Río Bravo, cuyos orígenes reclaman en Aztlán. También, a través de la inserción de la experiencia total de este sujeto femenino, negativa y positiva, llama a transformar su posición en el mundo y el futuro que pueda afectar, particularmente desde su dominio de la profesión de la escritura. La propuesta de Anzaldúa es: toma lo que te va a hacer mejor y plena, bajo tus propias reglas, y rechaza todo lo que te coarte o anule.[11] La única medida es que cuando te mejores, lo hagas también para el mundo circundante.

¿Cómo cambiar el mundo desde la Academia utilizando la noción de movilización del paradigma mental que existe de la frontera? Los estudios de la frontera, de acuerdo a la misma Anzaldúa, tienen que tener el objetivo del cambio estructural y profundo de la sociedad y del mundo.[12] Sin embargo, en el mundo de la Academia, particularmente en algunas fronteras, todavía no se piensa en estos espacios como productores de cultura. No hay becas o incentivos para la investigación sistemática y metodológica de los productos culturales de la frontera. Se considera como una moda intelectual en los espacios donde no conocen realmente lo que se vive en la frontera, afirman los comités formados particularmente por angloamericanos, por hispanos cuasi asimilados a la cultura anglo, o latinos que no entienden estas zonas: de acuerdo a la concepción de la frontera de estos grupos, aquí, en la frontera sólo puede haber tráfico de drogas, violencia, ignorancia, estancamiento o muerte cultural e inmigración masiva de ilegales. Desde su óptica, los únicos productos culturales puedan ser quizá los narcocorridos; tal vez sólo la antropología y la sociología puedan encontrar aspectos de estudio en la cultura de la frontera. Una y otra vez todo lo que tenga que ver con peticiones de fondos para el estudio de la frontera, desde la frontera, de aspectos transnacionales y globalización partiendo de la frontera, la literatura de las y los escritores fronterizos, o la cultura de los aspectos limítrofes de la frontera mexicana, los barrios no urbanizados, historia de vida y salud de trabajadoras sexuales, etc., es obviado por estos comités universitarios a favor proyectos "de mayor envergadura" como un viaje a España a estudiar archivos de Indias, estudios sobre escritores de la generación del 28, o incluso la literatura contemporánea peninsular, o temas serios sobre las cartas escritas en la Francia del Siglo XVII y XVIII, los niveles de pobreza en áreas norteamericanas centrales, etc. ¿Cómo esta nueva mestiza que se ha construido como tal ideológicamente va a hacer su aportación en un mundo que no transige con lo que considera "regionalismo" o "localismo," implicando la carencia de un valor universal? Evidentemente, esto se traduce en pocas oportunidades de publicación y difusión, a menos que venda su alma al diablo, o sea, a los valores que trata de denunciar y cambiar, o que se pueda autopublicar, incluso fundar una editorial. Las otras avenidas pueden considerarse como "tokenismo,"[13] práctica que existe desde tiempos antiguos,[14] y a veces se debe tomar ventaja para utilizarla como foro.

La otra opción más viable y menos drástica es a través de la unión entre escritoras, académicas y mujeres de todos los estratos sociales en la comunidad. Existen ya este tipo de agrupaciones, aunque se den por breve espacio de tiempo, por ejemplo las que se crearon a raíz de la desaparición y asesinato de jóvenes mujeres en Cd. Juárez, en México. La obra de teatro *Mujeres de arena,* con la dirección de Humberto Robles y el apoyo y colaboración de la ONG *Nuestras hijas de regreso a casa*, es un buen ejemplo de la unión de intelectuales y comunidad por una causa común. Ya se ha llevado esta denuncia a muchas partes de México e incluso han viajado a Turín, Italia. Este proyecto nació del colectivo Movimiento Cultural Techo Blanco y tiene el formato de los *Monólogos de la Vagina*, con el propósito de difundir, diseminar la información para que el resto del mundo nos enteremos de lo que ha pasado. *El silencio que la voz de todas quiebra: mujeres y víctimas de Ciudad Juárez*, 1999, surgió de un taller de narrativa y fue publicado por Ediciones del Azar. Su objetivo también es diseminar la información a través de testimonios, utilizando la ficción narrativa. Este es un texto con un formato al que se puede acceder por Internet e imprimirlo si así lo desean, no hay derechos de autor o regalías, lo cual en sí rompe con los paradigmas tradicionales en cuanto a las leyes editoriales. Otros trabajos producto asimismo de la colaboración entre académicas y comunidad son los siguientes estudios críticos y documentales sobre el mismo tema: Marcela Lagarde, Olga Bustos, Mayela García y Ángela Alfarache presentaron el 28 de noviembre del 2007 los libros *Feminicidio: La política del asesinato de las mujeres*, y *Feminicidio: Una perspectiva global*, con el apoyo de la UNAM, en el marco de su Programa de Investigación Feminista y el Colegio de Académicas Universitarias. También el libro de Diana Washington Valdés, *Cosecha de mujeres, safari en el desierto*, publicado por Editorial Océano en el 2005, se pensó con el objetivo de denunciar la ineficacia de las autoridades a todos los niveles para resolver y detener esta ola de asesinatos. A Washington Valdez le ha valido recibir numerosos premios por su periodismo comprometido, además, tiene un blog en el que continuamente denuncia e informa sobre los problemas o adelantos en cuanto a las investigaciones sobre los feminicidios. Las ONGs son otra avenida más para las colaboraciones entre academia y comunidad, aunque las que más proliferan en la frontera son las ambientalistas, de acuerdo a Miriam Alfie Cohen, pero de allí se derivan otros intereses sociales que pueden desembocar en programas sociales novedosos y audaces, como lo manifiesta la investigadora en su análisis del 2002 (educación ambiental, planes de seguridad laboral, registros de contaminantes generados por las maquilas, elaborar planes de cooperación y entrenamiento con los Estados Unidos, etc.).

La desventaja de estas organizaciones es que no pueden recibir un presupuesto y solamente tienen acceso a fondos cuando se coordinan con organizaciones estadounidenses, y aquí es donde se pueden empezar a cuadrar y formar nuevas agendas entre la academia y la comunidad.[15]

En la frontera noreste mexicana es difícil iniciar luchas y compromisos. El sistema político es todavía fuertemente caudillista y el método más utilizado es el clientelismo. En ese sentido desanima a la comunidad a participar activamente en organizaciones que busquen el bien social. Existen varias ONGs en la frontera, una es el *Centro de Estudios Fronterizos y de Promoción de los Derechos Humanos* en Reynosa, Tamaulipas (CEFPRODHAC).[16] También está *Casa YMCA del Menor Migrante* (Ciudad Juárez, Chihuahua, México). Asimismo, en Juárez está *Ciudad Juárez Center for Information and Migration Studies* (Chihuahua). Todos estos organismos tienen sus objetivos principales que son: la defensa y promoción de los Derechos Humanos en la región fronteriza noreste de México, así como la difusión de mecanismos existentes en pro de los derechos económicos, políticos y sociales. La ONG de La Denuncia Pública de las Violaciones a Derechos Humanos, da asesoría jurídica y promueve los estudios e investigaciones relacionados con la problemática de esta parte de la frontera con la principal potencia militar y económica del mundo. Por supuesto, existe una fuerte intención en la promoción y educación sobre los Derechos Humanos. También actúan como un Centro de Documentación sobre migración, medio ambiente, situación laboral, situación penitenciaria, narcotráfico, procuración de justicia violencia física y sexual contra mujeres y niños y atención médica y sicológica a víctimas de la tortura y sus familiares. Sin embargo, de acuerdo al estudio de Cohen, el número de quienes se involucran es muy bajo (22).

Mi opinión después de haber leído una vez más el ensayo fundamental de Anzaldúa es que su intención inicial y central fue y es la construcción de un mundo más equitativo a través sobre todo del mejoramiento de la propia persona, alcanzando su máximo potencial primero como un ser humano. Yo creo que las mujeres en el ámbito académico que la estudiamos y la enseñamos estamos logrando de entrada su objetivo, pero todavía hay mucho más que podemos hacer si iniciamos enlaces y proyectos con la comunidad y continuamos utilizando sus planteamientos teóricos, transformándolos en praxis.

**Notes**

1 Anzaldúa misma lo declara en *Interviews/Entrevistas*: son muchos los aspectos que todavía no se estudian sobre su obra, pero que ya aparecen en *Borderlands* y que luego se han extendido en sus demás textos y entrevistas (268).

2 En "Speaking in Tongues: A Letter to Third World Women Writers." En *Women Writing Resistance: Essays on Latin America and the Caribbean* (89).

3 "On Being Shorter: How Our Testimonial Texts Defy the Academy." En *Women Writing Resistance: Essays on Latin America and the Caribbean* (181).

4 Anzaldúa lo absorbe y lo modifica, tal y como Foucault lo propone, a través de la diseminación de la versión de una identidad.

5 "Introduction" a *Making Face, Making Soul/Haciendo Caras: Creative and Critical Perspectives of Feminist of Color*. San Francisco: Aunt Lute Books, 1990. 25-26.

6 Saldívar-Hull, "Introduction to the Second Edition of *Borderlands*," 2-3.

7 Esta novela fue publicada en 1980 por Joaquín Mortiz y la generalidad de la crítica sobre la obra de Elena Garro concluyen que es una crónica ficcional del exilio/deportación que vivió a causa de sus declaraciones en contra del rol que los intelectuales habían tenido en el Movimiento Estudiantil de Tlatelolco en 1968.

8 *El Laberinto de la Soledad* 59-80. Tercera edición. México: Fondo de Cultura Económica, 1989.

9 Elena Poniatowska prologa *El asesinato de Elena Garro: periodismo a través de una perspectiva biográfica*. México, D. F.: Editorial Porrúa; Universidad Autónoma del Estado de Morelos, 2005, escrito por Patricia Rosas Lopátegui. De acuerdo a Christopher Domínguez Michael, Poniatowska desautoriza la devoción de Rosas Lopátegui en el prólogo a este texto. ("El asesinato de Elena Garro, de Patricia Rosas Lopátegui." Letras Libres, Octubre de 2006. www.letraslibres.com. Mar. 12, 2007).

10 "Introduction" a la segunda edición de *Borderlands/La Frontera* (2).

11 "Culturas que traicionan" en *Borderlands* y "Speaking in Tongues: A Letter to Third World Women Writers," en *Women Writing Resistance*, 79-89.

12 "Speaking in Tongues: A Letter to Third World Women Writers," en *Women Writing*

*Resistance*, 79-89.

13 No, no ha sido incluido el término en el *Diccionario de la Real Academia*, pero se utiliza ya en análisis antropológicos en español y se ha incorporado ya al portugués.

14 José en Egipto es uno de los ejemplos que puedo recordar en relación al acceso al círculo del poder de un grupo minoritario, pero seguramente debe de haber más ejemplos.

15 "Imágenes de ONGs ambientalistas en la Frontera México-Estados Unidos," 28. Análisis de 35 hojas sobre la situación de las ONGs en la frontera, publicado por la revista académica *Frontera Norte*, del Colegio de la Frontera Norte, en Tijuana, México.

16 Cuentan con programas en materia de derechos de la niñez, educación policial y militar, incidencia legislativa y derechos de los migrantes y refugiados.

**Works Cited and Consulted**

Anzaldúa, Gloria. *Borderlands/La Frontera: The New Mestiza*, 3rd edition. San Francisco: Aunt Lute Books, 2007. Print.

Anzaldúa, Gloria. *Friends from the Other Side/Amigos del Otro Lado*. San Francisco: Children's Book Press, 1993. Print.

Anzaldúa, Gloria, Ed. *Making Face, Making Soul/Haciendo Caras: Creative and Critical Perspectives of Feminist of Color*. San Francisco: Aunt Lute Books, 1990. Print.

Anzaldúa, Gloria. *Prietita and the Ghost Woman/Prietita y la Llorona*. San Francisco: Children's Book Press, 1995. Print.

Anzaldúa, Gloria. "Speaking in Tongues: A Letter to Third World Women Writers." *Women Writing Resistance: Essays on Latin America and the Caribbean*. Jennifer Browdy de Hernández, Ed. Cambridge, MA: South End Press, 2003. Print.

Anzaldúa, Gloria. "(Un)natural bridges, (Un)safe spaces." *This Bridge We Call Home: Radical Visions for Transformation*. Gloria E. Anzaldúa y AnaLouise Keating, Eds. New York: Routledge, 2002. 1–5. Print.

Anzaldúa, Gloria E., y AnaLouise Keating, Eds. *This Bridge We Call Home: Radical Visions for*

*Transformation*. New York: Routledge, 2002, 1–5. Print.

Anzaldúa, Gloria E., y Cherríe Moraga. *This Bridge Called My Back: Writing by Radical Women of Color*. New York: Kitchen Table, Women of Color Press, 1983. Print.

Cantú, Norma E. *Canícula: Imágenes de una niñez fronteriza*. Trad. 1995. In *Canícula: Snapshots of a Girlhood en la Frontera*. Nuestra Visión: U.S. Latino Literature Series. Boston: Houghton Mifflin, 2001. Print.

Cervantes, Lorna Dee. *Emplumada*. Houston: Arte Público Press, 1981. Print.

Cervantes, Lorna Dee. *From the Cables of Genocide: Poems on Love and Hunger*. Pittsburgh: University of Pittsburgh Press, 1981. Print.

Cisneros, Sandra. *El arroyo de la Llorona y otros cuentos*. Trad. Liliana Valenzuela. New York: Vintage Books, 1996. Print.

Cohen, Miriam Alfie. "Imágenes de ONGs ambientalistas en la Frontera México-Estados Unidos." *Frontera Norte: Estudios ambientales, culturales, de población, de administración pública, económicos, sociales* 14.027 (2002): 1–35. Print.

Cotera, Marta. *Diosa y Hembra: The History and Heritage of Chicanas in the U.S.* Austin, Texas: Information System Development, 1976. Print.

Cotera, Marta. *The Chicana Feminist*. Austin, Texas: Information System Development, 1977. Print.

Domínguez Michael, Christopher. "*El asesinato de Elena Garro*, de Patricia Rosas Lopátegui." *Letras Libres,* Octubre 2006. March 12, 2007. Available at: www.letraslibres.com

Garro, Elena. *Andamos huyendo, Lola*. Joaquín Mortiz, 1980. Print.

Garro, Elena. *Mi hermanita Magdalena*. Monterrey, Nuevo León: Ediciones Castillo, 1998. Print.

Garro, Elena. *Reencuentro de personajes*. México, D. F.: Grijalbo, 1982. Print.

Garro, Elena. *Testimonios sobre Mariana*. México, D. F.: Grijalbo, 1981. Print.

Garro, Elena. *Un corazón en un bote de basura*. México: Joaquín Mortiz, 1996. Print.

Garro, Elena. *Un traje rojo para un duelo*. Monterrey, Nuevo León: Ediciones Castillo, 1996. Print.

Hempel, Julie. *Faces, Bodies, and Spaces: Differential Identity Construction in Mexicana and Chicana Narrative*. Ph.D. dissertation. University of Michigan, 2004. Print.

Hinojosa, Rolando. *Estampas del Valle*. Tempe, Arizona: Editorial Bilingüe, 1994. Print.

Keating, AnaLouise. "Shifting worlds, una entrada." *EntreMundos/AmongWorlds: New Perspectives on Gloria Anzaldúa*. AnaLouise Keating, Ed. New York: Palgrave Macmillan, 2005, 1–12. Print.

Keating, AnaLouise, Ed. *Gloria E. Anzaldúa: Interviews/Entrevistas*. New York: Routledge, 2000. Print.

Méndez, Miguel. *El sueño de Santa María de las Piedras*. México, D.F.: Editorial Diana, 1993. Print.

Michaelsen, Scott, y David E. Johnson, Eds. *Teoría de la frontera: Los límites de la política cultural*. Barcelona: Gedisa Editorial, 2003. Print.

Monsiváis, Carlos. "Prólogo." *Visiones de frontera: Las culturas mexicanas del suroeste de los Estados Unidos*. Carlos G. Vélez Ibáñez. Trad. Katia Rheault. México: Porrúa, 1999. Print.

Nieto-Gómez, Ana. "La Feminista." *Encuentro Femenil* 1:2 (1974). Print.

Paredes, Américo. *With His Pistol in His Hand: A Border Ballad and its Hero*. Austin: U of Texas P, 1971. Print.

Paz, Octavio. *El laberinto de la soledad* (1950). 3rd edition. México: Fondo de Cultura Económica, 1989. Print.

Poniatowska, Elena. "Prólogo." *El asesinato de Elena Garro: periodismo a través de una perspectiva biográfica*. Patricia Rosas Lopátegui. México: Editorial Porrúa; Universidad del Estado de Morelos, 2005. Print.

Rosas Lopátegui, Patricia. *El asesinato de Elena Garro: periodismo a través de una perspectiva biográfica*. México: Editorial Porrúa, Universidad del Estado de Morelos, 2005. Print.

Rosas Lopátegui, Patricia. *Testimonios sobre Elena Garro: biografía exclusiva y autorizada de Elena Garro*. Monterrey, Nuevo León: Ediciones Castillo, 2002. Print.

Rosas Lopátegui, Patricia. *Yo sólo soy memoria: biografía visual de Elena Garro*. Monterrey, Nuevo León: Ediciones Castillo, 2000. Print.

Russell, Diana E., y Jill Radford, Eds. *Feminicidio: La política del asesinato de las mujeres*, y *Feminicidio: Una perspectiva global*. México: UNAM, 2007. Print.

Saldívar-Hull, Sonia. "Introduction to the Second Edition." *Borderlands/La Frontera: The New Mestiza*. San Francisco: Aunt Lute Books, 1999. 1–15. Print.

Vidal, Marta. "Chicanas Speak Out. Women: New Voice of La Raza." In *Feminism and Socialism*. New York: Pathfinder Press, 1972. Print.

Washington Valdez, Diana. *Cosecha de mujeres: Safari en el desierto mexicano (el dedo en la llaga)*. México: Océano, 2007. Print.

Wittig, Monique. *Les Guérrillères* (1971) Trad. David Le Vay. Boston: Beacon Press, 1985. Print.

# PART 2

## ANZALDÚA AND QUEER STUDIES

# 4

# WHAT GLORIA SAID ABOUT LA VIRGEN'S HANDS

*AMELIA M.L. MONTES*

The first time I met Gloria Anzaldúa was at a conference in San Francisco in the early 1990s. I was between panels, walking through a crowd in a narrow hall. It was a rounded hallway so you could not see individual faces too far ahead—just many bodies coming at you or around you. There was much chatter and laughter. A woman as short as I am but walking at a less frenetic pace suddenly faced me. We may have shared a similarity in height, but our choice of dress differed. She wore sandals, a brown linen tunic, loose pants—she carried nothing. I was in academic suiting: black skirt and jacket, blue shirt, heels, and I carried a briefcase. She stopped in front of me, more due to the crowd hemming us in than seeking my attention. I knew immediately who she was and had often wondered during my readings of *Borderlands/La Frontera* and *This Bridge Called My Back* if I'd ever meet her.

Maybe she expected a simple greeting from me—"*Quíubole*" or "*Saludos*"—something just to acknowledge our presence in front of each other. Instead, what came out of my mouth surprised me: "I never looked at la Virgen de Guadalupe's hands clearly until after I read your book. Her hands are tied." She looked at me intently. In those few seconds, I wondered if she cut her own short locks of hair. It didn't look unprofessional, just an inch of uneven bangs and only if one were really close to her, like I was at that moment, would one notice. Her eyes were half-moon-shaped like my Tia Chala's eyes. She leaned in closer as if wishing to whisper in my ear. I obliged and turned my head a little. She said forcefully in clear syllables: "Untie her hands." The crowd parted and she walked past me.

* * *

Two years later, I was to see her again. This time I was attending a small Latina conference at St. Mary's Univeristy in San Antonio. The conference was called "*Hijas del Quinto Sol*: Studies in Latina Identity." Before the conference, I had heard she hadn't been well. When I arrived, word spread quickly that she was there. As in the meeting in San Francisco, her appearance carried a strong energy despite looking slimmer, more fragile than the day I first met her. She sat in front of us on an elevated platform. We were a small group, no more than forty. Gloria Anzaldúa began speaking by first acknowledging the people she knew in the audience. I was amazed that she could remember so many people by name, even those she hadn't seen for a long time. She was very candid in her talk with us. She spoke of her struggles with diabetes, of identity, of *familia* and its difficulties. She also spoke of her latest and future projects: children's books, a new edition of *This Bridge Called My Back.* The writing of children's books, she said, was a responsibility to the next generation, to educate them early, to make sure teachers have bilingual books in their classrooms offering Chicana perspectives of stories such as that of *Malintzín* or of *familia.* She said she was happy to be feeling better and with us that day—that it felt good to be among friends, those who understood her work.

Later, I stood in line to have her sign two copies of the *Borderlands/La Frontera* books I had brought with me. One was somewhat worn already but the other was new. The conference was also selling lovely poster prints of a painting by Chicana artist Nivia González, created before her car accident, which would leave her with short-term memory loss. It would take Nivia many months of rehabilitation to recover, but when she did, she would tell everyone that it was her art that helped bring her back. All the writers there were autographing Nivia's posters as well as their books: Judith Ortiz Cofer, Marjorie Agosín, Carmen Tafolla, Mary Helen Ponce, in addition to Gloria Anzaldúa. Nivia's poster, entitled "Accompanied Beneath Descending Light/*Acompañada Dentro Luz Descendiente*," centers on one woman, a *Mestiza* looking intently at the viewer. Coral and cerulean blue colors are behind her. Hanging above her is abundant green foliage that makes a shadow on the cerulean-colored wall. A gecko looks like it's going to crawl up into the foliage, its little lizard body dark in the shadows of the leaves. I bought a poster print and Nivia, Carmen Tafolla, and Judith Ortiz Cofer gladly signed it. I slowly made my way to Gloria's side of the table, greeting her as if we had never met. After all, we really hadn't. I couldn't see counting a few seconds as any type of meeting. I smiled and gave her the two books to sign as well as Nivia's print.

While I watched her sign the books, she looked up at me and asked, "Are you untying la Virgen's hands?" I was startled. She remembered those few seconds, and the even fewer words we had exchanged two years before. All I could say was, "It's not easy." She smiled and then I watched her draw in the book what Chicana historian and fiction writer Emma Pérez has described to me as a "plasmagormic" figure, which Emma told me pleased Gloria every time she drew it. I gave her Nivia's print and Gloria happily (like a child) drew the figure on that one too. I like Emma's description of Gloria's little figure. Its head, body, and arms are merely simple rounded lines. Plasma is, after all, a distinct state of matter. Plasma does not have a defining shape or volume but can form various structures depending on the environmental fields around it, whether these fields are matter or energy. I thought it was interesting that in each drawing, her signature moved into and out of the figure, giving this plasmagormic character a fluidity of movement. After many years of thinking about Anzaldúa's drawings, it seems to me they are very much linked to her idea of "*la conciencia de la mestiza*" when she writes, "*Soy un amasamiento,* I am an act of kneading, of uniting and joining that not only has produced both a creature of darkness and a creature of light, but also a creature that questions the definitions of light and dark and gives them new meanings" (103). Every time I have seen one of her creatures, it is not the same—it is always different.

* * *

After this second meeting, I never saw Gloria Anzaldúa again. A few years later, in 2000, I received my Ph.D. and took a job at The University of Nebraska-Lincoln. The Midwest was definitely a culture shock from my hometown of Los Angeles. I quickly learned, however, that some of that shock came from my own (and others') stereotypes and generalizations of the Midwest. What helped me was knowing that Gloria Anzaldúa was no stranger to the Midwest. In an interview with Karen Ikas, she recounts her years as a high school teacher. Anzaldúa says, "For one summer I even traveled with the migrant families who were on their way from Texas to the Midwest. By doing so I became a liaison between the migrant camps and the regular school teachers for one year. Later, they hired me to be the bilingual and migrant director of the full state of Indiana" (228). Anzaldúa's presence in the Midwest was instrumental to her writing, and at the same time she was an instrument of change for the students she taught. Chicana writer Alicia Gaspar de Alba first heard Anzaldúa when she was a graduate student in Iowa—a life changing moment for Gaspar de Alba as well.

To think of Gloria as a Chicana lesbian in the Midwest helped me to think about Nebraska, the Great Plains, and the other Chicana lesbians who could be here. I decided to conduct interviews with Chicana lesbians and this led to a publication in *The Journal of Lesbian Studies.* During this journey, I met Latina and Chicana lesbians whose lives and self-perceptions in the Midwest reveal a very complex picture of Nebraska, Kansas, Iowa, Illinois—very different from dominant narratives that subvert and erase individual voices. Some *mujeres* told me they wouldn't live anywhere else but in Nebraska. They felt completely "themselves" and supported in the Midwest. Others felt isolated and wished very much that their presence in the Midwest could be acknowledged rather than ignored or erased because of the overwhelming scholarship and popular writing of Latina lesbians from the West and East Coasts. Still others focused their conversations on identity formation and how they struggled with being lesbian and Latina. Susanna and Lorena wished they had learned about their Latina heritage earlier. They had taken a Chicana literature course at The University of Nebraska and it had opened their eyes to a part of their culture they had not known before. Susanna talked about how proud she was, for the first time, of her indigenous past. Combining what they now knew of their indigenous past with their pride in their sexual identity made them feel powerful. My conversations with writer and scholar Norma Cantú also affirmed the importance of Chicanas in the Midwest. Cantú lived in Lincoln, Nebraska, for a number of years as a graduate student. She received her doctorate at the University of Nebraska-Lincoln, and it was there, she said, that the Great Plains tribes connected her to her indigenous self. She said, "they [the Great Plains tribes] come down even now...[to] South Texas" (31). What Cantú and Nebraska have indeed given me is a broader context of the Midwest: the indigenous presence and my own connections to my lost indigenous *raíces.*

My lost indigenous *raíces* go back to the Purepecha peoples of Michoacán. I grew up with pictures of *mi bisabuela* Adelaida. The story my family tells is that José Antonio Carrillo, a *criollo* (a Spaniard with one-eighth or less indigenous ancestry), had taken in a woman from the Purepecha as his maid, then as his lover. She gave birth to Adelaida Carrillo, who later became Adelaida Carillo de Rodríguez after she married José Encarnación Rodríguez. These are all Spanish names. I have never known the Purepecha names of my great-grandmother's family. Her pictures show a stern elderly woman with sharp eyes, a thin mouth, dark smooth skin. My mother says she remembers her as quiet and strict. Pictures I have of the family from 1920 in Torreón, Coahuila, reveal mixed bloods: dark skin, lighter skin, thick hair, high cheekbones in some. I have read about the Purepecha tribe, have heard the Purepecha language and music. Yet, as an outsider, I cannot claim to be Purepecha. They would never recognize me. As it is, when I am in Oaxaca, Coahuila, Guanajuato, or Michoacán, people tell me, *"Hablas Español muy bien—pero el acento es del Norte. Se nota."* (You speak very good Spanish, but your accent is from the North. It shows.) I am, as Gloria Anzaldúa describes, "at the confluence of two or more genetic streams" (100). It is futile to focus on claiming something I am not and that "something" is only a construction.

Instead, I find it important to read the Purepecha history, to find out that the Purepecha have a distinct language and were able to successfully resist Aztec conquest. When the Spanish arrived, they continued to resist, albeit in creative ways. Historian James Krippner-Martínez says of the Michoacán Spanish conquest, "Resistance involved a number of strategies, including an attempt to accommodate at least one faction of conquistadores, a refusal to recognize the legitimacy of Spanish direct tribute claims, flight, and armed attacks that resulted in Spanish deaths. This reality challenges dominant representations of the conquest of the region, which have emphasized Indian passivity and the rapid acceptance of Spanish colonial rule" (20). They were able to pick and choose their assimilation strategies: for survival and for retention of their culture. Colonial narratives since the sixteenth century in Mexico as well as in North America have worked to shape a one-sided perspective of the colonized: the narrative of Malintzín, the myth of Juan Diego, the image of la Virgen de Guadalupe whose hands are tied. Anzaldúa early on saw the makings of a "new consciousness." She saw it in the South, the Southwest, and the Midwest. The fact that her work has been translated into more than ten languages tells us that a constant evolving of consciousness has been and is presently occurring nationally and internationally. When Anzaldúa writes, "The *mestizo* and the queer exist at this time and point on the evolutionary continuum for a purpose. We are a blending that proves that all blood is intricately woven together," (107) she is recognizing all colonized peoples who are, as the Purepecha did, creating new strategies of resistance. I am on a continuum of consciousness, which brings me images of untying hands.

* * *

On a beautiful May morning in 2004, I received the news that Gloria Anzaldúa had died. At the time I was a visiting professor at the University of Illinois in Urbana-Champaign continuing to write about Latina and Chicana presence in the Midwest. After I heard the news, I got on my bicycle and took a ride out of the city. I passed a number of empty fields already planted or being prepared for planting, empty and dilapidated barns, a couple of road kill: raccoon and skunk. My fast speed made the browns, tiny greens, and cerulean sky meld together in a dry brush stroke, leaving crisp and hard-edged color lines in my periphery. On the way back, I noticed the Mexican restaurant on the edge of town announcing a combo special: enchiladas and tacos with a tamale, rice, and beans. As I followed the road through the school's arboretum, I noticed crocus and daffodils open and facing the sun. People were out because it was so warm, the worst of winter over. I was sad to think that Gloria was gone, that she hadn't finished. She had told Karin Ikas, "I will probably die before I have finished or realized all my plans and projects. You know, with my diabetes you never know, because with people who suffer from diabetes mortality is very unsure. But I hope I am lucky and get as much done as possible" (246). Then I remembered how she had looked at me the day I met her. I could hear the sound of her voice, "Untie her hands."

Yet I do not believe her words are a charge for me to untie "her" hands. I see the Virgen image and "her" hands as mine. Each of us is charged with the responsibility to revisit ourselves and unravel our own complicit restraints within societal, familial, sexual constructions. It is a continual exercise, this untying, and one that takes a lifetime. Later that year, I returned to the University of Nebraska with a renewed sense of commitment to teaching Chicana and Latina literature in the Midwest, in being in a place where I am not as likely to be expected.

* * *

Three years passed. On a warm June day in 2007, I took a quick hour drive north from Lincoln to Omaha. I wanted to visit The Antiquarium Bookstore downtown. After thirty-seven years, this bookstore was moving. What a loss to Omaha. This bookstore had been a landmark downtown, a huge warehouse-type bookstore: four floors which included a space for "peace" gatherings and community organizing. There was a rare books section, a vinyl records section, a huge literature section, and old-fashioned disappearing bookshelves. One could find anything there. During an inventory, owners Tom Rudloff and his sister Judy counted 100,000 books. Imagine! They called the bookstore *The Antiquarium* with an "m" at the end to blend the German word *antiquariat* (meaning secondhand) with the English word *antiquarian* (antiquities). When I first heard this, I thought it another symbol of "continuum" and I liked the bookstore even more. Now they were closing and I wanted to join with the crowds who were coming to mourn and to see what they could find among the close-out sale.

I was there for a while, looking through the literature, the geography, the poetry section. I had almost forgotten about looking at the anthologies until I came upon the handwritten sign, "Anthologies and Some Criticism." In the middle of one of the bookshelves, I recognized the title, *Making Face, Making Soul: Haciendo Caras*: *Creative and Critical Perspectives by Feminists of Color,* edited by Gloria Anzaldúa. I immediately picked it up and flipped through it. I ended up at the end, re-reading María Lugones' piece, "Playfulness, 'World'-Travelling, and Loving Perception." I looked around me in the bookstore and noticed I was pretty much alone, so I began to read Lugones's words out loud:

> Playfulness is, in part, an openness to being a fool, which is a combination of not worrying about competence, not being self-important, not taking norms as sacred and finding ambiguity and double edges a source of wisdom and delight. So, positively, the playful attitude involves openness to surprise, openness to being a fool, openness to self-construction or reconstructions and to construction or reconstruction of the "worlds" we inhabit playfully. …In attempting to take hold of oneself and of one's relation to others in a particular "world," one may study, examine and come to understand oneself. One may then see what the possibilities for play are for the being one is in that "world." One may even decide to inhabit that self fully in order to better understand it better and find its creative possibilities. All of this is just self-reflection and it is quite different from resigning or abandoning oneself to the particular construction of oneself that one is attempting to take a hold of. (401)

To "take hold" of a particular construction is key to continually untying oneself. I kept flipping through the book, reading various sections until I arrived at the beginning. Suddenly, I noticed writing on the very first page after the cover. It was Gloria's signature and a drawing! She wrote, "*Contigo*, Gloria S. Anzaldúa 10-17-96." She had held this book nine years before, perhaps somewhere here in the Midwest, perhaps in Nebraska. The drawing was not the plasmagormic figure she had drawn in my book or on the print that was now hanging in my school office. Instead it looked like a codex, a pictograph of a moving circle ending with a pointed arrow facing down. Then two horizontal lines were under it. Below the lines was another moving circle ending with a pointed arrow almost turning upward, not quite. Movement of line frozen in time. One could interpret the two lines in-between the circles as a river, water, borders, a road, even two strings or rope unraveled and laid out. However, the "*contigo*" was clear. She had written the word in my other books and she wrote it on the print. *Contigo. Contigo. Contigo.* I see her in the hallway stopping for just a few seconds. I see her mouth the words, her breath becoming little particles swirling in between us. I see her walk past me.

**Works Cited**

Anzaldúa, Gloria. *Borderlands/La Frontera: The New Mestiza*, 3rd edition. San Francisco: Aunt Lute Books, 2007. Print.

Anzaldúa, Gloria. "Interview with Karen Ikas." *Borderlands/La Frontera: The New Mestiza,* 3rd edition. San Francisco: Aunt Lute Books, 2007. Print.

Krippner-Martínez, James. *Rereading the Conquest: Power, Politics, and the History of Early colonial Michoacán, Mexico, 1521–1565.* University Park: Pennsylvania State UP, 2001. Print.

Lugones, María. "Playfulness, 'World'-Travelling, and Loving Perception." *Making Face, Making Soul/Haciendo Caras: Creative and Critical Perspectives by Feminists of Color.* San Francisco: Aunt Lute Books, 1990. Print.

Montes, Amelia María de la Luz. "Tortilleras on the Prairie: Latina Lesbians Writing the Midwest." *Journal of Lesbian Studies,* 7 (2003): 31. Print.

"Patricia." Interview by Amelia M.L. Montes. July 3, 2002.

"Susanna." Interview by Amelia M.L. Montes. July 3, 2002.

# 5
# QUEER FEMINIST BORDERLANDS

*ELLIE D. HERNÁNDEZ*

Gloria Anzaldúa's critically acclaimed collection of poetry and essays, *Borderlands/ La Frontera: The New Mestiza* (1987), shed new light on life along the U.S./ Mexico border, and while the larger critical concerns about the geopolitical epistemologies of national borders have been influential to the development of cultural studies in the United States, Latin American and global perspectives, the proper contextualization of Anzaldúa's borderlands eludes recognition as a paradigmatic feminist book.[1] The elusiveness of the feminist project remains a concern in understanding the basis of Anzaldúa's larger theoretical project, which is to show how gender difference, or, "new mestiza consciousness," is critical to understanding the philosophical dynamics of the U.S./Mexico borderlands.

Of the cultural studies projects that have illustrated the perspective of feminist trajectory, Norma Alarcón's "Anzaldúa's Frontera: Inscribing Gynetics," ascribes Anzaldúa a place among cultural studies and notes the incorporation of a female agent/subject in borderlands evident in Anzaldúa's claim of an indigenous female (border) subject.[2] The border/frontera geopolitical region (gash, wound, vagina) refers to the absence of female narrative production within the nation(s), as Alarcón demonstrates in her essay, the framing of the female in relation to the nation as necessary as a repossessing the land and territory. In Alarcón's assessment of Anzaldúa borderlands, the desire to reclaim symbolic territory is necessary to the construction of its gynetics.

The point of my analysis, however, is to call attention to the need to "repossess" the land, especially in cultural nationalist narratives, though scenarios of origins that emerge in the self-same territory be it the literary, legendary, historical, ideological, critical, or theoretical level producing in material and imaginary terms "authentic" and "inauthentic," legal and illegal subjects.

Anzaldúa's work provides a very strong example of the border as a counter-hegemonic discourse. Its framing of gender and racial embodiments allows for a much broader conceptualization of border life, beyond the nationalist narrative. Yet, despite its many successes, Anzaldúa's *Borderlands* rarely finds a feminist interpretation in many cultural studies offerings. This is true even though its more celebrated borderland terminology, "border crossing," "mestiza consciousness" and third space, advance the feminist gender-sex binary by providing the lexicon of the new age of globalization. That part of the book remains consistent even twenty years after its publication.

But the broader goals of Anzaldúa's project offer significant and intriguing outlets for the feminist voice in other interpretative analysis, especially the varied dimensions of her work. In many Third World countries, it is common to have female or goddess representations that are darker and intentionally grotesque. Some implications of the "border" identity consider feminist construction of voice and figurative embodiment. Part of Anzaldúa's overall project, however, to develop a theory of feminist practice that expresses relevance to a postmodern and cultural studies model clearly offers the feminist in trajectory as a much needed critique of globalization. For example, Anzaldúa's notion of a liminal subject, drawing from postcolonial terminology, takes from a tradition that theorizes *mestizaje* (meaning racial but also cultural mixing) as a basis for thinking about marginal citizenship. *Borderlands/La Frontera*, like the theories of *mestizaje*, alludes to the feminine principle and ultimately rests upon a nostalgic desire for wholeness which can easily slip into the centering of the subject in the Anglo-American hegemony and Western philosophy sense.[3]

Anzaldúa's feminist project begins with the concept of border culture and the displacement of binary oppositions within the nation such as "center and periphery," or, in the case of the American Southwest, "Mexican and Anglo" (just as in some parts of the American South, social and cultural category confound the more common United States binarism of black and white). But the border identity is nevertheless informed by these oppositions. As such, it is subversive only in a context where the traditional binaries still hold sway. Once a notion of national binaries falls apart, the configurations of power within the heterogeneous "border" space all create a separate but intriguing new outlook which Anzaldúa regards as the new *meztiza* consciousness. My brief discussion of the origins of the mestiza tradition is intended to provide some concrete examples of these problems present to nationalist constructions of the woman of color feminist.

Once again, I recast the concepts of hybridity, *mestizaje* and liminality as possible starting points for the construction of a counterhegemonic feminist subject. This is particularly important given that a number of scholars in current transnational studies, including (but not limited to) Néstor García Canclini, Sonia Saldívar-Hull, Maria Josefina Saldaña, and Arturo Aldama, who have done important work on cultural hybridity in some of its concrete forms and as a conceptualization. The work of these contemporary scholars also shows how concepts of *mestizaje,* hybridity, and feminism, which were deployed as countering hegemonic motivations, have now been reworked in the last thirty years to cast feminism as a "border" space in which an alternative and more democratic modernity might be elaborated. Especially in this intellectual context, it is, to say the least, insufficient for critics to only point to hybridity, *mestizaje*, and border culture without consideration of the feminist project.

Anzaldúa draws from cultural *mestizaje*. Here Anzaldúa cites Mexican writer,

José Vasconcelos (1882-1959), who is best-known for his book *La Raza Cósmica (The Cosmic Race*, 1925). This publication celebrates the *mestizo* as harbinger of a mixed race that transcends the nation by alluding to a "cosmic" or divine order. The *mestizo* incorporates all the positive characteristics of all previous disseminated tribes of Mexico into one unified people with a common goal. Because he saw *mestizaje* as a spiritual advancement of socialist Mexico, *La Raza Cósmica* was important in one of its original historical contexts, that of resistance to neocolonial domination, as it was again in the early days of the Chicano movement. Important indeed to the formation of a racial and ethnic critique of the nation, Vasconcelos is however, limited in his conclusions about the place of women and the role of gender. As I have noted, such affirmations are subversive in the context of white supremacy, which depends on strict racial divisions and fears amalgamation. At least as important to Vasconcelos as this challenge to racial and gender hierarchy is the idea that the creation of the "cosmic race" will signal the worldwide advent of a new, aesthetically- and spiritually-oriented age. Vasconcelos' text takes part in a colonial modernist tradition which, as Iris Zavala puts it, posited "a third way out between European colonialism and North American imperialism" and created "a hegemony of cultural formalization founded in the logic of identity, while bringing into question modern forms of capitalist expansion" (5). In this sense, it can be (and has been) said that *La Raza Cósmica* is a philosophical essay and utopian projection rather than a program to be used critically. I wish to bring attention to the terms in which Vasconcelos casts his hopes, for the sake of what this reveals about the problems inherent in them and thus, in the unexamined acceptance of the "hybridity" concept.

I also wish to point out that Vasconcelos was head of the National University of Mexico and Minister of Education during the presidency of Alvaro Obregón (1920-24). In this post-revolutionary period, *mestizaje* was a state ideology wielded to strengthen citizens' adherence to the nation-state in a program that included the deculturation of indigenous peoples (Lomnitz-Adler 281). Vasconcelos developed his theories of *mestizaje* in this national context, where their meaning is explicitly hierarchical. Deployed in this way, *mestizaje* is a strategy of management and containment of the tumultuous post-revolutionary period and not of transgression of culture, as one may be led to conclude.

Anzaldúa is careful to point out that her ideas are a "takeoff" on Vasconcelos' (91); she is interested in him, she says, for his "inclusivity" (as opposed to white America's ideology of racial purity) and his defense of hybrid being as superior, rather than inferior (77). So Anzaldúa's use of Vasconcelos is evocative rather than literal. Vasconcelos himself, however, strongly privileges the Caucasian element in his program for a "fifth universal race" (7) whose creation, he says, is the "transcendental mission" (7)—and, I point out, the justification—of what he considers to be the spiritual purpose of European, and in particular Iberian colonialism. Consider the attitude towards Native and African-Americans expressed in this passage:

> North Americans have held very firmly to their resolution to maintain a pure stock, the reason being that they are faced with Blacks, who are like the opposite pole, like the antithesis of the elements to be mixed. In the Ibero-American world, the problem does not present itself in such crude terms. We have very few Blacks, and a large part of them is already becoming a mulatto population. The Indian is a good bridge for racial mixing. Besides, the warm climate is propitious for the interaction and gathering of all peoples. (24)

To be fair to Vasconcelos, we must recognize that *La Raza Cósmica* in its happier moments is an attempt to formulate a program that looks like what now might be called "multiculturalism." For instance, the *mestizo* synthesis is articulated in part as a mobile configuration of differences.[4] Yet, at the same time there is a recognition of the other, the *mestizo* and the indigenous, as the effeminate form of the national consciousness, the exclusion of gender as a facet of the nation-of-difference draws with it the ideology of the 19th century to distinguish and classify people according in racial and ethnic terms. This gesture secures the predominance of masculinity and heterosexuality in the formation of the Mexicano and Chicano national consciousness. Ironic indeed but plausible because despite the fact that the Mexican nation is so marked as female, *la patria*, the motherland, and derives its spiritual consciousness from the Virgin de Guadalupe, the role of female is relegated to the symbolic and the unconscious. The place of the unconscious is clearly outlined in her references to the goddess

Coatlicue, who is represented as a dark and fierce figure. Anzaldúa, unlike Vasconcelos, inscribes the female back into the language of the borderlands. The future race will not be a fifth, or a sixth race, destined to prevail over its ancestors. What is going to emerge out there is the "definitive race, the synthetical race, the integral race, made up of the genius and the blood of all peoples and, for that reason, more capable of true brotherhood and of a truly universal vision" (18). Yet in his text as a whole, the subject-position with the greatest weight is male and Anglo-Caucasian and the logic of fragmentation and unity supersedes the logic of difference(s). Despite its power, Vasconcelos' paradigm is here at best an "oppositional" stance to the United States.[5] Even if we justify it, as is possible in some of its contexts, as a form of "strategic" essentialism, its flaws are serious enough to call into question the implications of its use. It is my contention that Vasconcelos' model is not simply retrograde or unsophisticated but rather a strikingly clear illustration of certain risks that inhere in latter day nationalist models as well. Some of these risks, as should be clear by now, are that hybridity and liminality as models for counterhegemonic identities fossilize all too easily into new unities, and that this privileging of hybridity and liminality as universalized theoretical concepts may gloss over the telling of specific histories and consciously formulated particularities. This is important because, despite Anzaldúa's invitation to meet her at the border, and despite the parallels a theorist like Jean-Luc Nancy (1994) draws between his own "mixed" history as a twentieth-century Frenchman and the Chicano experience, we are not all *mestizos* now. Some choose to enter the borderlands, but others are irrevocably there, whether they like it or not.

Theories of heterogeneity develop partially out of the desire to overcome the limitations of a politics based on essentialized identities. But they themselves substantially risk idealizing the liminal subject, and in this way come to constitute the creation of a new, unitary subject. In this essay I have tried to show how theories of heterogeneity, which appear to undermine the self/other paradigm by positing a non-unitary subjectivity, bring the two terms into contact (the "new *mestiza*" is a bridge between unities) but do not necessarily call the oppositions which define selfness and otherness into question or undermine their construction as mutually exclusive. An example of this is Anzaldúa's figuration of the "*new mestiza*" as a bridge between unities (e.g. Mexico, "white America," male, female). Her text wants to corrode these unities and call into question the neatness of their separation and hierarchization. But when it conceives the "borderlands" in terms of oppositions and their reconciliation, it reinstalls dualistic thought and the hierarchies that dualisms force us to replicate. I have added to this that the language used to describe heterogeneity, in Anzaldúa's text and elsewhere, often reveals the slippage between a theory which affirms multiplicity and a theory which creates a new hegemony, a new, unitary subject, and thence, perhaps, a recurrence of the myth of cultural "purity." I have also criticized the idealization of the "borderlands," which may just as easily be a space of deracinated incoherence as of celebratory heterogeneity. Because they can mean loss without gain, the borderlands, though they offer opportunities to rethink and reshape identities, cannot be construed as a space of free play. Anyone who has inhabited an actual border zone can attest to the difference one's papers and one's looks make there.

Another problem deriving from what I have called the "slippage back to wholeness" in Anzaldúa's text is that her use of the Chicana lesbian as supreme example of both multiple oppression and "border" identities may in fact reinstall racial and sexual hierarchies—albeit inverted ones. The "*new mestiza*" in *Borderlands/La Frontera* occupies a combination of the most abject subject-positions this text imagines, and because of her position between worlds, she becomes, in the logic of this text, an ideal agent of social change. But the presentation of any single constellation of subject-positions as the "most" abject or the "most" liminal easily functions to obscure other subaltern positions. For instance, the "*new mestiza*," marginalized though she may be, speaks English and holds a United States passport. In these aspects of her social positioning she is privileged in relation to, say, the undocumented Mayan worker who also crosses the border, but who knows no English and speaks Yucatec Maya better than s/he does Spanish. A further implication of the reinstallation of hierarchies in Anzaldúa's text and in some other theories of hybridity is that it may assign the heaviest tasks of social change to those most marginalized, those most discriminated against. In Anzaldúa's context, that subject is the multiply oppressed *mestiza*. In contexts where the liminal or hybrid subject is not a figure of multiple oppression but one of conciliation, the assignation of primary revolutionary work to liminals actually functions to obscure subaltern representation. Whether "border" identities are necessarily radical ones is another pertinent question here. Though Anzaldúa's book is based on the notion of radicalizing experience, it does not address the failure of experience to provide radical consciousness. For example, when Anzaldúa asserts a type of natural bond between the gay and the *mestiza,* she denies the existence of racism in the gay community. Where does the gay white Republican fall on the revolutionary continuum? If experience in itself radicalizes, how do we account for Richard Rodríguez' rejection of bilingualism? Alma García (1997) describes how the Chicano Movement failed to take gender oppression into account; this lack of attention to Chicanas and their needs "gave rise to a parallel movement of ideological opposition"—Chicana feminism (3). She describes this as a further development of chicanismo itself, enlarging its ideals to include a focus on gender as well as race oppression (3). As described by Alma García, these Chicana activists did not reject the idea of Aztlán, but rather enlarged it to include a feminist focus. Developing a new Chicana feminism that worked to bridge the gap between feminism and the Chicano Movement, García cites Anzaldúa as one of several Chicana writers who were equally disenfranchised by the patriarchal and homophobic Chicano movement and the often racist and predominantly Anglo-American women's movement of the same era (19). *Borderlands/La frontera* along with her groundbreaking 1981 anthology which she co-edited with Cherríe Moraga, *This Bridge Called My Back: Writings by Radical Women of Color*, became the founding texts of a new Chicana feminism, a feminism which reaches out to the Chicano community, remaking the Chicano movement as it seeks to include those female and queer voices silenced in movement discourse, and also to other ethnic and progressive communities in the United States, seeking to achieve many of the aims of the original Chicano movement through a process of dialogue and coalition-building. García describes this shared struggle, which focused on "the multiple sources of oppression generated by race, gender and social class" (4). Through the work of Chicanas and other women of color feminists, the Chicano Movement could thus be re-envisioned as part of a larger struggle for civil rights and economic and social justice for people of color in the United States, one that included the civil rights struggle of African Americans, the feminist movement and the anti-Vietnam war movement. García concludes: "Thus, a Chicana feminist movement represented a struggle that was both nationalist and feminist. Ultimately, the inherent constraints and cross-pressures facing Chicana feminists within the Chicano movement led to the broader development of Chicana feminist thought" (4). It is no accident that Alma García opposes nationalism to feminism in this passage. By reaching out to the possibility of dialogue and coalition with other feminists, both inside and outside the United States, Chicana feminists opened up the cultural nationalist focus of the Chicano Movement to create an increasingly transnational Chicana feminism. These feminists re-imagined Aztlán, exchanging its isolationism and sexism for a new, broader interpretation of a Chicano homeland.

The problem here may be that Anzaldúa's text bears witness but cannot theorize nationalist prerogatives to unify a people (13). Her feminism, which is poetically evocative of a historical situation in Anzaldúa's text, functions differently when the same geographical context of the border initiates a theoretical model for transnational studies which then loses its feminist critique. At that point, feminism begins to conceal the contradictions it was initially invoked to expose and celebrate the female emancipation from national and capitalist structures. Feminism and hybridity, initially considered transgressive, are shaded into figures of conciliation that obscure conflict and difference. It is here that *Borderlands/La Frontera* invites universalizing readings, idealizations of *mestizaje* and hybridity, and emulations of the "new *mestiza*" by more privileged subjects who might better spend our time doing concrete political work. It is when Anzaldúa emphasizes feminism as *mestizaje* that she best shows how we might, in Toni Cade Bambara's words, "fearlessly work towards potent meshings" (vii). It demonstrates above all else the workings of a feminist project that is conscious of differences from various positions.

Such blending is most effectively made when specific histories and local knowledge are not glossed over. How to conjugate local knowledge and a postnational universalism that might contest the increasing marginalization of already marginal subjects in the current global order is perhaps the most important question in Leftist theory today. In *Borderlands/La Frontera,* Anzaldúa addresses this question by bringing into view a Chicana history and a lesbian subjectivity within it. She then reveals how these stories are connected with those of a dominant culture that tries not to see how closely its own history is imbricated with that of its others. She shows how, particularly along the United States-Mexico border, these others are in fact only barely foreign, "different" though they may be and temporary though their residence may seem. "Their" difference challenges "our" unity. But this difference predates that unity, and does not attack it from the outside so much as corrode it from within. That this corrosion may be a good thing for the mythical body it attacks is one of Anzaldúa's more important theses. I am more interested in her feminist text when it speaks a language of inclusivity that is formed in a history of colonization. I look at the "new mestiza" as a postmodern theory that is a necessary precondition for coalition-building in women of color politics. I would like to suggest that if *Borderlands/La Frontera's* feminism and multiple differences slips sometimes towards a wholeness that is problematic, because it may invariably obscure such subaltern positions on the one hand, and on the other enable more privileged subjects to identify all too easily with the transnational "borderlands." As Anzaldúa tells us, a number of her commentators emphasize, the bilingualism of this text confounds both English- and Spanish-language purity. Unevenly divided between the several idioms in which it is written, *Borderlands/La Frontera* shifts tongues unpredictably (14). Although she provides English versions for some of the Spanish-language sections and explanatory footnotes for others, Anzaldúa never implies an easy translatability of tongues, and some sections are not translated at all. She uses bilingualism as a device of non- conformity, this is to say that this text offers no single, easily accessible common language in its coding. Its various tongues cut against each other, running both together and apart. In this way it presents a serious challenge to the monocultural reader, and interdicts any facile access to the borderlands. Through their languages, these borderlands show layer upon layer of history to those who follow their tangled paths, or in Anzaldúa's metaphor, their forking tongues. This is an intertwining of differences that does not take recourse in myths of commonality, imperial-humanist or otherwise. Nor does it allow assertions of difference that avoid addressing what there is of a common history. Anzaldúa's linguistic thickets also engage the reader in a way that blocks the easy pluralism which, as Joan

Scott puts it, "is seen as a condition of human existence rather than as the effect of difference that constitutes hierarchies" (5). Rather, her use of language(s) works to show a historical interconnectedness, and to reveal the ways in which difference and conflict structure that history. These borderlands take serious, life-changing work to enter: a hegemonic "we" cannot simply expand to include all those who see potential in the practice of living on the margins. Anzaldúa's book does want to show that that hegemonic "we" is small and limited compared to the global pluralism that is likely to emerge in this new millennium.

By addressing a nostalgia for wholeness, I do not mean to diminish the importance of forging an identity and claiming a voice—articulated in terms of wholeness and centering at some points in Anzaldúa's text—for subjects who, as Nancy K. Miller puts it, are not "burdened by too much Self, Ego, Cogito" (106). It seems to me, for instance, that the search for a mythic home that in some ways structures the text reflects a desire for spiritual sustenance, not for a centered subjectivity in the Cartesian sense. I do not mean to simply identify essentialism, overt or covert, in Anzaldúa's work. As Diana Fuss has shown, to discover essentialisms may be less useful than it is to inquire what motivates them and to examine their uses, "strategic" or otherwise (Spivak 205). While I may look at some ways in which *Borderlands/La Frontera* may invite essentializations of *mestizaje* and/or liminality, I do not want to suggest that it is Anzaldúa's project to do this. On the contrary, *mestizaje* is a term Anzaldúa must privilege in order to articulate the politics of her own feminist location, and which it is her explicit intent to reconstruct as a mobile configuration that opens out towards the future. Growing from a tradition of Chicano/a texts that address issues of historical and cultural hybridity and represent shifting positionalities (Chabram-Dernersesian), *mestiza* consciousness as a theoretical stance in Anzaldúa is not a unitary essence but the awareness and negotiation of multiple and sometimes contradictory subject-positions.[6] Like Chela Sandoval's "differential consciousness" (1991), it is a strategy for perception and action at least as much as it is the representation of an identity (4). In this sense I concur with Norma Alarcón's assessment that Anzaldúa's writing does not want to "remain at rest" in taxonomies of hybridity and syncretism but to "make a bid for new discourse formations bringing into view new subjects-in-process" (136-

37), and with Judith Raiskin's, that the synthesis Anzaldúa proposes through the figure of the *mestiza* is not designed to provide "unity or stasis" but to "embod[y] a continual confrontation of difference" (163).[7] To restate my claim, I am not arguing against the value of marginal models of the subject, and particularly not in the specific contexts of the United States-Mexican border and Anzaldúa's feminist project. Nor would I criticize every form of wholeness or unity that is waged in the name of revolution. What I advocate is that criticism and theory not idealize multiplicity, nor remain at rest with the discovery and invocation of the marginal space. In saying this I am in part critical of universalizing readings of *Borderlands/La Frontera*—readings that appropriate its metaphors for theoretical and political projects sympathetic to but not necessarily the same as Anzaldúa's. This criticism of decontextualized readings of Anzaldúa has been advanced by Yvonne Yarbro-Bejarano (9-10) and cannot be emphasized enough.[8] Unlike some critics, I do think there are moments in *Borderlands/La Frontera* that invite such readings. I will also suggest here that the current emphasis on plural identities, and the use of this text to bolster that emphasis, may obscure subaltern positions that do not exhibit hybridity or liminality as their most salient characteristic.

To underscore these arguments, I call attention to the tropes of hybridity and liminality in post-Independence Latin American cultural debates. Although Anzaldúa herself invites such a connection by her references to this context, my intention is not to claim that this is the "proper" or natural context for her work, which corresponds most specifically to Chicano/a culture. But Anzaldúa also extends her project to address the creation of radical American (and not just North American) identities. To do so, she draws on traditions whose roots lie farther south, and it is worth excavating this layer of meaning in her text. I also suspect this exercise may be useful in a more general way. While liminality and hybridity are relatively new terms in English studies, the Latin American tradition on which Anzaldúa partially draws is much older, and has had a chance to reveal some of the impasses that inhere in the conceptualization and deployment of hybrid selves. Some of these impasses may be instructive to those of us working to construct counterhegemonic identities elsewhere. Like a number Latin American authors, of a variety of ideological persuasions and subject-positions and at a variety of historical moments, Anzaldúa invokes mixed identities as salutary antidotes to ideologies of purity.[9] But at the levels of race, ethnicity, and culture (and I do recognize that Anzaldúa's *mestizaje* refers to more than this), the discourse of hybridity has also functioned in Latin America to maintain social divisions (Graham, Lomnitz-Adler). Patricia J. Williams notes that the current United States interest in mixed ethnicities risks replicating this problem. She writes:

> We must guard against replacing a two-story system of racism...with a multileveled caste system. We will end up only with something like what plagues parts of Latin America: whole skyscrapers of racial differentiation, with "white" still living in the penthouse, the "one drops" just below and those with buckets of black blood in the basement or out in the street. (9)

So I raise the Latin American context to make the point that we must think hybridity and liminality rigorously if we are to avoid falling into a similar trap. I also raise this context simply to point out that it *is* one of Anzaldúa's, who, tellingly enough, does not provide English versions of every Spanish section of her text. The open smuggling of this language—the much denied other tongue of our hemisphere—into the United States cultural scene may be *Borderlands/La Frontera's* most radical intervention, although that topic lies outside the scope of this essay.

There are at least two overlapping but often conflicting discourses which shape the question of subaltern representation. One is the post-structuralist critique of the unitary subject as a construct which both denies and essentializes difference. The other is the politics of identity, which asserts the necessity of positing a subject with voice and agency. The split between these two discourses creates a double bind: the oppressed subject and the intellectual who theorizes her are caught between choosing subjectivity within the terms of the dominant discourse, or relinquishing the possibility of representation. Describing this double bind, Gayatri Spivak writes:

> The radical intellectual in the West is either caught in a deliberate choice of subalternity, granting to the oppressed that very expressive subjectivity

which s/he criticizes, or instead, a total unrepresentability. (209)

Anzaldúa offers a way out of this impasse by positing an identity politics of the already divided/multiple subject, a subject between cultures, languages, and races. She theorizes this state of betweenness as a physical and psychic territory that she calls the borderlands. The inhabitants of the borderlands are defined by their divergence from hegemonic racial, cultural, and sexual identities:

> *Los atravesados* live here: the squint-eyed, the perverse, the queer, the troublesome, the mongrel, the mulatto, the half-breed, the half-dead; in short those who cross over, pass over, or go through the confines of the "normal." (3)

Anzaldúa describes the Chicana as "cradled in one culture, sandwiched between two cultures, straddling all three cultures and their value systems" (78). She herself has grown up "between two cultures, the Mexican (with a heavy Indian influence) and the Anglo (as a member of a colonized people in [their] own territory)" (Preface). Her text throws into relief the complex identifications that cross the Chicana subject, divided not only between Mexican and Anglo culture but also between the expectations of gender inherent in both. Since the *mestiza* can identify with neither a dominant culture nor a single, unified minority group, the unitary subjectivity poststructuralism critiques is never available to her. Anzaldúa emphasizes the pain of speaking a "border tongue" (55), of feeling "orphaned" by her native language and therefore culturally deficient (58). The border, "this place of contradictions," is "not a comfortable territory to live in[.] Hatred, anger and exploitation are the prominent features of this landscape" (Preface). But precisely because she is in so many senses an outcast at the cross-section of cultures she inhabits, the Chicana is in a position to draw on the strengths of several cultures and to use each of these cultures to critique the other(s) from the point of view of an insider. Anzaldúa writes,

> The new *mestiza* copes by developing a tolerance for contradictions, a tolerance for ambiguity. She learns to be an Indian in Mexican culture, to be Mexican from an Anglo point of view. She learns to juggle cultures. She has a plural personality, she operates in a pluralistic mode.... Not

> only does she sustain contradictions, she turns the ambivalence into something else. (79)

Lesbianism marks Anzaldúa's deviance from the heterosexual imperative of Anglo, Mexican and Chicano cultures (18-20), as well as her identification with liminal subjects of different cultural backgrounds. She says,

> Being the supreme crossers of cultures, homosexuals have strong bonds with the queer white, Black, Asian, Native American, Latino, and with the queer in Italy, Australia and the rest of the planet. We come from all colors, all classes, all races, all time periods. Our role is to link people with each other.... (84)

This formulation may risk essentializing the lesbian of color as a necessarily revolutionary class—a problem to which I return below. Anzaldúa, however, insists that life in the borderlands is a practice, not an essence. Her

> *Mestiza* puts history through a sieve, winnows out the lies, looks at the forces that we as a race, as women, have been a part of. *Luego bota lo que no vale*... This step is a conscious rupture with all the oppressive traditions of all cultures... She communicates that rupture, documents the struggle. She reinterprets history and, using new symbols, she shapes new myths.[...] She surrenders all notions of safety, of the familiar. Deconstruct, construct. (82)

Finally, Anzaldúa's association of psychic unrest, writing, and the borderlands (72, 73), together with the heterogeneity of her implied audience and her explicit invitations to non-Chicanas to meet her at the border (Preface), suggests that few of us escape the pain of the borderlands, and calls us to participate actively in their work. The title of one poem, "To live in the Borderlands means you" (194, emphasis added), insists we recognize the multiple communities to which we belong and examine the conflicts, as well as the connections among them. This poem ends,

> To survive the Borderlands

you must live *sin fronteras*

be a crossroads. (195)

Anzaldúa thus transforms the borderlands from a space in which she is caught among conflicting loyalties and overlapping oppressions into a space in which she remaps and revises her cultural identity. In the fifth chapter of Borderlands, "How to Tame a Wild Tongue," Anzaldúa describes the evolution of Chicano Spanish in the Borderlands. She consistently differentiates between Chicanas and Latinas, a difference that begins with language itself: 'Their language was not outlawed in their countries. They had a whole lifetime of being immersed in their native tongue; generations, centuries in which Spanish was a first language, taught in school, heard on radio and TV, and read in the newspaper' (58). In contrast with the Latinas that Anzaldúa describes as growing up immersed in Spanish, she describes Chicanas as speaking as many as eight different languages (55). Calling language a homeland, she insists upon the validity of each one, insisting "I am my language" (59). In a later passage, she again insists upon the specificity of her Chicana identity, describing people who use other labels, such as Spanish, Hispanic, Spanish-American, Mexican-American, Latin American and Latin as "copping out"—acculturating and thus denying the particularity of their Chicano identity (62). Although Anzaldúa does state that the "Latinoist movement is good" she also insists that it is not enough, focusing instead on the historical and cultural specificity of Chicanos in her new inclusive theory of Aztlán (86).

In conclusion, in *Borderlands/La Frontera: The New Mestiza*, the idea of Aztlán moves from Chicano nationalism directly to a feminist model without losing its emphasis on the values of home and family so sacred to early Chicano movement activists, but enlarges its own definition to address the issues of global migration, transnational capital and shifting identities, insisting always on the fluidity and impermeability of categorizations and definitions. This Aztlán is not the same Aztlán presented by Rodolfo "Corky" Gonzales at the Chicano National Liberation Youth Conference in 1969. Instead it is a vision of Aztlán for all the linguistic, cultural and spiritual border-crossers that Anzaldúa addresses in her work. As a metaphorical palimpsest (Cooper Alarcón 1997), Aztlán will continue to change and be redefined by succeeding generations of Chicano scholars, never completely erasing its earlier definitions.

**Notes**

1 This essay originated from many discussions over the framing of gender across the U.S. Mexico borderlands. The aim of this essay is to illustrate the feminist orientation in Anzaldúa that directs us toward an examination of gender as a critical aspect of her book.

2 See Norma Alarcón's,"Anzaldúa's Frontera: Inscribing Gynetics" in *Chicana Feminisms: A Critical Reader* ed. Gabriela Arredondo, Aída Hurtado, Norma Khahn, Olga Nájera-Ramírez and Patricia Zavella, Durham, NC: Duke UP, 2003.

3 For some recent and quite varied critiques of hybridity, *mestizaje*, and transculturation as ideologemes in the discourse of Latin American culture, see Beverley, Lomnitz-Adler, Moraña, and Moreiras.

4 "Difference" is a loaded term which needs further explanation. In this sentence I am using it to signify the imagining of identities that are neither unified nor fragments of a supposed unity.

5 By "oppositional stance" I mean identities which oppose the "norm" and therefore risk strengthening the power of the norm as such, as well as reinstalling such binary oppositions as black/ white, male/female, etc. See Chela Sandoval (1991) on the distinction between oppositional identities which reproduce the dominant social order and the counter hegemonic "tactical subjectivity" (14) she calls "differential consciousness." Recent examples of work which employs and celebrates liminal and "hybrid" models include Benitez-Rojo (1992), Hicks (1991), Pérez Firmat (1989), and Saldívar (1991).

6 See Chabram-Dernersesian, Angie. 1992. "I Throw Punches for My Race, but I Don't Want to Be a Man: Writing Us—Chica-nos (Girl, Us)/Chicanas—into the Movement Script." *Cultural Studies*. Ed. Lawrence Grossberg, Cary Nelson, and Paula Triechler. New York: Routledge. 81-95.

7 Unlike Judith Raiskin, who speaks to Anzaldúa's intentions more than to the way her text actually works, I do not think *Borderlands/La Frontera's* postmodern reworking of nineteenth-century racial classifications frees itself of their contradictions. See Raiskin p.162.

8 There are some distinctions between Sandoval's theory and Anzaldúa's. See Yarbro-Bejarano 7-8. Yarbro-Bejarano, Yvonne. (1994). "Gloria Anzaldúa's *Borderlands/La Frontera*: Cultural

Studies, 'Difference,' and the Non-Unitary Subject." Cultural Critique (Fall): 5-28.

9 Anzaldúa's choices of Latin American points of reference—pre-Columbian deities and canonical authors like José Vasconcelos and Octavio Paz—are interesting, since there are in Latin America a number of "minority" traditions both contemporary and older, whose texts parallel more closely the sense of hers.

**Works Cited and Consulted**

Alarcón, Norma. "Conjugating Subjects: The Heteroglossia of Essence and Resistance." *An Other Tongue*. Ed. Alfred Arteaga. Durham: Duke UP, 1994. 125-138. Print.

Alarcón, Norma. "Anzaldúa's Frontera: Inscribing Gynetics." *A Critical Reader: Chicana Feminisms*. Ed. Gabriela F. Arredondo et al. Durham and London: Duke UP, 2003. 354-369. Print.

Anzaldúa, Gloria. *Borderlands/La Frontera: The New Mestiza*. San Francisco: Spinsters/Aunt Lute, 1987. Print.

Bambara, Toni Cade. Foreword. *This Bridge Called My Back: Writings by Radical Women of Color.* Ed. Cherríe Moraga and Gloria Anzaldúa. New York: Kitchen Table: Women of Color Press, 1983. vi-viii. Print.

"The Search for Cultural Identity." *Problems in Modern Latin American History*. Ed. John C. Chasteen and Joseph Tulchin. Wilmington, DE: Scholarly Resources, 1994. 168-98. Print.

Chabram-Dernersesian, Angie. "I Throw Punches for My Race, but I Don't Want to Be a Man: Writing Us—Chica-nos (Girl, Us)/Chicanas—into the Movement Script." *Cultural Studies*. Ed. Lawrence Grossberg, Cary Nelson, and Paula Triechler. New York: Routledge, 1992. 81-95. Print.

Christensen, Kimberly. "'With Whom Do You Believe Your Lot Is Cast?' White Feminists and Racism." *Signs* 22:3 (1997): 617-48. Print.

Fernández Retamar, Roberto. "*Caliban*." Fernández Retamar, *Caliban and Other Essays.* Trans. Edward Baker. Minneapolis: U of Minnesota, 1989. 3-45. Print.

Fuss, Diana. *Essentially Speaking: Feminism, Nature, and Difference*. New York: Routledge,

1989. Print.

Canclini, Nestor. "Cultural Reconversion." Trans. Holly Staver. *On Edge: The Crisis of Contemporary Latin American Culture.* Ed. George Yúdice, Jean Franco, and Juan Flores. Minneapolis: U of Minnesota, 1992. 29-43. Print.

Gordon, Linda. "On Difference." *Genders* 10 (1991): 91-111. Print.

Graham, Richard, ed. *The Idea of Race in Latin America, 1870-1940.* Austin: U of Texas, 1990. Print.

Hicks, D. Emily. *Border Writing: The Multidimensional Text.* Minneapolis: U of Minnesota, 1991. Print.

Jaén, Didier. Introduction. José Vasconcelos. *La Raza Cósmica/The Cosmic Race.* Trans. Didier Jaén. Los Angeles: Centro de Publicaciones, California State University at Los Angeles, 1979. xi-xxxiv. Print.

Kaplan, Caren. "Deterritorializations: The Rewriting of Home and Exile in Western Feminist Discourse." *The Nature and Context of Minority Discourse.* Ed. Abdul JanMohamed and David Lloyd. New York: Oxford UP, 1990. 357-68. Print.

Prakash, *After Colonialism: Imperial Histories and Postcolonial Displacements.* Princeton: Princeton UP, 1995. 241-75. Print.

Kutzinski, Vera. *Sugar's Secrets: Race and the Erotics of Cuban Nationalism.* Charlottesville: UP of Virginia, 1993. Print.

Laclau, Ernesto, and Mouffe, Chantal. *Hegemony and Socialist Strategy.* London: Verso, 1985. Print.

Larsen, Neil. Foreword. D. Emily Hicks, *Border Writing.* Minneapolis: U of Minnesota, 1991. xi-xxi. Print.

Lomnitz-Adler, Claudio. *Exits from the Labyrinth: Culture and Ideology in the Mexican National Space.* Berkeley: U of California, 1992. Print.

Mackey, Eva. "Postmodernism and Cultural Politics in a Multicultural Nation: Contests over Truth in the *Into the Heart of Africa* Controversy." *Public Culture* 7:2 (1995): 403-31. Print.

Martí, José. "Our America." *The America of José Martí.* Trans. Juan de Onís. New York:

Noonday Press, 1953. 138-52. Print.

Mignolo, Walter. "Linguistic Maps, Literary Geographies, and Cultural Landscapes: Languages, Languaging, and (Trans)nationalism." *Modern Language Quarterly* 57:2 (1996): 181-96. Print.

Miller, Nancy K. "Changing the Subject: Authorship, Writing, and the Reader." *Feminist Studies/Critical Studies.* Ed. Teresa de Lauretis. Bloomington: Indiana UP, 1986. 102-120. Print.

Mouffe, Chantal. "Radical Democracy: Modern or Postmodern?" *Universal Abandon: The Politics of Postmodernism.* Ed. Andrew Ross. Minneapolis: U of Minnesota P, 1988. 31-45. Print.

Mouffe, Chantal. "Democratic Politics and the Question of Identity." *The Identity in Question.* Ed. John Rajchmann. New York: Routledge, 1995. 33-45. Print.

Nancy, Jean-Luc. "Cut Throat Sun." *An Other Tongue.* Ed. Alfred Arteaga. Durham: Duke UP, 1994. 113-23. Print.

Pérez Firmat, Gustavo. *The Cuban Condition.* New York: Cambridge UP, 1989.

Piedra, José. "Literary Whiteness and the Afro-Hispanic Difference." *New Literary History* 18:2 (1987): 303-32. Print.

Pratt, Minnie Bruce. "Identity: Skin Blood Heart." *Yours in Struggle: Three Feminist Perspectives on Anti-Semitism and Racism.* Ed. Elly Bulkin, Minnie Bruce Pratt, and Barbar Smith. Brooklyn: Long Haul Press, 1984. 11-63. Print.

Raiskin, Judith. "Inverts and Hybrids: Lesbian Reworkings of Sexual and Racial Identities." *The Lesbian Postmodern.* Ed. Laura Doan. New York: Columbia UP, (1994). 156-72. Print.

Saldívar, José David. *The Dialectics of Our America: Genealogy, Cultural Critique, and Literary History.* Durham: Duke UP, 1991. Print.

Sandoval, Chela. "U.S. Third World Feminism: The Theory and Method of Oppositional Consciousness in the Postmodern World." *Genders* 10 (1991): 1-24. Print.

Scott, Joan W. "Multiculturalism and the Politics of Identity." *The Identity in Question.* Ed. John Rajchmann. New York: Routledge, 1995. 3-12. Print.

Sommer, Doris. *Foundational Fictions: The National Romances of Latin America.* Berkeley:

University of California Press, 1991. Print.

Spivak, Gayatri Chakravorty. "Subaltern Studies: Deconstructing Historiography." *In Other Worlds: Essays in Cultural Politics*. New York: Methuen, 1987. 197-221. Print.

Vasconcelos, José. *La Raza Cósmica/The Cosmic Race*. Trans. Didier Jaén. Los Angeles: Centro de Publicaciones, Department of Chicano Studies, California State University at Los Angeles, 1979. Print.

Yarbro-Bejarano, Yvonne. "Gloria Anzaldúa's *Borderlands/La Frontera*: Cultural Studies, 'Difference,' and the Non-Unitary Subject." *Cultural Critique* (1994): 5-28. Print.

Zavala, Iris. *Colonialism and Culture: Hispanic Modernisms and the Social Imaginary*. Bloomington: Indiana UP, 1992.

# 6

# GLORIA ANZALDÚA: BRIDGING THE ACADEMY

*RUSTY BARCELÓ*

When I think of Gloria Anzaldúa, I think of transformation. We have all been changed by her, and so have the worlds we inhabit. She gave us new ways to understand our struggle and the realities we have faced as *mujeres*, living the contradictions and ambiguities of *mestizaje*. And I, for one, will be forever indebted to her.

As a Chicana higher education administrator, I have often turned to Gloria for the courage and strength to overcome barriers I have encountered in the academy. For me, Gloria's influence goes far beyond the personal. It goes to the heart of my work as a chief diversity officer. Since my first reading of *Borderlands/ La Frontera* twenty years ago, I have gone back to it, and to every new edition, again and again. Hardly a day has passed when I haven't wanted to ask Gloria, "What would you do?"

As vice president for equity and diversity, I have fashioned from Gloria's words a vision for institutional transformation. I brought the meaning and spirit of her writings into my own life, and then into the privileged spaces of the academy, in an attempt to reconstruct those spaces according to new architectural principles, using Gloria's conceptual tools.

I realize that educational administrators aren't necessarily known for literary and scholarly sensibilities—and so I was especially honored to be invited to join this company of scholars and writers, first at the symposium and now in this volume celebrating the 20th anniversary of *La Frontera*. What I bring to this volume is not the top-down perspective of a vice president cast in the traditional institutional mold. I am an insider who is still an outsider. I bring the borderlands of my world into the academy as a prototype for change driven by diversity. I am a Chicana lesbian who sees my institutional leadership role as a builder of communities, in the Anzaldúa mode.

I remember realizing, as I thought about my remarks for the symposium more than a year ago, that we would be coming together around the time of Día de los Muertos, and as I was revisiting Gloria's work I came across a passage in *This Bridge Called Home* that has particular resonance for me:

> May the roaring force of our collective creativity
> heal the wounds of hate, ignorance, indifference
> dissolve the divisions creating chasms between us
> open our throats so we who fear speaking out raise our voices
> by our witnessing, find connections through our passions,
> pay homage to those whose backs served as bridges.
> We remember our dead:
> Pat Parker, Audre Lorde, Toni Cade Bambara, Barbara Cameron,
> *y tantas otras*. (576)

"*…y tantas otras*"—and so many others. How ironic that Gloria, who asked us to "remember our dead," crossed that final bridge to join them so soon after sharing these words with us. And so, in a "roaring force of collective creativity," we gather in this collection to raise our voices in tribute to her, honoring as well those others "whose backs served as [our] bridges." In doing this, we share the Gloria we knew: the ways her spirit runs through us, and the ways her words became written on our psyches, shaped our professional and personal lives, and transformed our scholarship, our teaching, our understandings, our relationships with each other, our work and activism, and our institutions of higher education.

Every time I revisit those powerful metaphors, *la frontera* and *la puente*, I am struck by their enduring capacity to help me make sense of the worlds we inhabit as Latinas, both within and beyond the academy. And I find myself thinking in new ways about those shifting and ambiguous spaces that Gloria described as "physically present wherever two or more cultures edge each other, where people of different races occupy the same territory, where under, lower, middle and upper classes touch, where the space between two individuals shrinks with intimacy" (*Borderlands/La Frontera*, 19).

Those of us who dwell in these borderlands and inhabit racialized and gendered spaces in every part of our lives have developed an uncommon capacity to "read" the converging cultures and to negotiate the borders between them. That capacity is especially important in the academy, which for so long kept us on the margins and where for so long we "chafed" against what Gloria called the "thin edge of barbwire" between cultures (3). With Gloria leading us, we've learned how to step over that edge and bridge the divide—to move in and out of the margins with a certain agility without abdicating the spirit of resistance that fuels our movement. This is how we've survived—not by capitulating or surrendering but by learning to straddle the fences.

In *La Frontera*, Gloria wrote about the "new *mestiza*" in a way that speaks to all of us who have made it our life's work to navigate the sometimes forbidding terrain of the academic borderlands. We begin, she says, locked in a "counterstance"—"stand[ing] on the opposite river bank, shouting questions, challenging patriarchal, white conventions." But we've learned that we also need to move beyond that reactive, oppositional stance, or we become, in a way, complicit with and determined by those who seek to dominate us. We become immobilized by our sense of injury and injustice. As Gloria says,

> A counterstance locks one into a duel of oppressor and oppressed; locked in mortal combat...both are reduced to a common denominator of violence. [This is] a step towards liberation from cultural domination. But it's not a way of life. At some point, on our way to a new consciousness, we will have to leave the opposite bank, the split between the two mortal combatants healed so that we are on both shores at once and, at once, we see through serpent and eagle eyes. (100)

As an educational administrator, I find that this is perhaps my greatest challenge: to see and to act from different vantage points, to balance my formal institutional role with my role as an advocate. If I want to be heard and be effective, I can't just be confrontational. I need to mediate my personal and institutional identities, my "insiderness" and "outsiderness." And like the new *mestiza*, I must develop "a tolerance for contradictions, a tolerance for ambiguity":

> [The new *mestiza*] learns to be an Indian in Mexican culture, to be Mexican from an Anglo point of view. She learns to juggle cultures. She...operates in a pluralistic mode—nothing is thrust out, the good the bad and the ugly, nothing rejected, nothing abandoned. Not only does she sustain contradictions, she turns the ambivalence into something else. (101)

As academicians and Latinas, we all carry those contradictions within ourselves. That "something else"—that vital "new consciousness," that new third way of being and knowing, of straddling and mediating worlds, is uniquely ours, and we bring it to the academy as a creative and transformative force. Indeed, it underpins a guiding principle of my work: Institutional transformation begins at the most personal level. First we claim and affirm our identities, and then we form vital alliances around those identities to create change. We bring our new consciousness to the academy, and transfuse that consciousness into the institutional culture.

Chicanas/Latinas have always experienced in a very personal way the edging of majority and minority cultures. We have been pierced and wounded by the "thin edge of barbwire." We have experienced the occupation of territory, the oppressions of mind, spirit, and body. But we also know that a borderland is a dynamic site of engagement, learning, and growth for all of us across divides of race, ethnicity, class, gender, sexuality, and disability. It's a place of transformation, "where the Third World grates against the first and bleeds. And before a scab forms it hemorrhages again, the lifeblood of two worlds merging to form a third country—a border culture" (23). That border culture is a prototype for the modern university we are working to create—a place where disparate ideas, cultures and identities, and knowledge systems collide and are reborn.

Gloria understood that borderlands are dangerous and often wounding places to be. It's no accident that bleeding and blood appear so often as metaphors in her work, especially her early work. But the blood here is "lifeblood." It's the blood of birth. Change is born in struggle. It hurts. But it's also necessary. We *must* engage in the difficult, searching, sometimes painful conversations at the edges and intersections of our identities if we want to go somewhere new. As Latinas and as academicians, we've always had those conversations. But it's Gloria who gave us the language to fully express and resolve our feelings of dislocation, the contradictions and disjunctions of our lives in the unsettled terrain of the borderlands.

Working in the academy, in such close proximity to the dominant academic and administrative culture, we Latinas have internalized that culture so that it coexists with other parts of ourselves, so that we have become both part of, and not part of, that culture. As Gloria said in a 1996 interview,

> Now there's no such thing as the "other." I can't disown the white tradition, the Euro-American tradition, any more than I can the Mexican, the Latino, or the Native, because they're all in me.... We are mutually complicitous: us and them, white and colored, straight and queer, Christian and Jew, self and other, oppressor and oppressed.... (*Interviews/Entrevistas*, 254)

This proximity makes it all the more difficult to resist the powerful institutional pressures to assimilate into the dominant culture—to check pieces of ourselves at the door as if they were mere accessories, or shoes caked with mud, or even weapons. That pressure has, at times, pushed many of us into a proud and defiant counterstance. But we know that we cannot stay there for long, or we become further marginalized. The "new consciousness" enables us to move out of that counterstance and cross the threshold without yielding to pressure to assimilate. We channel our resistance into efforts to create fundamental institutional change by *owning* our multiple identities and by affirming and embracing differences—a concept that is central to my work.

In the 1980s, it was Gloria's concept of the new *mestiza* that allowed her to break through the gendered and racialized dualities imposed on her and construct a coherent and powerful Chicana lesbian feminist consciousness:

> I am visible—see this Indian face—yet I am invisible. I both blind them with my beak nose and am their blind spot. But I exist, we exist. They'd like to think I have melted in the pot. But I haven't. We haven't. (*La Frontera*, 108)

We were there with her, migrating between the constantly shifting sides of ourselves, shouting across that river. But it was in that cry of self-affirmation—"I exist, we exist"—where the movement began. The bridges were already under construction.

Back then, caught between a white culture that shunned and devalued us and the Mexican culture that was our ancestral home but also a site of oppression, many Chicanas joined Gloria in a kind of counterstance: "If going home is denied me then I will have to stand and claim my space, making a new culture—*una cultura mestiza*—with my own lumber, my own brick and mortar and my own feminist architecture" (44), Gloria said. With her, we searched for "a homeground, where [the dark-skinned woman] can plumb the rich ancestral roots into her own ample *mestiza* heart" (45). And we certainly didn't find that homeground in the academy. We found it only within ourselves. And we were isolated and marginalized.

But as we continued to revisit the "extremes of our cultural realities," we forged from our "cultural sensitivities to differences" a "hybrid consciousness" that would help all of us "navigate the switchback roads between assimilation/ acquiescence to the dominant culture and isolation/preservation of our ethnic cultural integrity" (*Interviews/Entrevistas*, 254). We would come to occupy a new reality that was rooted in the homeground but grew and branched into multiple communities.

Even as recently as 1996, such thinking was considered pretty radical in its resistance to the overwhelming forces of cultural dominance and assimilation. In the academy of that time, diversity was studied by scholars and reflected in the curriculum, and it was named as a priority in institutional planning documents, but it had yet to become a core value. The work of advancing student, faculty, and staff diversity was still often done on the institutional margins; "diversity" was understood by administrators mostly in quantitative terms; and many still believed that excellence and diversity were at odds.

For those of us who knew better, who understood diversity as intrinsic to institutional excellence, and who sought comprehensive climate change on our campuses, the concept of "hybrid consciousness" offered a powerful new paradigm for a holistic and integrative approach to diversity at a critical time in the academy.

Today, it is in the emerging multicultural spaces of the 21st century academy that my colleagues and I do our institutional work around equity and diversity, bridging the contradictions by affirming and embracing them. Of course, the cracks remain, and the barriers persist. One of the chief sources of resistance to this work is the belief that diversity is a problem to be solved, and that the solution to that problem is to focus on the sameness among cultures. But Gloria's work has taken us on a different path, toward the recognition that while uniting around our commonalities may seem sensible and practical, the more important work of diversity is to find understanding and connection across our differences.

Assimilation not only erases who we are, it erases what we contribute—our knowledge and understandings, our ways of knowing. It undermines the very idea of the university as a diverse intellectual and cultural ecosystem, as a place where diversity *drives* discovery.

Diverse cultural perspectives have long worked their magic in the academy, but their transformative role was mostly unrecognized until fairly recently. Until the past few decades, diversity meant recognizing differences only within a "context of commonality" (*This Bridge Called Home*, 2). The only differences that were valued were theoretical and disciplinary variations on Eurocentric perspectives. What we needed was a framework that would bring a broader understanding of diversity to the institutional center as a core value that would be recognized as intrinsic to the academic enterprise.

*La Frontera* gave us some of the tools for building that framework. But we needed to become institutional insiders in order to create real change, even while we resisted assimilationist pressures that sought to make us invisible. Wielding Gloria's conceptual tools, we were able to work on the inside without losing our edge of resistance and activism. We could begin transforming the Eurocentric model of the academy into one that is vibrant, multicultural, multiethnic—one that supports and models the hybrid consciousness that is so essential to our work of advancing equity and diversity.

As leaders in higher education, we women of color have come to realize that if we are to transform our institutions, we must become bridges within our institutions and across higher education and our communities. And as I have said, we begin in the most personal of places, inside ourselves:

> The struggle is inner: Chicano, indio, American Indian, mojado, mexicano, immigrant Latino, Anglo in power, working class Anglo, Black, Asian—our psyches resemble the bordertowns and are populated by the same people. The struggle has always been inner, and is played out in the outer terrains... Nothing happens in the real world unless it first happens in the images in our heads. (*La Frontera*, 109)

What connects those worlds within us, and also connects our inner and outer worlds, is *el puente*. The full richness of that concept in my own life was dramatically revealed to me in 1991, when I gave the official welcome at the University of Iowa's Annual Gay Pride Rally. Although I was an out Chicana lesbian in my daily life, that June day marked my first public statement as an assistant dean about my multiple identities. The "outing" was covered on the front pages of Iowa newspapers and in television newscasts, even in the *Chronicle of Higher Education*.

I had taken a pretty big risk. But it was a defining moment. Speaking publicly about the identities that constituted my *whole self* not only made me more whole, but also advanced my understanding of diversity within a multicultural framework as something richer, more complex, and more holistic than race *or* gender *or* sexual orientation *or* something else. And in declaring my multiple identities, I became a bridge to multiple communities. Ultimately, I became a more effective leader. By changing the image in my head, I was able to create change in the "real world." Indeed, not long afterward, I began working with Iowa's GLBT faculty and staff in their successful campaign for domestic partner benefits.

Today, I continue to draw upon the richness of my multiple identities and my "hybrid consciousness" to inform the work that I so often describe as bridging communities. And that consciousness has enabled me to work with people across the University of Minnesota system to develop and implement a vision framework for *reimagining* equity and diversity. And yet even as a member of the executive leadership team, I cannot and will not claim full insider status. As a Chicana lesbian, I inhabit the institutional borderlands even as I do my work from the center. And the bridges are still under construction.

I believe that we all must share in the work of constructing those bridges. We must all take personal and institutional responsibility for advancing equity and diversity in the academy. And we must begin by recognizing all parts of the self as interconnected. As Gloria said,

> The lesbian is part of the writer, is part of class, gender, is part of whatever identity you have of yourself and I have of myself. There's no way we can put ourselves through this sieve and say "Okay, we're only going to

> let the lesbian part out, and everything else will stay in the sieve." The sieve and all the different identities we're supposed to sift are part of the lesbian. (*Interviews/Entrevistas*, 130)

As my colleagues and I have done this work over the years, our understanding of diversity has become both more complex and more "pliant," to use Gloria's word. We have moved "beyond separate and easy identifications, creating bridges that cross race and other classifications among different groups via intergenerational dialogue" (*This Bridge We Call Home*, 2). Indeed, our whole vantage point has shifted. As Gloria described this evolution of understanding,

> Twenty-one years ago we struggled with the recognition of commonality within the context of commonality. Today we grapple with the recognition of commonality within the context of difference... This book intends to change notions of identity, viewing it as part of a more complex system covering a larger terrain, and demonstrating that the politics of exclusion based on traditional categories diminishes our humanness. (2)

As our definitions have become more elastic, we have broadened our circles of inclusion and begun dissolving boundaries not only between disciplines but also between and among identity groups, so that our work embraces multiple identities, hyphenated identities, all of the complex realities of people's lives as cultural beings in that "in-between space, [the] unstable, unpredictable, precarious, always-in-transition space lacking clear boundaries" (*This Bridge Called Home*, 1). We are breaking the "stalemate" between women of color and other historically marginalized groups by "gathering people from many geographies in a multicultural approach." This, said Gloria, "is a mark of inclusivity, increased consciousness, and dialogue... [reflecting] the hybrid quality of our lives and identities—*todos somos nos/otras*" (3). And it reflects the transformed academy that we are struggling to build.

In *This Bridge Called Home*, Gloria affirmed what has become a central principle of my work: We advance diversity not by segregating ourselves, on the one hand, or "glossing over" our differences, on the other. It is in living and giving voice to our differences, and also bridging those differences, that we form truly inclusive multicultural communities. "Though most people self-define by what they exclude," she says, "we define who we are by what we include—what I call the new tribalism" (3).

Some women of color may still yearn for the separatist world of *This Bridge Called My Back*, viewing it as "a safe space, as 'home.'" But in her later work, Gloria insisted, "There are no safe spaces." In fact, she issued a challenge to us all:

> Staying "home" and not venturing out from our own group...stagnates our growth. To bridge means loosening our borders...opening the gate to the stranger, within and without.... To bridge is to attempt community, and for that we must risk being open to personal, political, and spiritual intimacy, to risk being wounded. Effective bridging comes from knowing when to close ranks to those outside our home, group, community, nation—and when to keep the gates open. (3)

Gloria lived long enough to witness the growing climate of fear and the closing of ranks following September 11, 2001. But even as the fences went up, she saw possibilities for "transformation." "Ultimately," she said,

> It's about doing away with demarcations like "ours" and "theirs." It's about honoring people's otherness rather than punishing others for having a different view, belief system, skin color, or spiritual practice. Diversity of perspectives expands and alters the dialogue, not in an add-on fashion but through a multiplicity that's transformational. (*This Bridge Called Home*, 4)

Our struggle continues in the borderlands of higher education. And even though Gloria is no longer with us as a physical presence, her spirit remains—the fierce, passionate new *mestiza*, the brave pioneer who explored and defined *la frontera*, the visionary architect of *la puente*, the poet and scholar whose hybrid consciousness gave us all a new conceptual home. We know that the world is made better by our fully realized differences, and it is precisely at the flash points of intersecting differences that there is potential for transformation through multiplicity.

As a higher education administrator, I have brought Gloria's vision into a place once closed to us, the privileged sphere of higher education administration. I think she would approve, as she watches us shepherd our institutions across *los puentes*, beyond access, beyond boundaries, beyond restrictive definitions, beyond traditional structures and conceptual frameworks to create new ways of being, acting, teaching, learning, and knowing. We transform the academy in her name.

*Special thanks to Eugenia Smith, who collaborated in the editing and research for this piece, and helped me take my thinking further. Together, we have come to know Gloria even better.*

**Works Cited**

Anzaldúa, Gloria. *Borderlands/La Frontera: The New Mestiza*. San Francisco: Spinsters/Aunt Lute, 1987. Print.

Anzaldúa, Gloria, and AnaLouise Keating, Eds. *This Bridge We Call Home: Radical Visions for Transformation*. New York: Routledge, 2002. Print.

Anzaldúa, Gloria E.. *Interviews/Entrevistas*. Ed. AnaLouise Keating. New York: Routledge, 2000. Print.

Moraga, Cherríe, and Gloria Anzaldúa, Eds. *This Bridge Called My Back: Writings by Radical Women of Color*. New York: Kitchen Table/Women of Color Press, 1981. Print.

# PART 3

## ANZALDÚA AND INTERNATIONAL PERSPECTIVES

# 7

# TRANSNATIONAL BORDERLANDS: GLORIA ANZALDÚA'S EPISTEMOLOGIES OF RESISTANCE AND LESBIANS "OF COLOR" IN PARIS

*PAOLA BACCHETTA*

## SITUATIONS, POSITIONINGS, INTER-RELATIONALITIES

I would like to begin by multiply, albeit briefly, situating my comments. I will first put forth a few words about my relation to the subjects, theories and practices I discuss here. Next, I will locate Gloria Anzaldúa's work in relation to France and to a range of feminist and lesbian subjects "of color,"[1] before moving on to engage with her epistemologies of transnational resistance.

First, briefly, about my own location here. I am lesbian of mixed background out of three continents. Beginning in 1979, I lived in Paris for fifteen solid years, first as an undocumented subject, later as a documented student, still later as an academic, before moving to the U.S. Since then I have returned to Paris very regularly, sometimes for months at a time, sometimes for shorter periods, often several times a year. I have been deeply engaged in feminist, lesbian, pro-immigration, and anti-racism movements for a long time. Currently I work with two groups: one is an autonomous pluralist lesbian "of color" group; the other an alliance of lesbians "of color" and Franco-French lesbians. I hope to speak "near and with" the groups in which I do and do not participate (Trinh 1989). Specifically, I do not claim to speak for, or even fully about, the groups. They are extremely heterogeneous, comprised of many different voices, and open to many possible types of interpretation. They cannot be summarized by any one person, any part of the collectivity, or any one axis of analysis. Moreover, we have not held any elections; I cannot and do not wish to represent anyone else. This said, my way of thinking about the world, including about Gloria Anzaldúa's work, is deeply indebted to conversations and collective work with lesbians "of color" in Paris over many years.

Second: Gloria Anzaldúa and/in France. Outside of a small circle of feminists and lesbians "of color," her work is practically unknown in France. The two main obstacles for its dissemination and availability are language and power. There is not one French translation of her work in existence. In fact, beyond Gloria Anzaldúa's work, to date no Chicana feminist or Chicana lesbian work at all has ever been published in translation in French. Gloria Anzaldúa's writing is also not easily accessible in English in France. There are very few feminists and lesbians "of color" in the academy in France, thus the university avenue of access to articles or books in English is quite blocked for feminists and lesbians "of color." I did not become aware of Gloria Anzaldúa's work through French publishing circuits, universities or bookstores. I was introduced to her writings in 1989 only thanks to a U.S. friend who gave me a copy of *Borderlands/La Frontera*, two years after its publication. Since then I've been reading her work, and sharing it with others around me. Obviously this mode of diffusion is extremely limited. But, in March 2008 I began, with a colleague, to do the first translations of Gloria Anzaldúa's work for publication in France.

Beyond the language issue, there is, of course, the deeper, wider question of historical, contextual power. In France we are faced with a specific formation of a dominant grid of intelligibility that operates as a filter to determine which conditions, subjects, theories and practices do and do not count as viable. In France, a sizable mainstream publication circuit has been constructed for French feminist theories that presume the exclusive existence of what Norma

Alarcón (1990) has critically identified as the "unitary subject" of feminism (the category of feminist subject defined in white, middle class feminist terms) and what we can term by analogy the "unitary subject" of queer. In contrast, there is no established publication route in France for writing by French lesbians "of color" that would severely complicate dominant notions of feminism, lesbian and queer, of the subject, of theory, of practices, of power and of France itself.

To date the only such publication is a self-published pamphlet, with no formal diffusion outlet, produced by one collective, the *Groupe du 6 Novembre: lesbiennes issues de l'esclavage, le colonialisme, et la migration* (6 November Group: Lesbians Begotten Of/Out Of Slavery, Colonialism and Immigration).[2] It contains group and individual analytical essays, poetry, and art. This pamphlet is of monumental importance for lesbians "of color" in France, for it is a means of communicating directly with each other without the mediation of voices that distort and filter. As one group writing in the *Groupe du 6 Novembre*'s pamphlet states about the reception of lesbian "of color" analytics in "white" feminist and queer milieux: "Our words (parole)" are "considered an immense brouhaha, the cry of savages, incoherent and inconsistent screams" (Bêtes Noires 26). They are "perceived as stammerings of fragmented words that as soon as constructed are already deconstructed" (Bêtes Noires 26). Yet, "Our words are reflections about and on our multiple oppressions. They are analysis, anger, tools for a situation…" (Bêtes Noires 26).

Over the past 30 years, even as French feminist and queer "of color" critical theorizing continues to be under erasure in France, whole books of "unitary" feminist and "unitary" queer theories from the U.S. have been translated and diffused in French feminist, university and mainstream publishing circuits. Some of these works have contained insights that are extremely useful, including for feminists and lesbians "of color." However, as N. Doumia points out in the *Groupe du 6 Novembre*'s pamphlet, the now intense international traffic in feminist and queer theories that do *not* engage with intersections, has enabled large-scale alliances among "race"-racism,[3] slavery and post-slavery, and colonialism and postcoloniality amnesiac feminists and queers across national borders (5). In France, an effect of this situation has been to further reinforce the erasure of contextually specific (to France) theories and practices in which gender, sexualities, "race"-racism, class, slavery and post-slavery, and colonialism and postcoloniality are inseparable. Gloria Anzaldúa identifies a similar mechanism in the U.S. where white queers "occupy theorizing space, and though their theories aim to enable and emancipate, they often disempower and neo-colonize.... They theorize, that is, perceive, organize, classify, and name specific chunks of reality by using approaches, styles and methodologies that are Anglo-American or European. Their theories limit the ways we think about being queer" (265).

In the past year, a shift seemed to occur when a French feminist publisher produced an anthology of writings by some selected U.S. Black feminist academics entitled (in the singular) *Black feminism: Anthologie du féminisme africain-américain, 1975-2000* (*Black Feminism: Anthology of African-American Feminism, 1975-2000*). The very idea of such a volume in French was a welcome change for feminists and lesbians "of color" in France. Yet, many pointed out a number of the texts selected for the anthology are directly addressed to white (U.S.) feminists (such as Hazel Carby's "White Woman Listen!"), while several others engage centrally with relations between white and black feminists. The anthology seemed to set up white French feminists as a primary audience and to inscribe Black feminisms in an exclusive black/white binary.

The publicity (in poster, print and electronic form) and the back cover of *Black feminism* announce: "Why, in France, an ex-colonial power, hasn't the equivalent of this black feminism existed? These texts, thanks to their vitality and political shrewdness, invite us to ask this question and to interrogate ourselves differently about republican universalism and the blind spots of French feminism." Many of us were pleased to observe in these sentences the call (to "ourselves" presumably meaning white French feminists) to interrogate the particularist notion of French universalist republicanism and the "blind spots" of ("white") French Feminism. It was exciting to see that the analyses of Black feminists (from anywhere) were actually considered in France to be what they are: important theoretical works. We noted that the publicity made a connection between France and colonialism, even as we wondered why there was no mention of French practices of slavery.

By placing the title in English (*Black feminism*) did the editors hope to mark its difference, the foreign origin of the texts, in the French context? But above all there was one claim in the book's publicity that was particularly astonishing: that there have been no French Black (not to mention Arab, Asian, Latina, and mixed) feminist and lesbian theories and practices in France. This invisibilization of historical and current feminist and lesbian "of color" theories and practices seemed to reinforce the very "blind spots" from which both universalist republicanism and (white) French feminism have long been interrogated. Gloria Anzaldúa described a similar procedure in the U.S. in *Borderlands/La Frontera* when she wrote:

> It is okay to listen to a black man like Homi Bhabha from Britain—import him to the United States and listen to his thoughts about post-coloniality—rather than take somebody from California who is a Chicano/a and who has experienced some other things. If you are very exotic, like being from Australia, Africa, India, et cetera, this legitimates you more than being an internal exile. We still don't receive much attention and often aren't listened to at all. (243-44)

At the same time, the book *Black feminism* is having a variety of constructive effects in France, some of them perhaps unpredictable. It has inspired some "white" French feminists and queers to think seriously about issues of racism. But moreover the book is being read against the grain of its potential for "racial fragmentation" by Black French feminists and lesbians and other subjects "of color" who are finding useful analytics, inspiration, energies, and possibilities for transnational alliances in its pages (Alexander and Mohanty 1997). I am reminded of what Gloria Anzaldúa wrote in *Making Face/Making Soul*: "if we have been gagged and disempowered by theories, we can also be loosened and empowered by theories" (xxvi).

## READING GLORIA ANZALDÚA, RETHINKING RESISTANCE, IN FRANCE

To be "loosened and empowered by theories." This brings me to the question of how exactly to read Gloria Anzaldúa's theories productively, ethically, in France, across the differences between the U.S. and French contexts. I have been deeply inspired by her work as have many others. But how do we avoid the dangers of pulling her work into a French contextual grid of intelligibility, including into the "blind spots" some of us inhabit, which are, for all their various gradations of subalterneity, very distant from the site of Gloria Anzaldúa's textual production? How do we respect Gloria Anzaldúa's specificities while finding in her work a plethora of ideas, perspectives, modes of analysis, and concepts that are useful in France? How can we read Gloria Anzaldúa where she is, even as she is multiply located? We will necessarily read her from our elsewhere, even if we are also multiply located. These are not only questions about translation (in a sense wider than linguistic). They are questions about building constructive, inspiring inter-subjectivities together. I think they demand some intense reflection and will not be resolved easily.

In the meantime, Gloria Anzaldúa herself provides many insights on how to receive her writing. It will be good to meditate on her thoughts. She states that she prefers that her work be read as a whole, not quoted out of context. She tells us we all need to form our own categories and points of reference. She says she wants her work to be useful across all kinds of contexts. With this in mind, I will point to one area of conversation between Gloria Anzaldúa's work and the work of lesbians "of color" in France: epistemologies of transnational resistance.

Resistance is, of course, a very wide concept encompassing a myriad of relations within and to formations of power. In the U.S., the term resistance lost much of its productive capacity as it became associated in dominant liberal scholarship with humanist notions of a free liberal subject as agent-with-choice. In France, resistance is not always already connected to such associations. It is deployed across a range of scholarship, including poststructuralist. In my own work on France, I have thought about psychic, transgressive, oppositional, interruptive, and non-oppositional resistances. But here I will concern myself only with transnational psychic resistance.

Psychic resistance is a central pre-occupation for nearly every lesbian "of color" group I have ever been in or engaged with in France. Like other subjects, lesbians "of color" are caught up in the powers that are part of our formation. To imagine effective resistance it is necessary to decolonize one's self. But even that is something we might also resist. Relatedly, Pile points out that for the francophone theorist Franz Fanon "resistance" has two main meanings: psychic resistance in the sense of Freud and resistance in the sociological sense of acts against power (24). In order to arrive at (sociological) resistance, Fanon proposed that the colonized would first have to overcome (psychic) resistance to resisting (2001 [1959]). That is, for Fanon and for Pile, the colonized would have to conquer themselves (psychically) if they wished to liberate themselves. To decolonize, the colonized must identify and neutralize the colonizer's fantasies that participate, and get internalized, in the very formation of the colonized as subject. This form of resistance can be thought of as transnational. For, the dominant grid of intelligibility, the official history that makes sense within it, the colonial practices that are officially legitimized within it, are all produced, variously, through transnational relations of power in which gender, sexuality, "race"-racism, slavery and post-slavery, colonialism and post-coloniality, and immigration operate inseparably. But also, the resisting subjects in question and all their modalities of resistance too, are formed in and through, even if against, this same transnational context.

Now let us move back closer to Gloria Anzaldúa, and listen to her insightful engagement with psychic resistance. In *Interviews/Entrevistas* she opens up the question to a multi-register and multi-scale interrogation. Among many other things, she states: "Decolonizing oneself [...] is both personal and political, inner and outer" (Anzaldúa 200). She explains that, for her, decolonization is linked to *conocimientos*, which she defines as "an overarching theory of consciousness, of how the mind works. It's an epistemology that tries to encompass all dimensions of life" (177). To engage with *conocimientos* implies a range of questions, such as: "How do we know? How do we perceive? How do we make meaning? Who produces knowledge and who is kept from producing it? Who distributes it and who passes it on? Who has access to it and who doesn't? Is there such a thing as counter-knowledge, and if so, who constructs it and how?" (178). And further, she tells us:

> I use the idea of outlawed knowledge to encourage Chicanas and other women and people of color to produce our own forms, to originate our own theories of how the world works. I think those who produce our own *conocimientos* have to shift the frame of reference, reframe the issue or situation being looked at, connect the disparate parts of information in new ways or from a perspective that's new. (*Interviews/Entrevistas*, 178)

Gloria Anzaldúa's insights about decolonization, *conocimientos* and the creation of "outlawed knowledge" can be placed into conversation with processes of transnational psychic resistance that groups of feminists "of color" and lesbians "of color" have enabled and enacted in France (*Interviews/Entrevistas*, 178). Here I will address only some of the inter-related fragments: the construction of a critical relationship to official historiography, the re-conceptualization of genealogies of the present that are relevant to feminist and lesbian "of color" subjects-in-process, and the politics of auto-designation or self-naming.

## COGNITIVE DECOLONIZATION, CONOCIMIENTOS, OUTLAWED KNOWLEDGES, AND AUTO-DESIGNATIONS

Gloria Anzaldúa begins *Borderlands/La Frontera* by re-writing her own histories, on her own terms, and *in* her own terms, with *el otro méxico*, the *Aztecas del norte* and the border as points of departure. In doing so she appropriates for herself the right to create her own vision of the context of her life. She draws some components of her historical narrative from official historiography, but unravels them, re-interprets them, re-signifies them, re-arranges them. She makes present some historical elements that are absent from official historiographies. As she proceeds, page after page, she pauses here and there to demarcate, take apart, and re-define concepts that have otherwise crystallized into common sense notions (such as "border" itself, see *Interviews/Entrevistas*, 25-26). She shifts between her personal histories and the larger histories of her peoples (which she defines in the plural). Her re-conceptualizations cannot be contained in any one genre. She inscribes them multiply, weaves them together: paragraphs publishable in academic journals, personal narratives, poetry, fiction, dream sequences. Together they make for some intense theorizing.

In France, too, feminists and lesbians "of color" have carried out multi-faceted deconstructive and constructive labor for quite some time, and have produced in each phase of its unfolding new subjects who speak together, hear each other, enact together, and inscribe their analytics in a variety of genres. The forms of subject-production have been deeply contextual, and they are marked by attempts at self-naming.

## NATIONAL ATTACHMENTS AND THE POLITICS IN/OF NAMING

Over the past 35 years many postcolonial, post-slavery, immigrant feminist (and lesbian) groups in France have self-identified and dis-identified in relation to cultural-national and regional belonging. These forms of attachment are signaled in the names of some early groups, such as *Groupe femmes Algeriennes* (Algerian Women's Group), *Mouvement des femmes Noires* (Black Women's Movement), *Groupe femmes Tunisiennes* (Tunisian Women's group), among others. These groups, and the subjects who comprised them, the first generation of women immigrants in France, were often deeply connected both personally to their families and politically to social movements in their countries of origin. Such attachments were not the effect of free-floating choices; rather they were deeply situational. Many of the founders and members of these groups were highly politicized subjects who had directly participated in the national liberation struggles that ended French colonialism in their home countries. In France, they were faced with the continuation of France's colonial divide and rule policy by other means. In the postcolonial period this policy was manifested in the form of bi-lateral treaties regulating immigration with France's individual post-colonies. In that context, national-centric groups were in fact a most efficient means of participating in the fate of one's postcolonial nation, but also of organizing for immigration rights in France.

## (DOUBLED) NATIONAL DETACHMENTS AND "RACE"-RACISM IN FRANCE

By the 1980s the situation had shifted greatly. A second generation of subjects of immigrant origin, who were born and raised exclusively in France, came of age. The gap between the context of their formation, the exigencies of French universalist republicanism, French dominant hailings to assimilate, and the impossibility, given their particular positionalities, of assimilating, worked to deeply politicize this generation. This process was also provoked by a rise in anti-immigrant violence and its coverage by the French press, conditions of poverty, and youth unemployment. By the early 1980s, second generation youth had formed a number of groups in the *banlieues* (urban slums), the sites of their greatest concentration, to demand both material equality (better schools, freedom from civil and police racist violence, employment) and the recognition of difference as a means to halt the imperative to become a blank slate for assimilation. Though this is not the place to provide a full account of the 1980s, I want to mention that the second generation created a massive social movement that deeply affected French society and politics for generations to come. It also produced some lasting contributions to (pluralist) French cultures, mainly in literature and music.

During those momentous times, the subjects of the second generation invented auto-designations that signaled a certain detachment from the national-normativities of their parents' countries of origin and from dominant France itself, a process that Rosello (1993) has called *double départenance* (a double detachment from forced belonging), and they did so even as they remembered ethnicities, racializations and cultural difference. These auto-designations include such terms as *Beur* and then *Rebeu,* both of which signify "Arab" in *verlan,* a language developed in the *banlieues. Beur* and *Rebeu* do several kinds of political work at once. They signal the second generation subjects' recognition of their parents not via national attachments (such as to Algeria, Tunisia, etc.) but rather via a common ethnicity and culture (Arab). They establish an inter-generational relation of continuity (in the reiteration of the referent Arab) but also of difference (in the variants *Beur* and *Rebeu*). Similarly, in the 1980s the term *Black* (in English) was self-adopted in the *banlieues* to signify a shift from the dominant terms deployed against, but also by and for, earlier generations in France: *Noir* (Black) and *Africain* (African). The reiteration of *Black* (in English) did a range of political work, too. It attached the pride in Blackness associated with Black power movements in the U.S. to *Black* youth in France. And it de-isolated *Black* youth in France by positioning them as transnational subjects who belong to a wide and vibrant diaspora.

As these creative auto-designation processes were in full bloom, some younger lesbians "of color," mainly in Paris, proposed to self-identify as *lesbiennes ciblées par le racisme* (Lesbians Targeted by Racism). The creation of this term was primarily a move to focus directly on conditions of racism that all lesbians "of color," albeit variably, are faced within France. At the same time, perhaps inadvertently, the term de-emphasized nations of origin, French national normativity, and the new categories of "race," ethnicity and culture that were operative at the time (*Black*, *Beur*, *Rebeu*, etc.).

The term "Lesbians Targeted by Racism" might best be understood in relation to the historical particularities of wider analytics of "race"-racism in France. It emerged through discussion, including in the context of the *collectif féministe contre le racisme et l'anti-sémitisme* (Feminist Collective against Racism and Anti-Semitism) at the *Maison des femmes de Paris* (Paris Women's Center), at a time when several of us were immersed in reading histories of productions of "race" categories and of racist practices in Fance. I remember a specific desire to resist the bio-chromatic criteria on which eighteenth and nineteenth century scientific racist categorizations were based. (In contrast, also for reasons of context, the bio-chromatic referents surface, albeit re-signified, deeply oppositionally, in the U.S. term "of color" and in the analogous overall British term "Black").

In France, the work of Franz Fanon for some, and the publicity allotted to the post-World War II UNESCO scholarly deconstruction of eighteenth and nineteenth century scientific "race" theories for others, produced a kind of general social aversion to discussions of "race." Fanon had remarked early on that France's colonial universalist assimilationist project required a shift from essentialist bio-chromatic referents to cultural ones if the colonized were to be seen as incorporable into the body of the French nation. The civilizing mission, indeed, depended upon a notion that the natives could in fact eventually be civilized. When the UNESCO scholars exposed "race" categories as fictions, this seemed to confirm French notions of the universal human, and progress towards civilization. Later, Collette Guillaumin (1972) would refer to the form of racism that drew on cultural instead of bio-chromatic criteria as "civilizational" racism; today, Etienne Balibar (1991) calls it "neo-racism." Importantly, Fanon had maintained that, throughout this shift, the bio-chromatic referents did not disappear but rather left their trace in sedimented forms in "cultural racism."

In this context, the term "Lesbians Targeted by Racism" was to emphasize the *political* effects of "race" (as fictive categories) and of (materialized) practices of racism, that is, violence and potential violence against subalternly racialized lesbian bodies.

## REMEMBERING GENEALOGIES AND/IN ALLIANCES

By the 1990s, many politicized lesbians "of color" in France were seeking a mode of self-identification that would retain the notion of the politics of racism but also work to remember genealogies in slavery, colonialism and immigration. Thus a new term was configured: *lesbiennes issues de l'esclavage, le colonialisme et l' immigration* (Lesbians Begotten Of/Out of Slavery, Colonialism, and Immigration). It is rather clumsy in both French and English. Yet it does several kinds of important political work.

The phrase "Lesbians Begotten Of/Out of Slavery, Colonialism, and Immigration" is of course the subtitle of the *Groupe du 6 novembre*'s name. Together these words are signs of deep critical labor. The *Groupe*'s members are from Maghrebian, Sub-Saharan African, Afro-Carribean, Latin American and mixed racialized backgrounds. The very fact of their unity moves against French State divide and rule strategies. It directly confronts the French State's desire to forget its past, notably by naming slavery and colonialism. At the time that this term was configured the State refused to officially recognize France's role in slavery and it still imagined colonialism as a civilizing mission, a view that crystallized later in the 2005 Law stipulating that instruction on French colonialism in educational institutions place French colonizers and their allies in a positive light. The auto-designation Lesbians Begotten Of/Out of Slavery, Colonialism, and Immigration also counters invisibilizations of lesbians "of color" in imaginings of slavery (where enslaved women are individualized as the heterosexual property of masters) and of colonialism (where colonized women are fantasized as non-agents under colonized male control, or as hypersexed subjects desiring colonized men). It also pushes against the grain of French universalist assimilationism, insofar as the *Groupe*'s subjects resist interpellation as proper blank slates into Franco-French culture.

Indeed, as Nedjmam (2002), a *Groupe* co-founder and member remarks:

> How could we forget or deny the past histories of our communities since the effects are totally present? Hi/Herstories of deported, displaced, dispossessed people. Past and still very present hi/herstories of colonization. All these hi/herstories in which territories are at stake. These hi/herstories with which we have to re-compose our own herstory.

Nedjmam's poem both attaches and frees for its readers an analytic of the affective-political links across divergent yet related pasts and presents that resonate with the naming of slavery, colonialism and immigration in the *Groupe*'s self-designation. The "we have to re-compose our herstory" does not naively imagine that the past will disappear. Instead, it must be worked on and through, "re-composed" to create something else. This relationship takes up some of the terms thought through in the 1980s youth "of color" movements, that is, the aspect of *double départenanc.* Yet, Nedjmam's notion of re-composing "our own herstory" evokes a future that will not negate its genealogy in the present.

In the *Groupe*'s name the notion of *issues de*, or the "out of" of "nomad" and "lesbian" invoke circuits of escape through some sites of power's incompleteness or fissure. It signals that current conditions can be unlocked, and are unlocked, through movement. This movement is not independent of territoriality, does not exist in a presumed innocent utopia. Instead, *Groupe* subjects, while recognizing the territories of their historical production, refuse to be territorialized (as abstract space), fixed in the position of the properly postcolonial nationalized woman: as mother, wife, symbol of postcolonial culture and nation. And they refuse to embody the properly colonized/enslaved woman: object of the colonizer-master's desire, object of the colonizer-master's progress and savior narratives, object whom the colonizer-master imagines desires him. The notion of being of and with "territories" and the notion of "nomad" together depict the dynamics of what may be required of each subject to produce a liveable present and future.

This "out of" in relation to territories resists the essentialization of sites of slavery and coloniality and the fixing of subjectivities interpellated in and with them. It might also mark a moment of what Anzaldúa refers to as "homophobia" (as home-phobia) in the sense of "fear of going home" (*Borderlands*: 41-42). The *Groupe* posits multiple post-colonized sites as homes, as motherlands, which are always absent/present, and which *Groupe* subjects simultaneously reclaim (in the "begotten of" and in the evocation of communities, in the plural), even as they claim the right to move away from them (in the "out of" and in the notion that something new is to be "re-composed"). "Out of" also implies the desire to take leave of the power relations of both forced (Franco-French) assimilation and of (colonial, racialized and lesbian) difference. "Out of" evokes a sense of displacement, a sense of being forced out of place and time by relations of power that are named, of psychic labor to unfix oneself, to take leave, to reposition oneself, to bring oneself elsewhere, together.

The *Groupe*'s "out of" is not the material/metaphoric "out of the closet" that circulates among some lesbians in the west/north. Many *Groupe* subjects radically interrogate that particular "out of the closet"; they see it as a paradoxical scopic modality that risks further shadowing, invisibilizing and vulnerabilizing lesbians "of color." Currently in the dominant Franco-French grid of intelligibility the totalizing term "lesbian" often works to both erase and hypervisibilize "race." It does so mainly by positing a universalized lesbian subject to which no lesbian "of color" can correspond. Gloria Anzaldúa identifies a similar situation in the U.S. thus"When a [white] 'lesbian' names me the same as her, she subsumes me under her category ("To Queer the Writer": 263). I am of her group but not as an equal, not as a whole person- my color erased, my class ignored.[...] 'Lesbian' doesn't name anything in my homeland. [...]Yes, we may all love members of the same sex, but we are not the same." Relatedly, Hanan Kaddour, writing in the pamphlet by *Groupe du 6 Novembre* states: "The barriers between them and us are historical and political; these can not disappear simply because these *Waspiennes de France* (female WASPs of France) maintain that they love women.

Whether they love women, bees or red poppies will not in any way bring them nearer to working class lesbians from migrations" (34).

The *Groupe*'s self-designation in relation to "out of" extends to its publishing company, founded in 2000, called *Nomades Langues* (which has been translated by the *Groupe* itself as both Nomadic Languages and the two juxtaposed nouns Languages Nomads).

## THE "L" IN COLORS

Finally, one recent lesbian "of color" designation is: *les "L" en couleurs* which translates roughly as "*The 'L' in Colors.*" It is difficult to render the poetry of this term in translation. It includes multiple metaphors and evokes several transnational associations. The letter "L" stands for *Lesbiennes* (Lesbians), but phonetically it is also the French word for both "she" (elle-s) and "wings" (aile-s) in the singular and plural. The word "colors" operates as a sign of pluralism; it evokes recognition of multiple bio-chromaticisms without directly attaching color to racialized (lesbian) bodies; yet it resonates in solidarity with transnational identifications around *of color* in some anglophone contexts including in the U.S. Like the phrase "out of," so can the term "L" (as wing-s, as she-s, as lesbians, as lesbians "of color" with wings) suggest the movement of flight beyond heterosexual community, national boundaries and the homogenizing assimilation-bound constraints of "unitary" communities.

In its openness, flexibility, playfulness with metaphor, The *'L' in Colors* seems particularly akin to, without being exactly the same as, Gloria Anzaldúa's mode of thinking about her auto-designation "mestiza." If we listen to her words in *Interviews/Entrevistas*, we find:

> I was trying to get away from just thinking in terms of blood—you know, the mestiza as being of mixed blood. The new mestiza is a mixture of all these identities and has the ability, the flexibility, the malleability, the amorphous quality of being able to stretch, and go this way and that way, and add new labels or names which would mix with the others and they would be also malleable. But it's hard to articulate. I'm trying to

> find metaphors—like the mountain range, the river, the mestiza—but they're not quite what I want. Maybe in the process of writing it'll come to me: some new way of talking about these things without cementing them, without fixing them forever in my own writing, Metaphors that have exits and entrances, an open door so things can come in and go out, so that other people can enter and exit. (133)

## SOME CONCLUDING REMARKS: OR WING PRINT TRACES

Gloria Anzaldúa once remarked: "Naming is how I make my presence known, how I assert who and what I am and want to be known as. Naming myself is a survival tactic" ("To Queer the Writer": 264). In France, where lesbians "of color" remain under erasure, are unheard (of), or when heard are unintelligible, self-naming is an equally vital enactment for life. Self-naming is how we recognize our selves and each other as subjects through the fog. The auto-designations that have been re-configured in every historical phase operate as signs with which to make new sense of one's self, inhabit the world differently (perhaps more gently), open what was closed off. In this process Gloria Anzaldúa's inscriptions are signposts scattered in a landscape, scattered in the wind, scattered in our psyches, hearts and minds, so many resting places, safe spaces, for which we can be, are and will be infinitely grateful.

**Notes**

1 I keep the terms "of color" (and later the term "white") in quotes when referring to the French context to signal that they are not used in France in the same way as in the U.S. The literal translations in French (without quotes) of "of color" (de couleur) and of "white" (blanc) are derogatory terms. I use "of color" and "white" here only while writing in English, as bridgework, insofar these terms may be useful to signify populations that are somewhat analogously positioned in relation to concentrations of power in the contexts of the U.S. and France. Below in the text, I present and explain the actual terms used by lesbians "of color" in France to self-designate, and explain the contextual problematics of bio-chromatic designations in France.

2 This and all other French to English translations herein are by the author.

3 I place "race" in quotes to signal the fictional character of "race" categories and the instability of their variant formations in different historical contexts, a point I explain farther below. I keep racism directly without quotes to refer to concrete materialized practices of targeting, oppression and repression. I attach the two terms together with a hyphen to signal their interdependencies and their operability as a unit.

**Works Cited**

Alexander, M. Jacqui and Chandra Talpade Mohanty. Introduction. In *Feminist Genealogies, Colonial Legacies, Democratic Futures.* Edited by M. Jacqui Alexander, Chandra Talpade Mohanty, ix-xiii. New York: Routledge, 1997. Print.

Alarcón, Norma. 1990. "The Theoretical Subject(s) of *This Bridge Called My Back* and Anglo-American Feminism." In *Making Face, Making Soul/Haciendo Caras: Creative and Critical Perspectives of Women of Color*. Ed. Gloria Anzaldúa. San Francisco: Aunt Lute Books, 1995. 356-369. Print.

Anzaldúa, Gloria. *Borderlands/La Frontera: The New Mestiza*. San Francisco: Aunt Lute Books, 1999. Print.

Anzaldúa, Gloria. *Interviews/Entrevistas*. New York: Routledge, 2001. Print.

Anzaldúa, Gloria. "Haciendo Caras, una entrada." In *Making Face, Making Soul/Haciendo Caras: Creative and Critical Perspectives of Women of Color.* Ed. Gloria Anzaldúa. San Francisco: Aunt Lute Books, 1990. xv-xxviii. Print.

Anzaldúa, Gloria. "To(o) Queer the Writer- Loca, escritora y chicana." In *Living Chicana Theory*. Ed. Carla Trujillo. Berkeley: Third Woman Press, 1998. 263-276. Print.

Balibar, Etienne. "Is There a Neo-Racism?" In *Race, Nation and Class: Ambiguous Identities*. Ed. Etienne Balibar and Immanuel Wallerstein. London: Verso, 1991. 17-28. Print.

Bêtes Noires. "Des lesbiennes blanches rêvent notre silence." In *Warriors/Guerrieres*. Ed. Groupe du 6 novembre. Paris: Nomades'Langues Editions, 2001. 25-30. Print.

Fanon, Franz. *L'an V de la révolution algérienne*. Paris: La Découvert, 2001. Print.

Guilaumin, Colette. *l'Idéologie raciste*. Paris: Gallimard, 1972. Print.

Groupe du 6 Novembre, Ed. *Warrior/Guerrieres*. Paris: Nomades'Langues, 2001. Print.

Kaddour, Hanan. La continuité de la vision coloniale dans la pensée et analyse de lesbiennes francaises. In *Warrior/Guerrieres*. Edited by Groupe du 6 Novembre, Paris: Nomades'Langues, 2001. 33-36. Print.

Nedjmam. Introduction: Terres natales, terres d'exil: à la recherche de nos territoires. Bint el Nas (7) 2001. www.bintelnas.org/07nativexile/contents.html

Pile, Steve. "Introduction: Opposition, Political Identities and Spaces of Resistance." In *Geographies of Resistance*. Eds. Steve Pile and Michael Keith. New York: Routledge, 1997. 1-32. Print.

Rosello, Mireille. "'The Beur Nation': Towards a Theory of Départenance." *Research in African Literatures* 24.3 (1993). Print.

# 8

# "LET US BE THE HEALING OF THE WOUND": ANZALDÚA'S POST-SEPTEMBER 11, 2001, TESTIMONIAL VISION

*CLAIRE JOYSMITH*

I would like to start by offering words of deep gratitude to Gloria. Gratitude because she and her words have changed my life and work *del otro lado de la frontera, on the other side of the border, en México.* This has shown me that a good karma is a good karma is a good karma, to very loosely paraphrase Gertrude Stein.

I first experienced Gloria's amazing *curandera cultural,* cultural healer power, in 1992 at the Universidad Nacional Autónoma de México (UNAM) in Mexico City where I heard her read, standing up to her fullest height—not sitting like other panelists at the multicultural conference she had been invited to—talking *con tanta fuerza*, with such strength, *con espíritu*, mesmerizing me. I interviewed her later that day; although she had recently been diagnosed with diabetes, she was amazingly generous with her time and energy. We talked for hours, *y hasta chismeamos.* We laughed about the ironies: here we were conversing in Mexico City in an admixture of English and Spanish; *yo, la gringa*-looking *"güera," mexicana*-born, and her, *una "prieta," chicana fronteriza*, considered in México—particularly Central Mexico, *centro del chilango*-centrism[1]—*como del otro lado, estadounidense, gringa, pocha* (as on the other side, gringa and pocha) ironically even *gabacha*-like for some, but not as a *mexicana*. The afternoon grew into evening; still she talked, still she was patient enough to open many windows for me. I later had to find the doors.

* * *

"In terms of evolutionary stages," Gloria Anzaldúa writes in her essay "Let Us Be the Healing of the Wound: The Coyolxauhqui Imperative—*La Sombra y El Sueño*," the world is presently between *el quinto sol y el sexto (the fifth and sixth sun)*. According to Maya knowledge, the sixth world starts December 2012. It is this Nuevo Mundo, this new order, we need to create with the choices we make, the acts we perform, and the futures we dream (99). And she adds: "We are the song that sings us. It begins with 'Let us fight no more but heal the wounds of nations. Let us be the healing of the wound'" (103).

In this singular cybertestimonio-essay, included in a cross-border Mexico-U.S. book publication entitled *One Wound for Another/Una herida por otra. Cybertestimonios de Latin@s in the U.S. Through Cyberspace (11 de septiembre de 2001–11 de marzo de 2002)*, Gloria responds movingly, poignantly, intensely, using the testimonial form, to what is commonly referred to as "9/11"; I choose to refer to it as September 11, 2001, in respectful deference to the September 11, 1973, CIA-backed bombings in Santiago de Chile, an event mostly forgotten through historical blurring and amnesia.

Gloria "speaks" passionately, yet with great temperance and wisdom, "from the wound's gash" (93), from the very heart-hurt of confusion and deep anguish experienced through the new wounds that bled at the time—that still continue to bleed.

What is perhaps most striking about this twelve-page cybertestimonio is the clarity of Gloria's vision at a time of pain and confusion that Native American poet Joy Harjo has referred to as "the magnetic field thrown off by grief"

(344) when words and discourses lost pre-September 11, 2001, significance/ meaningfulness.

Also striking about this cybertestimonio-essay is the way Gloria gathers the quintessential filaments of her theoretical-critical discursivity and iconography, contextualizing them for unexpected and different *nepantla* (as she calls it),[2] times, responding to the aftermath of September 11, 2001, con *"el corazón con razón"* (102), strongly, intelligently, with courage and great compassion—the markings, the *huellas* of a true *curandera cultural.*

Notable, too, is the flow of past-present-future visions that inform Gloria's response in which she creatively interweaves theoretical concepts and terms she developed throughout the years, through various texts, beginning with *Borderlands/La Frontera* twenty years ago.

It may be striking, yet by no means surprising, for Gloria's vision in her writings was uncannily visionary in several ways. Woven into all her writings, her seer-ways slid across temporal borders, voicing the myths of the ancient past, even as she wrote from and for each present moment, with the prophetic glimpse of what was in the making. It is this malleability she returns to once again in her cybertestimonio-essay, in which she upholds what can be seen as becoming a mantra of sorts: "Let us be the healing of the wound."

Her visionary perspective about the individual and collective creation of a Nuevo Mundo, of the "new order" she addresses in her cybertestimonio, emerges from a situated knowledge space, a post-September 11, 2001, *nepantla* space.

> A momentous event such as that of 9/11 es un arrebatamiento con la fuerza de un hacha. Carlos Castaneda's (sic) Don Juan would call such times the day the World stopped. The "world" doesn't so much stop as it cracks. What cracked is our perception of the world, how we relate to it, how we engage with it. Afterwards we view reality differently—we see through its rendijas (holes) to the illusion of consensual reality. The world as we know it "ends." We experience a radical shift in perception, otra forma de ver (99).

And she continues:

> Este choque shifts us to nepantla, a psychological, liminal space between the way things had been and an unknown future. Nepantla is the space in-between, the locus and sign of transition....Torn between ways, we seek to find some sort of harmony amidst the remolinos of multiple and conflictive worldviews; we must learn to integrate all these perspectives. Transitions are a form of crisis, an emotionally significant event or a radical change in status. During crisis the existential isolation all people experience is exacerbated. In nepantla we hang out between shifts, trying to make rational sense of this crisis, seeking solace, support, appeasement, or some kind of intimate connection. En este lugar we fall into chaos, fear of the unknown, and are forced to take up the task of self-redefinition. (99)

Gloria once again writes as she did in *Borderlands/La Frontera* twenty years ago of the urgent need for "the task of self-redefinition" as a personal and collective responsibility. It is the interaction between individual and a collectivity that becomes meaningful. Fully aware that "en estos tiempos of loss, fear and confusion the human race must delve into its cenotes (wells) of collective wisdom, both ancient and modern" (101), Gloria goes back again and again to the certitude that "we can transshape reality by changing our perspective and perceptions" (102), that "each of us can make a difference" (101), that we can heal ourselves as well as others, heal the world at large, as "world citizens." She does so by repeating *casi como estribillo,* a refrain, like a mantra: "Let us be the healing of the wound."

*Me acuerdo,* I clearly remember, when, shortly after September 11, 2001, Gloria was invited by Clara Lomas and me to contribute a cybertestimonio that was to be later published in *One Wound for Another/Una herida por otra.* The book, posthumously dedicated to her memory, owes much to her; for instance, the initial part of its title was borrowed—with her permission—from her cybertestimonio-essay. She almost didn't write the (essay) testimonio, almost pulled out after she had sent in the first draft, arguing it needed re-working, she had no time.... For the sake of many, I am glad I persisted, thankful she took the time to shape it so that she was happy with it, although she never actually got to see the final version in print. I did not realize at the time, of course, that this would be one of the last pieces Gloria would write or publish. Yet even on a first reading its power was immediately evident.

As she writes pain into the text, as she writes about the wounds, the *heridas*—so many of them open, *abiertas*—never forgetting to touch the underside of compassion, she also narrates her walk on the ocean front in Santa Cruz, a raging yet contained cry and whisper, fully footnoted with insightful data. Her meditative walk frames and sustains the entire piece. And as the moon and sea water keep her company, each and every paragraph gathers increasing strength, flowing towards her focal point: how to survive, how to compassionately help others survive, how to take action through a number of healing modes and strategies, towards "spiritual activism." It all flows towards the vital need in *nepantla* times to heal wounds: "Let us be the healing of the wound."

She (ad)dresses wounds directly, reminds us continually that each of "us" can become responsible in our own way. To this end she resorts to what she calls the Coyolxauhqui imperative, applying it to post-September 11, 2001, *nepantla* times.

> The Coyolxauhqui imperative is to heal and achieve integration. When fragmentations occur you fall apart and feel as though you've been expelled from paradise. Coyolxauhqui is my symbol for the necessary process of dismemberment and fragmentation, of seeing that self, or the situations you're embroiled in, differently. It is also my symbol for reconstruction and reframing, one that allows for putting the pieces together in a new way. The Coyolxauhqui imperative is an ongoing process of making and unmaking. There is never any resolution, just the process of healing. (100)

This continued process of healing is at the heart of Gloria's cybertestimonio-essay in which she expounds upon what she terms *conocimiento* (which she deliberately used in Spanish, thereby underscoring a distinction from the preloaded meanings of its linguistic translation in English).

> In trying to make sense of what's happening, some of us come into deep awareness (*conocimiento*) of political and spiritual situations and the unconscious mechanisms that abet hate, intolerance and discord. I name this searching, inquiring, and healing consciousness conocimiento. Conocimiento urges us to respond not just with the traditional practice of spirituality (contemplation, meditation, and private rituals) or with the technologies of political activism (protests, demonstrations, and speakouts), but with the amalgam of the two—spiritual activism which we have also inherited along with la sombra. Conocimiento pushes us into engaging the spirit in confronting our social sickness with new tools and practices whose goal is to effect a shift. (100)

Situated within the context of this cybertestimonio, *conocimiento* becomes the active and dynamic counterpart of "desconocimiento," what Gloria refers to as personal and collective "shadow beasts," on which she expounds by directly addressing a larger collectivity and a corresponding accountability.

> As I see it, this country's real battle is with its shadow—its racism, propensity for violence, rapacity for consuming, neglect of its responsibility to global communities and the environment, and unjust treatment of dissenters and the disenfranchised, especially people of color. As an artist I feel compelled to expose this shadow side which the mainstream media and government denies. In order to understand our complicity and responsibility we must look at the shadow. (93)

So whereas desconocimiento is "self-righteousness" and "creates the abyss," *conocimiento* "builds bridges across it" (100).

We are all no doubt familiar with Gloria as bridge-builder. And certainly none of us are unfamiliar with her well-known quote in *Borderlands/La Frontera*: "The U.S.-Mexican border *es una herida abierta* where the Third World grates against the first and bleeds" (3).

I would like to draw attention to a fascinating resonance between this quote born circa 1987 and what Gloria states in her March 2002 cybertestimonio, a vision for *nepantla* times that overflows with compassion, a vision of (re)new(ed) healing possibilities that also creates a bridge between several of her theoretical proposals: "We are all wounded but we can connect through the wound that's alienated us from others. When the wound forms a cicatriz, the scar can become a bridge linking people split apart" (2005:102).

It is this kind of language and post-September 11, 2001 vision that is so striking in this cybertestimonio-essay, for it speaks of and to the present, even as it is becoming the future. Gloria envisions this as an opportunity because "when we own our shadow we allow the breath of healing to enter our lives"; after all, "ultimately each of us has the potential to change the sentience of the world" (101). So she encourages her readers by stating:

> As we see beyond what divides us to what connects us, we're compelled to reach out beyond our walls of distrust and extend our hands to others and share information and resources. The survival of the human species depends on each one of us connecting to our vecinos (neighbors) whether they live across the street, across national borders, or across oceans. A calamity of the magnitude of 9/11 can compel us to think not in terms of "my" country or "your" nation but "our" planet. (101)

In this sense, the poignant, insightful, inspired and inspiring contents of this cybertestimonio-essay are of great value today, theoretically and as daily praxis. They are also of value for all readers who must "survive the Borderlands," "live *sin fronteras*" and become "a crossroads" (195), as "we" identify ourselves as survivors, too, of this new post-September 11, 2001, history-border. On a personal note, I see such wound-scar-bridge metaphors as one of Gloria's *bruja*-potions for the harsh post-September 11, 2001, *nepantla* times.

* * *

Gloria, *nepantlera,* selfless and compassionate *curandera cultural, has cruzado la frontera al reino de los muertos, pero continúas atendiendo las heridas de las otras, de los otros, compartiendo múltiples sanaciones.*[3] Her wisdom-words are ones we can hold as treasures in our hearts, in our minds.

She has given those to us. She has left them to us as her legacy.

But she has done her work. We must do ours.

We can offer her a *"gracias."* We can follow her dust-prints, find inspiration in

her words by also creating our own.

We can become "the healing of the wound."

We can, as she urges in the closing words of her cybertestimonio, "do work that matters."

**Notes**

1 Chilango is a synonym for a Mexico City dweller, used tongue-in-cheek, even self-deprecatingly, when used by insiders, and derogatively when used by outsiders. The term alludes to a geographical, political, cultural and ideological centrality that reflects, in turn, a term such as "Eurocentrism" that indicates a tendency to identify Europe as an ethnic and cultural norm/ideal.

2 Nepantla is derived from panotla (bridge) that translates into Spanish as tierra de en medio (land in-between or in the middle).

3 Translation: Cultural healer, you have crossed the border into the realm of the dead, but you continue to (ad)dress the wounds of others, sharing myriad healings.

**Works Cited**

Anzaldúa, Gloria. *Borderlands/La Frontera: The New Mestiza.* San Francisco: Spinsters/Aunt Lute, 1987. Print.

Anzaldúa, Gloria. "Let Us Be The Healing Of The Wound: The Coyolxauhqui Imperative—La

Sombra y El Sueño." In *One Wound for Another/Una herida por otra. Testimonios de Latin@s in the U.S. through Cyberspace (11 de septiembre de 2001–11 de marzo de 2002)*, eds. Claire Joysmith and Clara Lomas. Mexico City: CISAN/UNAM, Colorado College, Whittier College, 2005. Print.

Harjo, Joy. "When the World as We Knew It Ended." In *Speaking desde las*

*heridas. C(y)ibertestimonios (t)Transfronterizos/(t)Transborder (September 11, 2001–March 11, 2007.* Ed. Claire Joysmith. Mexico City: CISAN/UNAM, Whittier College, California, ITESM campus Toluca and Monterrey, Mexico, 2009, 2008. Print.

# 9

# UN ROSARIO DE GLORIAS: GÜERAS AND PRIETAS AT THE BORDERS: THE LATERAL NARRATIVES OF GLORIA ANZALDÚA AND ROSARIO CASTELLANOS

*MARISA BELAUSTEGUIGOITIA*

My analysis of Anzaldúa's work focuses on the construction of a politics of reading understood as a pedagogical approach to incorporate what is refused due to an excess of differences in national, gendered, racial, and sexual identities. I propose a strategy for the circulation of the work of border thinkers such as Gloria Anzaldúa in a transnational scene. This approach emerges from the reading of *Borderlands* by Gloria Anzaldúa and *Balún Canán* by Rosario Castellanos, from the conviction of their pedagogical values vis-à-vis hegemonic narratives. In this article I look at Anzaldúa's *Borderlands* and Castellanos' *Balún Canán* through Julio Cortázar's conceptual tools for writing in order to create an interplay of mirrors in which both works are reflected. In this way I link Cortázar's provocation in the way he reads nation, identity, and writing with that articulated by Anzaldúa.

With this pairing of authors, I seek to explore several questions. Is it possible to "make sense" of a narrative from a transnational reading? How are texts transformed by such an act of reading? What is similar and what is different about these writers born at the borders of what could be understood as the nation's limits? What emerges when writing from this location? What can be understood as a transnational reading?

These questions can be answered from at least two dimensions. The first is related to the construction and preservation of an activity that gives academia lasting meaning: the production of criticism. Julio Cortázar writes about that place from which writing is produced as criticism: "I write from an interstice.... I write to always be a little more to the left or a little deeper in the place where one should be for everything to come together satisfactorily" (*La Casilla*, 61).

Cortázar understands writing—critical writing, the one that de-centers criticism—as an act of "misplacement" that he dubs "lateral-ness," a term that means the sensitivity to alien, eccentric, peripheral situations, or "misplaced" situations. This sensitivity is called wonderment and leads to petrification that writing brings together, kneads and softens. From these "lateral" positions, from these two borders, and from these two misplaced writings, I will analyze the political and critical function of Anzaldúa's and Castellanos' narratives.

The writers Castellanos and Anzaldúa foster not only the rereading of the nation's exclusions but the construction of inter-related strategies for visibility and citizenship for women, Indians, and migrant communities. What emerges from *Borderlands* when placed alongside a narrative from the South such as *Balún Canán*? What becomes of the concept of the New Mestiza when circulated among well-installed Mexican narratives?

I have paired these authors for many reasons. Rosario Castellanos and Gloria Anzaldúa wrote about women and situated their writings on the border. As Cortázar says, "They are not completely there," in discipline, in mission, in genre, or in ideology ("El sentimiento," 60). Castellanos wrote from the South, Chiapas, and Anzaldúa, from the North, the border with the United States. Castellanos is today a national figure and has moved to the center, but her narrative often still represents the South. They wrote from the borders of the acceptable and from the borders of what could be enunciated. They produced lateral knowledge.

Both authors wrote from and about the crevices and breaks of our nation: the divisions and duels among classes, ethnic groups, and the sexes. One of their main themes was what inhabits the periphery, the excluded, the national impossible: indigenous, poor women, and migrants. Both have been bridges for racial, ethnic, class, and gender differences. Both have been translators and have been accused of betraying their feminine culture, the patriarchal culture, and hegemonic values.

The differences are equally illustrative: one (Castellanos) is read as *güera,* white or a fair-haired, fair-skinned woman; the other is read as dark-skinned or *prieta.* One is from the intellectual middle class, the other from the lower class, related to wetbacks and migrants. *La güera* is today a national icon and is widely known, while *la prieta* is only beginning to be understood. One writes about the South, the other about the North. One writes in Spanish, the other in "Spanglish," using code switching. One uses the tongue, the other the back as a tongue and as a bridge between worlds, countries, and sexes. One is heterosexual, the other homosexual. One is renowned, the other is barely being looked at.

What unites them or makes them objects of comparison is their writing from the limits of the nation, their lateralness, their misplacement, their eccentric meaning poured into writing that overflows as it makes national excesses visible in a body and language—migrants, indigenous, women. How to be a woman from those limits? What writing is produced with the back and the tongue wet?

Gloria and Rosario, North and South, *prieta* and *güera,* bridge as back and tongue contain and delimit new notions of identity and writing. For the past decade we have witnessed different events that define the nation on its two borders, north and south: *Zapatistas* and *maquiladoras*; *Zapatista's* revolutionary women's laws and speeches to the Mexican Congress from the southern border; feminicides, indigenous and migrants as objects, and sometimes subjects of the administration of justice and resistance from Chiapas to Ciudad Juárez. These two writers help us understand our transitions to democracy, to unexpected ways of fragile integration, to interculturalness, by unfolding those very painful and so radically unjust and exclusionary border scenarios.

Castellanos dedicated an important part of her work to making visible the southern border, the lives of indigenous people, particularly Indian women, and the way in which women relate to several private and public systems of exclusion: patriarchy, capitalism, modernity, tradition, customs, violence, the family, and education. She unfolded the role and lives of middle-class women in contact with the particular oppression of indigenous people. Castellanos formed a genealogy of women in contact, rubbing against all the systems that exclude them and take away their confidence, joy, and will. She wanted women to be subjects of respect and dialogue, of exchange of projects and dreams. One thing that connects Castellanos and Anzaldúa is that this respect had to be an effect of a very complex understanding of subalternity and exclusion, an understanding that also included the ways in which the indigenous people, women, or Chicanas were trapped by their own practices and relations of power and fears, carefully cherished by their own culture. In Castellanos' words:

> The meaning of the word is its recipient: the other who listens, who understands and who responds, turns its interlocutor into he who listens and understands, thus establishing a dialogue that is only possible among those who take each other into consideration and treat each other as equals, and is only fruitful among those who want each other to be free. (24)

Anzaldúa—the *prieta,* farm worker, writer, self-proclaimed Indian, and sixth-generation migrant, born in Texas in 1942—wrote about the life of Mexicans, Chicanos, and migrants in the United States, on the border. On the border as a wall and barbed wire, on the border with "pistols of ammunition and pepper," because, as Luis Ernesto Derbez asked, what is better, that they kill you or they just give you a few "biting stings," spattering you with little metal balls steeped in a little pepper?

Anzaldúa writes to make visible all the ways in which migrants and wetbacks pain themselves, feel sorry for themselves, leave the skin in order to not leave the back anymore, since the idea is to start sticking out their tongue. She undertakes the unfathomable task of exchanging the back for the tongue. Sweat for ink. In the first pages of her best-known text, *Borderlands/La Frontera: The New Mestiza,* she writes:

> In the fields, *la migra.* My aunt saying, "*No corran,* don't run. They'll think you're *del otro lao.*" In the confusion, Pedro ran, terrified of being caught. He couldn't speak English, couldn't tell them he was fifth generation American. Sin *papeles*—he did not carry his birth certificate to work in the fields. La migra took him away while we watched. *Se lo llevaron.* He tried to smile when he looked back at us, to raise his fist. But I saw the shame pushing his head down, I saw the terrible weight of shame hunch his shoulders. They deported him to Guadalajara by plane. The furthest he'd ever been to Mexico was Reynosa, a small border town opposite Hidalgo, Texas, not far from McAllen. Pedro walked all the way to the Valley. *Se lo llevaron sin un centavo el pobre. Se vino andando desde Guadalajara.* (4)

*Borderlands* is a hybrid text composed of fragments of essay, the development of conceptual categories, fiction, pieces of history in the mouths of the vanquished and counterposed to the official history, poetry, *corridos,* autobiography, sayings, and songs. Classifying it into a single genre is impossible because it navigates between essay, fiction, autobiography, and poetic narrative.

In *Borderlands,* Anzaldúa tenses racial, class, and sexuality differences to the limit by subjecting them to the category of being female, being poor, being Chicana, and being lesbian, living in English but thinking in Spanish. She unfolds being the female protagonist of all betrayals: of her Mexican culture because she writes in English, of the Anglo culture because she turns English into Spanglish, of women's culture because she renounces maternity, of the patriarchal culture because she rejects both femininity and heterosexuality. Anzaldúa's writing, body, and language are at the limits of any social and symbolic national/hegemonic system; her entire being falls within the periphery; her entire being is the product of lateralness.

Castellanos and Anzaldúa are mediators, translators, contemporary *Malinches* of their own peoples and of strangers and foreigners. They have been accused of betrayal because they offer scenes of conscience and liberation to women and men willing to misplace themselves, to displace themselves.

The consciousness or awareness their texts generate can be defined as a state acquired on crossing over from one emotion to another, from one territory to another, from one struggle to another. This transcendence of difference happens by crossing over and recreating the original meaning and making it coincide with the unknown or subordinate. Travelers of crossings, permanent crossers from the opposite to the different, weavers of what can knit a topographical change, bring those from below to the height of the gaze and lower "those from above" to the level of the back. But there are differences among them.

Castellanos' crossings lead to the awareness of one's loneliness, whose strength lies in the recognition of its labyrinths and the handling and contention of desires that spur complete surrender—to service, to the nation, to suffering, and to love and sexuality. Anzaldúa's crossings lead us, not shoulder-to-shoulder but back-to-back, to recognize a way of being Mexican, Chicana, Gringa, and a woman articulating all deficits—those of color (*prieta*); those of language (tongue-less); those of origin (Indian); those of sexuality (lesbian). This crossing builds us new and whole, face-to-face with the challenges of desire, power, and politics. Castellanos proposes an "us" that is alone, suspended and fragmented on the threshold of surrender, while Anzaldúa gathers the fragments, sutures them together, and suspends us as surrenders that rend us anew.

Both writers were prolific. Of their most widely read texts—*Balún Canán* by Castellanos and *Borderlands/La Frontera: The New Mestiza* by Anzaldúa—one of their great thematic similarities has been the representation of the indigenous border woman: the indigenous nana in Castellanos' narrative and the New Mestiza in Anzaldúa's. The nana and the New Mestiza are figures that both writers link to "the consciousness of crossing," the transition from difference and subordination to consciousness, as a result of the possession/position of the racial, sexual, or national differences, according to the ability of signification, not only of exclusion. While the capabilities they propose in their texts are very different, their interstitial and "misplaced" treatment is similar.

The nana and the New Mestiza share two common facets. One is the preservation of a visible, articulating indigenous supplement, a component that traces the body, the territory, and the indigenous language on the territorial defeat. This defeat has pushed the indigenous subject out of the story, that is, outside the power to make sense from its place and to do it in such a way that it circulates legitimately. Both return the indigenous representation of body and tongue to the text. The second facet has to do with an interstitial position, on the margins and outside the literary and sexual genres and their degrees of confrontation and union of gender, class, ethnic, and generational differences.

Castellanos' nana and Anzaldúa's New Mestiza speak of their 500-year-old solitude. They create a textual/sexual body. In her narrative, particularly in *Balún Canán,* Castellanos shows the ways in which identification with the margins, with indigenous subalternity is impossible. We perceive multiple reasons for our refusal to identify ourselves with that periphery. She shows these refusals without romanticizing the indigenous world and culture. In this case we do not speak of an identification that would make the indigenous identical or at least similar, but an identification that conceives of them as subjects of the same rights that we have as citizens.

Castellanos' novel deals with the life of a family on a hacienda in Comitán and its contact with and dependence on the indigenous world. The narrative is divided into three parts. The first and last, written in the third person, are told from the perspective of a seven-year-old girl. In Castellanos' words, "This childish world is very similar to the world of the indigenous where the action of the novel is situated" (13). A little girl and an Indian woman love, understand, and enjoy each other. A little girl who loves her Indian nana. How can she love the other, who is so radically different?

These two parts of the novel are constructed around the world of the girl and her nana, both communicating in their own language, murmuring, muttering, an indigenous world in contact with the white world of a girl who loves the "other." The narrative puts forward a return of the indigenous in two versions: the first in the contact and rubbing together of the margins (a girl and an Indian), the closeness and the love between the nana and the little girl, both invisible in the paternal household; the second based on the clash between what is Indian and what is "*caxtlán*" (white), between the world of identification and exclusion, the center and the margins, the Indian, the white, and the mestiza, the scenario of exploitation, discrimination and betrayal not only between Indians and mestizos. The second part of the novel clarifies the breaks between the Indian world and its own culture in contact with modernity and the vital capital economy of a hacienda.

The relationship between the nana and the girl punctuates the novel. They are one and they are different. We never know the name of either; they are anonymous and insignificant. In the margins, their worlds intertwine and their plots are woven. In the first part of the novel, we see the ways the nana and the little girl can relate and love each other from the margins of the family and society. The little girl has an older brother, Mario, who monopolizes their mother's attention as first-born and favorite child. The entire patriarchal world moves to the edges of the plot from where the girl and nana love and get to know each other, from where the nana fills the girl's ears and eyes with images and stories of her Indian world, a world that for the nana is also experienced in Spanish. Both live together in the limits of their worlds: the urban, the traditional, the patriarchal, and the indigenous.

> I am poking among the dishes…I like the color of lard and to touch the cheeks of the fruit and undress the onions. "Those are witches' things, girl; they eat everything. The crops, families' peace, people's health." I have found a basket of eggs. The spotted ones are turkey eggs. "Look what they're doing to me." And raising the *tzec,* the nana shows me a fresh, pink sore disfiguring her knee. I look at it with my eyes big with surprise. "Don't say anything, girl. I came from Chajtajal so they wouldn't follow me, but their curse reaches a long way." Why do they hurt you? "Because I love your parents, Mario and you." "Is it bad to love us?" "It is bad to love those 'who run things, those who own things.' That is what the Law says."

The beginning of *Balún Canán* is representative and announces the story's end on page two. The cherished relationship of the nana and the girl, so carnal, so oral, so loving, is described very early in the novel:

> "Finish up your milk." Every afternoon at five the Swiss cow vendor goes by, ringing his tin bell. (I have explained to Mario that "Swiss" means "fat.")...The maids come out of the houses and buy a glassful. And spoiled children like me make faces and spill it on the tablecloth. "God is going to punish you for wasting it," says the nana. I want to drink coffee. Like you. Like everybody else. "You're going to become an Indian." Her threat makes me shiver with apprehension. From tomorrow on. I won't spill the milk. (20)

The threat of becoming an Indian makes her shiver with fear. The nana threatens the little girl with being like the person she loves and trusts the most, with being like her. This should make her excited at the prospect, not shiver with fear. What pedagogical, disciplinary, and emotional processes do the nation and its systems (the family, the school, morality) trigger to create rejection of what is most intimate, to produce apprehension in place of pride at being like the person we most love?

Castellanos emphasizes the patriarchal subjection of both the indigenous and the European cultures, but it is in the figure of the nana that she establishes the transgressions of both universes, the Indian and the European. The nana is the bridge that translates the indigenous wisdom and the urban wisdom, the central and peripheral wisdoms. The nana is a kind of *Malinche*, the translator between an indigenous and a national culture, between the traditions of indigenous wisdom and modernity. She speaks Spanish and an indigenous language. She knows the customs of the *caxtlanes* and she does not forget her own. She is literally an interstitial, a border, a misplaced subject.

An excellent example of this wisdom is the explanation that the nana gives the little girl about who the poor are and why her mother visits an impoverished paralyzed woman. The story is a long one, going through the indigenous mythology that explains the creation of men, first out of wood and then out of gold:

> And day after day, the hardness of the heart of the man of gold cracked little by little until the word of gratitude that the four lords had placed in him rose to his mouth....That is why our law says that no rich man may

> enter into heaven if a poor man does not take him by the hand. The nana is silent. She carefully folds the garment she has just mended...and stands up to leave. But before she takes the first step that will separate us, I ask her, who is my poor nana? "You still don't know. But if you watch carefully, when you are older and understand more, you will know." (34–35)

The fragile possibility of a way forward accompanied by Indian and mestiza othernesses is perceptible at the threshold where reciprocity finally exists.

Gloria Anzaldúa works in reverse, the other way around: she points to the unfathomable breaks, that which separates us from that liminal identification with otherness to put forward the emergence of a new consciousness, the product of the breach and the recomposition of these racial, ethnic, sexual, and national differences. In the first paragraph of her preface to *Borderlands,* we read:

> The actual physical borderland that I am dealing with in this book is the Texas-U.S. Southwest/Mexican border. The psychological borderland, the sexual borderlands and the spiritual borderlands are not particular to the Southwest. In fact, the Borderlands are physically present wherever two or more cultures edge each other, where people of different races occupy the same territory, where under, lower, middle and upper classes touch, where the space between two individuals shrinks with intimacy.

A new awareness is born on the border between the United States and Mexico, born from the re-signification of exploitation, violence, and mistrust among Mexicans, Chicanos, Mexican-Americans, and Anglos.

*Borderlands* appropriates the history of the vanquished to their own tongue as a revealing discourse, but it also uses operations learned from shamans and from what is left of pre-Hispanic wisdom to visualize the ways in which Anzaldúa herself and her culture can be the reason for the disillusionment. It is as if Castellanos' nana were turned into a migrant, a wetback, to the northern border and were made to speak.

In the second chapter, *"Movimientos de rebeldía y culturas que traicionan,"* we read in Spanglish:

> *Esos movimientos de rebeldía que tenemos en la sangre nosotros los mexicanos surgen como ríos desbocanados en mis venas. Y como mi raza que cada en cuando deja caer esa esclavitud de obedecer, de callarse y aceptar, en mí está la rebeldía encimita de mi carne. Debajo de mi humillada mirada está una cara insolente lista para explotar. Me costó muy caro mi rebeldía-acalambrada con desvelos y dudas, sintiéndome inútil, estúpida e impotente...repelé. Hablé pa'tras. Fui hocicona. Era indiferente a muchos valores de mi cultura. No me dejé de los hombres. No fui buena ni obediente. Pero he crecido. Ya no sólo paso toda mi vida botando las costumbres y los valores de mi cultura que me traicionan. También recojo las costumbres que por un tiempo se han provocado y las costumbres de respeto a las mujeres.* But despite my growing tolerance, for this Chicana, *la guerra de independencia* is a constant. (15)

In Anzaldúa's book, the creation of consciousness does not only reside in laying the emotional, psychological, and economic states of migrants at the door of Anglo-Saxon culture, capitalist exploitation, or the abuse of power in U.S. culture. It also emphasizes the ways in which the culture of Mexicans and Chicanos operates to weaken them and undermine their abilities and sensations.

Anzaldúa is capable of proposing a consciousness-raising operation because she shares all the cultures, knows the languages and practices, and lives in those areas of Anglo power and of the weakening due to her sexuality, her class, and her Mexican cultural association.

> Because I, a *mestiza*
> continually walk out of one culture
> And into another,
> Because I am in all cultures
> at the same time,
> Alma entre dos mundos, tres cuatro,
> Me zumba la cabeza con lo contradictorio.

> *Estoy norteada por todas las voces que me hablan simultáneamente.* (77)

With Anzaldúa, the final product is the creation of a consciousness of oppression, not only of women, but of people of color, homosexuals, migrants, and the poor. She traces delicate equations that highlight the correspondences and equivalencies in these identity "deficits."

> *El choque de un alma atrapada entre el mundo del espíritu* y *el mundo de la técnica a veces la deja entullida.* Cradled in one culture, sandwiched between two cultures, straddling three cultures and their value systems, *la mestiza* undergoes a struggle of flesh, a struggle of borders, an inner war....Within us and within *la cultura chicana,* commonly held beliefs of the white culture attack commonly held beliefs of the Mexican culture, and both attack commonly held beliefs of the indigenous culture. Subconsciously, we see an attack on ourselves and on our beliefs as a threat we attempt to block with a counterstance. (78)

These deficits (poverty, wandering, femininity, being dark-skinned, indigenous, or Mexican, the "wrong" sexuality) constitute, together with all the "being on the sidelines," the mortar that creates the New Mestiza—the hybrid, interstitial, border, peripheral subject. They make up the New Mestiza as an effect of so many crossings and a life on the line of all the borders that articulates the impossibilities.

> The new *mestiza* copes by developing a tolerance for contradictions, a tolerance for ambiguity. She learns to be an Indian in Mexican culture, to be Mexican from an Anglo point of view. She learns to juggle cultures. She has a plural personality, she operates in a pluralistic mode—nothing is thrust out, the good, the bad and the ugly, nothing rejected, nothing abandoned. Not only does she sustain contradictions, she turns ambivalence into something else. (79)

The transits between different identities that Anzaldúa establishes, the tension that she demands of the cross-over between different subjectivities, produces a textuality full of crossings, of negotiations between opposites, with the aim of accepting, understanding, codifying the other.

Gloria Anzaldúa was a farm worker, a migrant worker in the United States, a sixth-generation Texan-American; her mother did not speak English. She traveled through different states with her family, renting herself out as agricultural labor. A wetback with a sharp tongue, educated in schools for poor migrants, self-identified as an indigenous, with indigenous features, but sixth-generation Texan.

In almost opposite ways, the two narratives make the sutures of the nation visible. Castellanos builds a bridge whose cracks are visible—a broken bridge among the lives of otherness. Anzaldúa offers her tongue as a bridge to substitute for the back and as a passage toward understanding differences and their re-elaboration. The nana-subject to the conscience of crossing, of the passage, ends up with sores, expelled and unrecognizable; the New Mestiza, a mixed subject, a subject from suturing together the fragments, lives in the most fragile areas of signification, on the borders. The nana ends up getting lost because "all Indians have the same face." And how does the New Mestiza end up? It is impossible to say in advance because the New Mestiza has barely been articulated. How does a subject end up who realizes her potential precisely based on her most fragile characteristics, a peripheral subject sexually, and in terms of nationality, gender, and class? We read in *Borderlands, "La oposición no es una manera de vivir. En un momento dado, en nuestro camino hacia la nueva conciencia de la mestiza, hay que abandonar la oposición.... Tenemos que aprender a accionar, no a reaccionar."* (78–79)

Anzaldúa and Castellanos give the border woman, the nana and the New Mestiza, the place of "synthesis," of being a bridge, of being translators. Anzaldúa bets on a very complex, adventurous synthesis, the fruit of all the deficits, of bringing together the peripheral.

When we realize that today more than twenty million Mexicans have migrated to the North, to the United States, and that in the South we have an ongoing indigenous rebellion, it becomes even more urgent to explore and more interesting to analyze the Anzaldúa/Castellanos, North/South, *prieta/güera,* homosexual/heterosexual, poor/middle class, academic/activist paradigm as bridges from and towards the other, as passages and inter-crossings from the geographical, sexual, ethnic, class, and discursive borders. Our greatest wounds and our abysmal problems come from these borders.

Gloria and Rosario, a glory of rosaries or a rosary of glories (as the names may be translated), glossaries that speak from and of the borders, from there build a different Mexico: the Mexico of the nana and the Indian woman who dissolves in the multitude, but whose knowledge and whose marks stay on the body and on the tongue of the girl, at the margins of whiteness and the nation unrecognizable but indelible; and that of the New Mestiza, that of the internal struggles with all their marginal markings.

The Indian woman in Mexico, the Chicana woman in the United States, the lesbian in the heterosexual world, the American in the Mexican tradition: from these places, both writers dismantle the binomials that radicalize and make the other banal, and build bridges. Rosario's Glory is to do it within the cracks in nation and language, Gloria's Rosary comes from the transformation of the back as tongue, with the back in her hand…writing. Back and tongue, language and nation are bridges and breaks, sutures and lines, that return migrants and indigenous to the periphery of the heart, to the center of our consciousness and our emotions.

Like the nana, the wizards of the north also punish our migrants, our nanas, servants, future New Mestizas, with sores. Border authorities answer that they are just a few stinging bites, buckshot with pepper, or Minuteman projects to get Mexicans to stop crossing borders, including the one that leads to consciousness. Which are the pedagogies, the forms of reading, the stories, the writing, that can "make sense of it all," that can create New Mestizas and not only nanas shriveled, vanished, and faceless?

*Acknowledgment: I am very grateful to Norma Alarcón from whom I got inspiration and many of the ideas included in this essay.*

**Works Cited**

Anzaldúa, Gloria. *Borderlands/La Frontera: The New Mestiza.* San Francisco: Spinsters/Aunt Lute, 1987. Print.

Castellanos, Rosario. *Balún Canán.* In *Obras Completas,* vol. I. Mexico City: Fondo de Cultura Económica, 1989. Print.

Cortázar, Julio. *La Casilla de Morelli.* Barcelona: Tusquets, 1973. Print.

Cortázar, Julio. "El sentimiento de no estar del todo." In *La Casilla de los Morelli.* Fondo de Cultura Económica: 1965. Print.

# PART 4

POETRY

## LA ESTRELLA

*de Dama infiel al sueño*

*MINERVA MARGARITA VILLARREAL*

Miedo del ruido de las sombras
del canto subterráneo que emerge de la noche
miedo del relámpago súbito de la esperanza hueca
de los piquetitos de conciencia
de la estrella que destrozó el gigante

Como cruel estribillo
como la letanía que descubre al silencio
como el padre nuestro de la infancia en desorden
o aquel librito del catecismo azul de las noches en vela
aquella lamentación aquel castigo
aquel cuerpo amoratado en llanto

La dejaron llorar la avergonzaron la enmudecieron
Hasta volver al lugar del crimen

la culpa
se desprendió en imagen beatífica y suprema
A ella obedeció y en ese instante ardió una niña
hasta fijarse en el firmamento
Sola en la oscuridad

## THE STAR

*from Dama infiel al sueño*

*MINERVA MARGARITA VILLARREAL*

*TRANSLATION BY NORMA E. CANTÚ*

Fear of the shadow's noise
of the underground song that emerges from the night
fear of hollow hope's sudden lightning
of conscience's little stings
of the star destroyed by the giant

Like a cruel refrain with its fine music
like the litany that coats silence
like the Our Father of childhood in disorder
or that little blue catechism book of sleepless nights
that lamentation that punishment
that bruised body in tears

Thus
they let her cry they shamed her they silenced her
they loaded her back with penance's grief
they made her remember returning to the scene of the crime
her guilt hidden

she detached herself into a supreme and devoted image
that obeyed her and in that instant a child burned
her ashes flew until they settled in the firmament
Alone in the darkness.

## EL DELIRIO

*from Pérdida*

*MINERVA MARGARITA VILLARREAL*

La noche inicia su rutina,
su lento y jorobado caminar
entre jardines y losetas: lápidas y rostros perdidos;
nada en el aire sino el agotamiento,
el *solitario solo* que deambula.

Decidiste quedarte entre sus flores
como si la marea, de tan alta, te hubiera tragado y devuelto
al sitio donde los ángeles duermen,
donde la ciudad cierra sus puertas.

La ciudad vela en tus ojos
sobre esas *dos piedras al fondo de una acequia vacía,*
tratando de extraerles un minuto de luz,
un instante donde la eternidad se suspendiera.

Pero regresa el vértigo
del hombre: el padre-dios lanza cuchillos
lacerando la carne,
la sangre de tu sangre en la traba del miedo:

niños insatisfechos de cigarros que incendian mariposas
    en la sequía del verano,
niños libélulas de pupilas tristes,
niños cucarachas del miedo acorazados,
niños de futuro vacío, ángeles de mirada turbia,
niños de fuego, niños, niños, niños.
Mis niños en el rincón del tiempo estacionados,
lágrimas que brotan de esos adolescentes
y la mujer vencida por los hijos del deseo:
nervios, hijos, ojos de hombres, ojos sombríos.

En el vaivén del tiempo
el delirio de tu trastorno
en el naufragio de una infancia
sobre la larga noche;
una y otra vez en la misma acera
pronunciándose el vértigo.

# DELIRIUM

*from Pérdida*

*MINERVA MARGARITA VILLARREAL*

*TRANSLATION BY NORMA E. CANTÚ*

The night begins its routine,
its slow and hunched walk
between gardens and tiles: tombstones and lost faces;
nothing in the air but exhaustion,
the *lonely loner alone* meandering,

You decided to stay among her flowers
as if the tide, being so high, had swallowed you and returned you
to the place where angels sleep,
to where the city closes its doors.

And you imagined, oh, how you imagined,
but the city sleeps in your eyes
upon those *two rocks at the bottom of an empty ditch,*
trying to extract a minute of light from them,
an instant where eternity would be suspended.

The vertigo of raped images returns,
Man: the father-god throws knives
lashing the skin,
the blood of your blood in fear's embrace:
children unsatisfied with cigarettes that light up butterflies
    in the summer's drought,

dragonfly children with sad pupils,
cockroach children armored by fear,
children of an empty future, angels with blurred vision,
children of fire, children, children, children.
My children parked in the corner of time,
tears that caress adolescents irises.
You stayed above,
clasped to the women beaten by desire's children:
nerves, children, men's eyes, gloomy eyes.

In the sway of time,
in the delirium of your madness:
the shipwreck of a childhood
over the long night of your demented walk;
time and again on the same sidewalk
the vertigo showing itself.

# HISTORIA

*GRISEL ACOSTA*

**Para todas las que me oyen y me reciben**
*Nuestra historia no la escriben*
*Pero vive en los arboles*
*Y en estrellas que iluminan las noches*
*Ella vive*
*Ella vive*
*Ella vive*
*Y volverá*
*Y volverá*
*Y volverá*

She invisibly walks on the streets
Her legs riddled with warm varicose veins
And she lingers in sheets
That have been scrubbed of their stains
Her smell is detected
When sand meets pine trees
And the texture of her calloused hands
Is found in fallen oak leaves
She began in an earthen pot
A mixture of herbs and river water
That laps back and forth in the cells of sons and daughters
Lulled to sleep by the
Comfort of her strokes
But who wake up in sweaty confusion
Not quite grasping the memory that chokes
And insists on the question:

"Where is she? Where is she?
Is it a person who we forgot?
Or is it not a person, just a mystery?"
She keeps calling from the
Fabric pulled over your shoulders
Whispering from the volcano's
Lava that smolders
Her rhythm beating out with
Every spin of rubber and iron on asphalt
The softness of her composure
Leaking out of milk and wheat and malt
Her grandeur yells! SCREAMS!
In the unified buzzing of insects and machines
Her glory pounds and Pounds and POUNDS
Tentacled dendrites in dreams
She is not written
She is not concrete
Holds everything yet owns nothing
She is not a member, she has no seat
But you breathe her from the sky
And give her back to us
With a sigh
Her work is hard in
Your muscles and bones
Her voice is the highest
And lowest of tones

Feel her vibrations in song…
*Feel her vibrations in song…*
*Where has she gone?*

She's here
You have always known
She isn't written
And as it should be
For written words are opinions
She lives in truth
Written words are man-made
And she was never man-made
She was glory-made
She is story-made
She is mud and rain and bloody pain
She lives in creation and in the inevitable result
She lives in death
She lives in death

And you will never understand
*Don't come back with how hard it is for you, too*
*Comparisons and conflicts are not what I choose*
*Still, that day you made me cry*
*Just for showing my pride*

*Para todas que me oyen y me reciben*
*Nuestra historia no la escriben*
*Pero vive en los arboles*
*Y en estrellas que iluminan las noches*
*Ella vive*
*Ella vive*
*Ella vive*
*Y volverá*
*Y volverá*
*Y volverá*

## DREAM WATER BREATH DEATH

*GRISEL ACOSTA*

She rests on a beach she is not allowed on. Her clothes are from a store she cannot afford. In her dreams she wakes up to a house that is larger on the inside than it is on the outside. The flies have turned into water lilies that flap like fans to cool the midday death sun. The family dog takes her on a tour of the church spires that Gaudi-twirl into the depths of the inner labyrinth. Books line the walls of the room at the end of the spiral darkness that illuminates the words she never sees. Brown stained carvings reach to her and guide her into the main hall escalator where students ignore her arrival. She gets lost looking for her locker which has a combination she cannot remember. Her platform shoes were not given to her so she walks barefoot in golden sandals. Red candles mimic the blood on her hands which belongs to the mother she did not murder. The bicycle she wished for is not hanging on the back stairs that she repeatedly walks down while holding a knife. She is in the room she cannot find again and the students appear and reappear. If she crawls out of the knick knack nook she will be in her house again which she is already inside of. Her mother buys cheap ornaments that are expensive. The house is transparent to sunlight when she crawls into the darkness of the church spires and book room and the modern school. The larger rooms are within the walls which are skinnier than she is because not even the walls have eaten. She smiles her sadness with closed lips to hide the cosmetic dentistry that hasn't been done. Her cousin doesn't send letters that she reads closely to connect with the outside world. Water fills the school and she underwater paddles through the columns and arches and banisters. When she wakes up she is in the ocean that is not hers and swims with dreams that salt the world inside her walls.

# MUJER

*ANALIESE TRUJILLO-ELLIS*

This is her home
this thin edge of
barbwire.
Gloria Anzaldúa

Soy Malintzin.

Ayudé a los que vinieron en barcos.

¿Por qué?

Ayudé a Hernán Cortés.

¿Por qué?

Ayudé a los españoles destruir mi cultura.

¿Por qué?

Porque me cambié bandos.
Porque fui traidora.

Porque fui vana.
Porque fui una mujer mala.
Porque fui capaz de matar a mis hijos.

*That's what people think.*

Soy Malintzin.

Ayudé a las tribus escapar.

¿Por qué?

Ayudé a mi cultura sobrevivir.

¿Por qué?

Ayudé a mi gente aprender un nuevo modo de vivir.

¿Por qué?

Porque fui esclava, vendida por mi mamá.
Porque podía hablar varios lenguajes.

Porque fui
inteligente.

Porque fui víctima de la ventaja de Cortés.
Porque fui una figura histórica en una situación imposible.
Porque estuve rodeada de desconocidos en ***mi*** tierra

Porque hice lo mejor que pude.

Soy Malintzin

VOLUME TWO

# EL MUNDO ZURDO

AN INTERNATIONAL CONFERENCE ON THE LIFE AND WORK OF GLORIA E. ANZALDÚA

Conference Proceedings, 2009

Edited by Norma Alarcón and Rita E. Urquijo-Ruiz

# PART 1

## NEPANTLA, SPIRITUALITY, AND CULTURE

*Religious Syncretism: Coatlicue, Guadalupe and Angela*
Jorge and Andrea Velásquez Collection
By ALMA GÓMEZ-FRITH

# 1

# SANTA NEPANTLA: A BORDERLANDS SUTRA PLENARY SPEECH

*RANDY P. CONNER*

First, I would like us, as Gloria has asked us, to "pay homage to those whose backs served as bridges./We remember our dead" ("now let us shift," 576).

At this conference, we especially recall the memory of Gloria Evangelina Anzaldúa.

In *Borderlands*, Gloria writes:

> A chicken is being sacrificed
> at a crossroads, a simple mound of earth
> a mud shrine for *Eshu*,
> Yoruba god of indeterminacy,
> who blesses her choice of path.
> She begins her journey. (80)

ABRE CAMINO! Let us open the road!

I want to thank Professor Norma Cantú, the Society for the Study of Gloria Anzaldúa, and the Women's Studies Institute at the University of Texas at San Antonio for inviting me to speak at this conference. I'm dedicating my talk to my partner of thirty years, David Hatfield Sparks, and to my friends Ariban Marta Chagoya, Cherríe Moraga, Liliana Wilson, and Dr. Laura Pérez, Nepantleras who are carrying on not only the intellectual work but also the heart-work and soul-work that Gloria assisted in birthing, and to Inéz Hernández-Ávila, who held a very special place in Gloria's life as an Opener of the Road.

I was a very close friend of Gloria's for thirty years. I assisted her in editing many of her works and was continuing to do so when she died. Thus, my relationship with her was both personal and literary; I was, despite my "race" and my genitalia one of her *comadres*, as was my partner David Hatfield Sparks, to whom she introduced me. Phoning me from Café La Bohème so many years ago, she told me, "I think I just met your lover. He's a poet and musician and he's radical, too."

"We're not supposed to remember ...otherworldly events," Gloria relates in *Borderlands*; "We're supposed to ignore, forget, kill those fleeting images of the soul's presence...We're supposed to forget that every cell in our bodies...has spirit in it" (36).

I would like to share with you this morning some memories I have regarding Gloria's spiritual beliefs and practices, as these, together with friendship and love, and literary and artistic kinship, formed a significant dimension of our bond.

I would also like to share with you this morning some thoughts I have regarding recent critiques of Gloria's work, especially in regard to the spiritual dimension. Some of these critiques are actually assaults on both her work and her person, the latter constituting, to be sure, *ad hominem*—or, I suppose, *ad mulierem* might be more appropriate—attacks. Brian Gollnick, for example, describes Gloria's "deployment of Latin American discourses of ethnicity and *mestizaje*" as "unself-critical" (110); Melissa Wright disparages her for "offer[ing] *an imaginative elixir* [italics mine] for a practical problem" (115); Scott Michaelsen and David E. Johnson, in *Border Theory: The Limits of Cultural Politics*, describe Gloria as a colonialist who "partak[es] of some of the most obvious of stereotypes about Premodern peoples" (13); in *The Revolutionary Imagination in the Americas and the Age of Development*, Maria Josefina Saldaña-Portillo portrays Gloria as a privileged U.S. Chicana who preys vampirically on the Indigenous (286); and Sheila Marie Contreras, in *Blood Lines: Myth, Indigenism, and Chicana/o Literature*, depicts Gloria as an imperialist and colonialist (9, 38, 122-123, 126, 131) who takes pleasure in "the looting of Indigenous material objects" (126) and also as an inventor of "fakelore"—reminiscent of the reaction to Gloria's early work on the part of the Good Ol' Boys of the UT Anthropology Department—her alleged spiritual experiences actually based on anthropology, archaeology, and folklore rather than being grounded in authentic revelatory encounters. In other words, Gloria's a huckster who sells snake-oil at the carnival (113-114).

In "*Canción de la diosa de la noche*," a poem dedicated to me because it was my nickname for Gloria when she would stand on her balcony long after midnight in her nightgown, deep in contemplation, blowing smoke-rings toward the moon, and because, when I was young, I reminded her of Dionysus, she chants, "To cast out the brute,/I shake earth, air, fire, and water" (*Borderlands*, 196).

Most of you here will know that Gloria was an activist in numerous sociopolitical movements, including the Chicano Movement, the Women's Movement, and the LGBT Movement. In 1980, becoming disheartened by separatist, anti-spiritual biases, and other issues in these movements, she founded *El Mundo Zurdo*, which began as a series of poetry and prose performances at Small Press Traffic in San Francisco by feminists, people of color, the differently abled, and Queer people. The concept of *El Mundo Zurdo* arose from the transformation of oppression into self-acceptance in regard to being left-handed; the association of the left with the political Left; the association of the left hand with esoteric wisdom, magical work that deals with both light and shadow, and the erotico-sacred path of Tantra; and the association of the left with her vision of a reborn Huitzilopochtli, the "Hummingbird of the Left," transformed from patriarchal warrior to spiritual warrior assisting in the overthrow of patriarchy. Determined, like numerous others in the San Francisco Bay Area and elsewhere, to bring together radical politics with an anti-hegemonic, earth-centered spiritual vision, she turned her efforts toward birthing a new "spiritual activism." "May the roaring force of our collective creativity," Gloria wrote, "heal the wounds of hate, ignorance, indifference/dissolve the divisions creating chasms between us" ("now let us shift" 575).

Gloria was a spiritual eclectic, but she was not a dilettante. She approached her study of transpersonal psychologies, esoteric philosophies, spiritual traditions, and healing, divinatory, and magical technologies *with the very same rigor* that she did her traditional academic studies.

In the 1970s and 1980s, Gloria devoted a great deal of time to studying Eastern philosophy and Western esotericism. She was deeply moved by the teachings of Sri Aurobindo, the Mother, their disciple Satprem, Gurdjieff, Krishnamurti, Ouspensky, Bhagwan Shree Rajneesh, and Swami Muktananda. Generally speaking, these were teachers who sought to interweave ancient non-Western epistemologies and contemplative technologies, such as various forms of yoga, with the notion of the "evolution of consciousness." This notion played a significant role in Gloria's spiritual vision, in regard to her belief in the increasing need for consciously evolved communities, which she referred to as "tribes," as many in the Bay Area did at that time, to perform acts of politico-spiritual activism in a rapidly approaching apocalyptic era, possibly culminating, as some accounts relating to the Maya suggest, in or near 2012 (Hernández-Ávila and Anzaldúa 193). The threat of nuclear war, the emergence of HIV/AIDS, and the ever-present threat of the "BIG ONE" were only a few of the reasons why apocalypticism became the order of the day in the Bay Area of the late Seventies and early Eighties. On June 8, 1983, Gloria wrote in a copy she sent to me of Satprem's explanation of the thought of Sri Aurobindo:

> *Querido Quetzal,*
>
> *Como te digo en la carta, you belong to the same Oversoul as Sri Aurobindo and the Mother. A little before 1986 the spirit of these two will "inhabit" your body though everything, your spirit, will remain the same. Do not get*

*scared, the process will be very gradual. It may have even started, as is the case with me, through dreams and night visions. [...] This book will help you prepare yourself. Don't let us kid ourselves—it will be work—sometimes very hard. [...] In June 1985 I will call a meeting of the Tribe to discuss what's coming down... [...] Randy, this is very important, I used my last few dollars to send you this—so you can see I am deadly serious.*

*Tu amiga siempre*

In regard to Western esotericism, Gloria studied alchemy, astrology, numerology, the I Ching, the Kabbalah, and the Tarot. Her study and practice of Tarot was strongly influenced by Angeles Arrien, a Basque professor who reformulated the Thoth or Crowley deck and who also first shared the meaning of Gloria's surname with her (Anzaldúa "*Noche y su Nidada*" 30). She also practiced candle magic. Oftentimes, especially in the days before she began writing at the computer, she would—as we were taught to do by the proprietor of the Candlelight Shop in the Mission in San Francisco—light an orange candle on one side of her paper and a blue candle on the other and then pass a bay leaf over the paper before beginning to write. In the early 1980s, we studied psychic development, including telepathy and lucid dreaming, with Tamara Diaghilev, one of the last living descendants of Sergei Diaghilev, the famed impresario of the Ballets Russes. Gloria was also inspired by the writings of Jane Roberts, a medium who channeled an entity named Seth, and by the works of Carlos Castañeda, whose work she considered metaphorically truthful. She also sought wisdom in dreams, trance meditation, and entheogens, particularly mushrooms. In regard to the charge that Gloria was a "New Ager," I think she put it best in an interview with AnaLouise Keating, that while many involved in New Age spiritualities are focused on transcending the body, she insisted that the body be taken into account in spiritual practice ("Last words?" 290). In this way, Gloria shared much more in common with present-day Wiccans, Witches, Neopagans, women involved in Women's Spirituality, and other practitioners of earth-centered spiritual traditions than she did with many aligning themselves with the New Age movement.

"I hate to call them goddesses," Gloria told Debbie Blake and Carmen Abrego in an interview in 1994. "I like to call them 'cultural figures'" ("Doing Gigs" 225). Yet she consistently spoke of La Diosa. Like Walt Whitman, Gloria was "large," she "contradict[ed her]self," she "contain[ed] multitudes" (Whitman, 96). For Gloria, as for Audre Lorde and other poet-priestesses, gods are simultaneously both living presences and metaphors. By metaphor, however, Gloria in no way meant "poetic device." Rather, she defined metaphor as philosopher Mary Daly does in *Pure Lust*, in which Daly argues that metaphors embody deep meaning and serve philosophically and spiritually to "transform…our perceptions of reality" and to "carry us toward knowledge of our future as they connect us with our…memories" (25-26). Likewise, when Gloria wrote of "constructing myths," of "myth-making," she did not mean to suggest, as social constructivist materialists hoped she did, that myths were lies or that divinities and spirits don't exist. She meant rather that, in order for us to share experiences of the ineffable or numinous with others, we utilize the language of symbol and metaphor, thus transforming an unmediated experience of the sacred into a mediated one. Myth-making, or the construction of myths, comprised one aspect of a process for her; its others, which until now, most academics have wanted to deny, were communication with, and embodiment of, the Divine.

In one of the last photos taken of the two of us together, Gloria and I are sitting on the couch in her living room in Santa Cruz on a sunny afternoon. Liliana's and Santa Barraza's beautiful paintings of goddesses, the Virgin, and strong women, together with the Huichol jaguar mask on the wall, wooden serpent staff, and copal incense Gloria has lit, give the room the feeling of a temple honoring ancient yet very much alive divinities.

Benjamin Alire Sáenz writes of Gloria:

> She firmly believes [in] *La diosa*…This is no solution. This is an escape… To return to…"traditional" spiritualities…makes very little sense. The material conditions that gave rise to the Aztecs' religion no longer exist. Anzaldúa's language…[is] ultimately completely mortgaged to a nostalgia I find unacceptable. The resurrection of the old gods…is a futile and

impossible task. To invoke old gods as a tool against oppression and capitalism is to choose the wrong weapon. (87)

Although I disagree with his viewpoint and find his attitude deeply pessimistic and extremely patronizing, Sáenz is correct when he argues that Gloria believed in the power of La Diosa to heal and transform humanity and the cosmos. When Gloria was still living in Austin in the mid-to-late 1970s, she came into contact with a number of women who had turned away from the patriarchal faiths in which they'd been reared, or else had begun to reformulate certain aspects of these faiths, in order to honor the Feminine Divine, whom they understood to be a Great Goddess, multiple goddesses, manifestations of the Virgin Mary—particularly the Virgin of Guadalupe, and female saints. In honoring this or these manifestations of divinity, they were—in abiding by the ancient principle of "as above, so below"—honoring their own femaleness, their own bodies, their sexuality, their relationships, their creativity, their work. Gloria was first published in an Austin journal, *Lady-Unique-Inclination-of-the-Night*, edited by folklorist Kay Turner, that grew out of this emerging spiritual movement. For a time, she lived as a roommate with a young Chicana lesbian who shared with Gloria a spiritual practice that mixed the feminist Witchcraft of Z. Budapest with veneration of La Virgen. During this period, she also read Merlin Stone's *When God Was a Woman*; after moving to San Francisco, Gloria became friends with Stone and participated in a women's workshop with the feminist Witch Starhawk, author of the immensely popular *Spiral Dance*. Gloria often spoke and wrote in her letters of her increasingly profound belief in the Goddess. On May 16, 1983, having moved to New York, she wrote to me from Brooklyn:

*Something weird happened to me in San Diego, Quetsy, I became this strong woman, I wasn't afraid to let my voice boom out and I realized that it wasn't coming from just me and that I was a channel for the Divine, my dear Shakti—some of it came from her. So now I feel myself changing, slowly letting out the real Gauri, the real Prieta, the real Gloria!*

A week later, she wrote:

> *All my energy has gone into meditation...I'm so excited. I'm on my fourth day of fasting! These days I've consecrated to the Divine and oh, Randito, I feel her presence so concretely. She is always with me. [...] I'm real tired. Last night was the worst (effects of fasting): shaky knees, stomach turning, slight diarrhea. This morning I felt so good that I didn't go to bed at my usual which is 7, 8 a.m. I stayed up till noon. It was great. I had intercourse with the Divine. That's what it...feels like when the meditation is real good. I was "locked" in to the Goddess...and physical cunt and heart synchronized with the "cosmic"...I felt a current running up and down my body...such intensity that I thought I was going to burst. No wonder monks take to solitary mountain caves.*

"Indigenous...cultural, social, religious, and political forms that constitute one as indigenous," Saldaña-Portillo writes,

> are not forms that exist in a kind of pastiche grab bag of Indian spiritual paraphernalia, as they seem to exist for Anzaldúa. Ultimately, Anzaldúa's model of representation reproduces liberal models of choice that privilege her position as a U.S. Chicana: she goes through her backpack and decides what to keep and what to throw out, and she chooses to keep signs of indigenous identity as ornamentation and spiritual revival. But what of the living Indian who refuses *mestizaje* as an avenue to political and literary representation? What of the *indigena* who demands new representational models that include her among the living? (286)

Contreras echoes: "I agree with Saldaña [regarding Anzaldúa's appropriation of Indigeneity, in that] I find *no engagement* [emphasis mine] with...American Indians [in her work]" (183, n. 16).

In *Borderlands,* in describing her intimate relationship with Nature, Gloria writes, "[T]rees whisper their secrets to Chrystos, a Native American." (36) Also in *Borderlands*, Gloria dedicates the poem "Cuyamaca" to Chrystos (182), a writer of Menominee heritage whom Gloria instructed in writing, and Beth Brant, a writer of Mohawk heritage, who thanks Gloria in her 1988 anthology *A Gathering of Spirit* for "teaching [her]...what being an editor means" (3).

When Gloria and Cherríe Moraga were co-editing *This Bridge Called My Back*, Gloria assisted several contributors of Indigenous heritage in shaping their pieces, including Barbara Cameron, an activist of Lakota-Hunkpapa heritage and Anita (now Max) Valerio, a writer of Blackfoot heritage who would return to contribute, now as a heterosexual male, to *This Bridge We Call Home*. In February 2002, Gloria wrote to me of her deep sadness on learning of the death of Cameron. In an interview with Inés Hernández Ávila and Domino Pérez near the end of her life, and also in an essay I was helping her edit when she died, Gloria spoke of her belief that all women and, indeed, all persons, having Indigenous heritage needed to come together in politico-spiritual alliances in order to struggle against devastating illnesses like alcoholism and diabetes, brought on or else dramatically escalated by the forces of imperialism and colonialism, and to struggle against the Right's virulent attack on Indigenous immigrants and Mexican and other Latino immigrants having Indigenous heritage. Her concern may have been rooted in the spiritual beliefs and practices of her ancestors, but this in no way hampered—indeed, if anything, it greatly enhanced—her commitment to align herself with the struggles of present-day Indigenous peoples (Anzaldúa "Geography of Selves" 23; Hernández-Ávila and Pérez 7-22).

I have previously mentioned that Michaelsen and Johnson disparage Gloria for, in their words, portraying Native American cultures as being "dominated by magic, shapeshifting, [and] healing"; they describe her "resorting to 'indigenousness'" as a "grasping at mythic-nostalgic straws" (13; 15). Similarly, Sáenz accuses Gloria of "fetishiz[ing] Aztec and Indian culture," adding, "Finding solutions (and identities) by appropriating indigenous mythologies is disturbing and very problematic" (85). Sáenz condescendingly presumes that because he has lost his connection to his Indigenous heritage, then it necessarily follows that Gloria has also lost hers, and it is his duty to tell her so (85-86). Cristina Beltran disapproves of Gloria's alleged theft of things Indigenous in terms of her appropriation of "pre-Cortesian feminist myths" and her desire to "return to indigenous approaches to cultural production (597). "Almost all of Anzaldúa's aesthetic references," she adds, "involve pre-Columbian symbols (beads, feathers, fur, twigs, clay, serpent, cactus)" (600).

When it comes to the issue of Gloria's relationship to certain Indigenous spiritual symbols, beliefs, and practices, beyond the fact that items and entities such as beads, feathers, and serpents also play significant role in African-diasporic and other spiritual traditions, it seems to me that Gloria's detractors are trapped within a binary that is utterly dependent upon a vast gulf existing between "pre-Cortesian myths" and the present, a gulf that no bridge could possibly span. It occurs to me that this perspective is governed and bound by a fence, a fence erected by colonizers and Christianizers, a fence to divide pagan past from Christian present, a fence which has proven not to be nearly as impenetrable as first imagined. More than a few border-crossers have gotten through. Over the centuries, border-crossers have embodied and enacted incessant innovation and metamorphoses of ancient traditions, as reflected in traditions including Curanderismo, Hechicería (Anzaldúa, Blake, and Abrego 225), Peyote Religion, Concheros dance troupes (Markman and Markman 156, 163, 165, 166), certain houses of Regla de Ocha (more commonly known as Santería) as practiced in Los Angeles, and other spiritual traditions practiced in Mexico and the U.S. Southwest. Indeed, in the Christian-hegemonic U.S. and Mexico, non-Christian beliefs and practices might be likened to an underground stream, and, as Gloria writes in *Borderlands*:

> The sea cannot be fenced,
> *el mar* does not stop at borders.
> To show the white man what she thought of his arrogance,
> Yemayá blew that wire fence down. (3)

Likewise, La Llorona is no respecter of fences. Gloria's favorite song was "La Llorona." She loved to hear it sung by Chavela Vargas, Joan Baez, Tish Hinojosa, Lila Downs, and the musicians at Mi Tierra when she and my partner David and I would eat *mole* there. She told me that during the Vietnam War, when the people of her town and the surrounding countryside heard La Llorona wailing, they knew that a beloved son had died. As Inés Hernández Ávila puts it in a 1991 dialogue with Gloria, "Tradition is not static, it's dynamic and it's always been dynamic. Otherwise it would have died" ("Quincentennial" 185).

Although Gloria was not formally initiated into the West African-based Yorùbá -diasporic religion, she became familiar with its beliefs and practices through her friendship with Luisah Teish, who, over the years Gloria knew her, became an initiated elder, an Iyanifa, in the Ifa/Orisha tradition, and who holds a chieftaincy title, Yeye'woro, from the Fatunmise Compound in Ile Ife, Nigeria (*Borderlands* 36). In the early 1980s, Gloria received a life-changing divinatory reading from Teish, which she mentions in her interviews. Although the bulk of this reading must remain secret, she was told, as she also mentions in the interviews, that she was watched over by both Yemayá and Oyá (Anzaldúa and Smuckler, 19). Over the thirty years I knew her, Gloria and I often visited *botánicas* and *yerberías*, including two in San Antonio and Cantú's in Austin, shops where religious supplies for this and kindred traditions are sold, many times. In the early 1980s, she interviewed two gay Latinos living on the East Coast who practiced la Regla de Ocha, Cuban and Puerto Rican expressions of this tradition, which eventually led to my partner and myself writing *Queering Creole Spiritual Traditions*. When Gloria and I were teaching at Florida Atlantic University in 2001, we would go to the beach and offer Yemayá cornmeal, molasses, and watermelons. Gloria's fascinations with horses and with *remolinos*, whirlwinds, which she of course witnessed many times growing up in South Texas, were enhanced on learning that one of those who guided her in life, Oyá, is the mother of whirlwinds and tempests, and that her wand is a whisk typically made of beads and horsehair. Perhaps most significantly for Gloria, encountering the *orishas*, and also within this tradition, the ancestors, assisted her, by way of the deployment of certain sacred technologies, in learning to recognize, contact, and invoke Mesoamerican divinities and ancestral spirits. When she died, Teish and her spiritual household, including Xochipala Maes Valdez, her spiritual name being Iyanifa Efunyemi Fakayode Fatunmise, a lesbian Chicana whom Gloria had instructed in writing, held a special funerary ritual to honor her; and Teish and another priestess, Uzuri Amini, an African-American woman whom Gloria had also instructed in writing, performed a public memorial rite in the Ifa tradition for her at a celebration of her life and work that my partner David and I held, together with Cherríe Moraga and her partner Célia Herrera Rodriguez, at the San Francisco Public Library.

It is especially unfortunate that so much effort has been wasted in trashing Gloria's so-called appropriation of Indigeneity, her belief in the Feminine Divine, and her so-called "New Age" tendencies when much more productive work might have been accomplished by exploring her experience of the sacred in relationship to relatively recent—historically speaking—pan-Indian spiritual traditions such as the Native American Church, or the Peyote Religion as it is otherwise known, as well as in relationship to African-diasporic spiritual traditions. As a prime example of this, Beltran (*Patrolling Borders* 597), Contreras (*Blood Lines* 118), and others disparage Gloria for what they see as her anti-historical, nationalistic, romantic, feminist reformulation of Coatlicue. Had they bothered to compare Gloria's understanding of Coatlicue and other divinities to understandings of sacred forces in the Peyote Religion, they would have discovered a remarkable resonance. As Joseph D. Calabrese II explains in "Reflexivity and Symbolism in the Navajo Peyote Meeting," for participants in the peyote ceremony, various kinds of forces that he calls "symbols" arise that include cultural ones as they are traditionally conceived; personal, private, or idiosyncratic ones; and ones that involve the transformation or metamorphosis of traditional cultural ones (499, 505-507). In Calabrese's terminology, "[I]ndividual symbols and interpretations become detached from their original relationships to generate a variety of new symbolic understandings…[and] radical ritual innovations" (518).

Likewise, where the *Yoruba*—diasporic religions of la Regla de Ocha and Candomblé are concerned, the goddess or *orishá* Yemayá held an important yet considerably less significantly lesser place in the pantheon as it existed in Nigeria than she does in the Americas, due to her coming to be seen as Protectress of those who were forced to cross the waters during the Middle Passage. Similarly, Babaluayé, ancient deity of death by illness rather than by violence or old age, Catholicized as St. Lazarus, has come to be the patron saint of persons with HIV/AIDS. In a similar manner, Gloria's beloved Santissima Muerte has in recent years become a patron of groups including transgendered prostitutes in Mexico and San Francisco, as well as, unfortunately, drug traffickers, because these groups take their lives in their hands whenever they hit the streets.

Beyond these comparisons, Gloria's conceptions of Coatlicue and other divinities might be compared to various conceptions of Jesus that emerged during the first four centuries of the construction of Christianity. Burton L. Mack, professor of early Christianity, writes in *Who Wrote the New Testament?*: "Each group" of early followers of Jesus, and there were at least five competing groups, "created Jesus" in its own image (46). Jesus was variously seen as a warrior-hero, a martyr, a sage, and a god who ascended to the heavens after dwelling on earth for a time (Mack 46, 70-71, 80, 93).

As Gloria tells us, "*Nuestra tarea* is to envision Coyolxauhqui, not dead and decapitated but with eyes wide open" (*Light in the Dark* vii).

Sáenz frustratedly describes Gloria's work as "all about...immers[ing herself] in a particular mythology (a non-European [one]...)" so that she can thereby "heal our sick body politic." He then adds, "*Healing* is a *totem* word for Anzaldúa [emphasis mine]" (86). He also adds that even if he agrees that our society is "desperately in need of healing," he "would not choose to use that language" (86). Michaelsen and Johnson view Gloria's focus on healing in her work as an attempt to cash in on stereotypes of Indigenous peoples (13). Similarly, Contreras is also deeply perturbed by Gloria's writing of "herself as psychic, as *curandera*" (126).

Although it's true that she spoke of illnesses she experienced, most of her readers and others who did not know her intimately were aware only of a fraction of the suffering she endured. From the time we first met, and from what I understood from conversations with her, her life was shadowed by periods of great suffering. During the years I knew her, she suffered from profoundly debilitating periods, carpal tunnel syndrome, insomnia, deep depression, uterine cancer, diabetes, high blood pressure, kidney problems, hypothyroidism, retinopathy, and neuropathy. What turned out to be our last conversations and correspondence focused heavily on illness and medications. She told me of taking Avapro, Cozaar, Flomax, Glucophage, Insulin, Levoxyl, Lexapro, Lovastatin, Premarin, and other drugs. Her sight was worsening to the extent that she was cautioned not to drive. Thus, her coming to bear an uncanny resemblance to the archetypal shaman as "wounded healer" wasn't something she planned as part of a heist to rip off Native cultures. I'm quite certain she would've been very happy indeed to have been relieved of that particular cup of poison.

She did not share with many people that one of her grandmothers—at least according to what she told me—had been a *curandera* and that she was destined to receive her wisdom. I remember once, within the last years of her life, we were walking along the sea cliff in Santa Cruz when she told me that at some point she'd decided to practice Curanderismo through her writing, but that, with her health declining rapidly, together with her disappointment in Caroline Myss and other "New Age" healers, she was thinking that maybe she'd made the wrong choice, that she should've chosen to become a *curandera* of traditional medicine.

When we were younger, however, Gloria had cured us of terrible colds with a heavy syrup of orange leaves from the Valley, and for quite a long time had cured our insomnia with certain herbs. Few beyond my partner David and I and her *comadres* knew that over the years she studied with a number of healers of Indigenous heritage. In the early 1980s, for example, she studied, as I did, Huichol shamanism as taught by the well-known Huichol shaman Don José Matsuwa, while in the late 1990s, she studied with Camila Martínez, a *curandera* of Mexican, German, and Hopi heritage who was herself apprenticed to Mazatec elder Doña Julieta Casimiro and who now heads the Institute of Traditional Native Medicine, the Maya Seed Ark Project, and the Maya Ecological Literacy Program.

Unfortunately, neither Western nor Indigenous medicine ultimately prevented her untimely and, in my view, tragic death. For those who say, "It was meant to be," I would say that in no small way, Gloria was a victim of the American health system during the Bush Administration. Since Gloria's passing, Suzanne Bost has treated this subject in her essay "Gloria Anzaldúa's Mestiza Pain: Sacrifice, Chicana Embodiment, and Feminist Politics."

Gloria has also been criticized for her depiction of Queer people as possessing *la facultad* (Beltran 606), a sort of psychic ability that appears to emerge from a complex of factors including one or more of the following: social oppression, division of labor, inborn traits, and divine embodiment. Gloria derived this belief from several places: first, during her childhood, local folklore attributed magical, although negative, hybrid- or were-like status to Queer people, referring to them as *mita-mita*; second, many of the lesbians, gay men, and bisexuals she encountered in Austin, San Francisco, and New York were practitioners of earth-centered spiritual traditions including Wicca and the Yorùbá-diasporic spiritual tradition or of the healing, divinatory, or magical arts, with many of the gay men being Radical Faeries; and third, she read many works by Paula Gunn Allen, Will Roscoe, and others on "Two-Spirit" people and became friends with some over the years. By the end of her life, I believe that she had become a bit less optimistic—as I have—when it came to thinking that, as Harry Hay imagined it, if you scratched a Queer person hard enough, you would find a shaman or a fairy just waiting to be released. Still, she continued to believe that certain people could develop this skill if they desired to do so.

In "Born Under the Sign of the Flower: Los *jotos* in Ancient Mexico and Modern Aztlan," an unfinished manuscript begun in the 1980s and continually worked on into the mid-1990s, written for an anthology which she and my partner David and I proposed but which unfortunately failed to materialize, Gloria addressed the relationship of queer men to Indigeneity as she saw it, especially in regard to present-day Chicanos, Mexicanos, and those she considered to be their spiritual forebears and divine patrons. Grounding the essay in her friendships and alliances with Chicano and Latino gay men including Juan Pablo Gutierrez and Francisco Alarcón, she suggests that gays who are "spiritually inclined" should create altars to "Tezcatlipoca, Tlazolteotl, [and] Xochiquetzal" and propitiate them with offerings (21). In the essay, which exists only as a very rough draft, she writes,

> I remember how Ronnie Burk, a Tejano *joto*, reacted to my reading of a Tlazolteotl poem [taken from the anthology *Shaking the Pumpkin*] in a bar in San Antonio. Gay men and goddesses. There is an affinity. (5)

Gloria dearly loved Ronnie Burk when he was young. He flamed BIG-TIME in his coat of many colors. I remember that when Gloria and he and I attended a United Farmworkers meeting near Austin, he charmed everyone there. He also charmed the likes of Allen Ginsberg and William Burroughs, and it's my understanding that Ana Castillo became good friends with him later on. Unfortunately, Gloria and David and I lost track of him. He became an activist struggling against HIV/AIDS and died of complications from the illness a number of years ago. He was a marvelous post-Beat poet and a very spiritual person.

When I first met Gloria, she was fascinated with Tezcatlipoca, especially in his manifestation as the "Smoking" or "Obsidian Mirror," which she linked to scrying, or divination by mirror-gazing, as practiced by the Elizabethan magus John Dee, who himself used an obsidian mirror (Markman and Markman 105). Although I can't recall if she ever had an experiential encounter with him, I know that she believed in Tezcatlipoca as a living deity. It is of course Tezcatlipoca who opens the "path of the red and black ink," resonating in this task with the Yorùbá *orishá* Eleggúa, in Catholic iconography, the Niño de Atocha and the Anima Sola, whose primary colors are red and black, with black signifying night, death, rebirth, and esoteric knowledge, and red signifying blood, the life-force, and creativity, that which the Yorùbá call *ashé* (Anzaldúa *Borderlands* 65ff, Markman and Markman 4, 31, 137, 138, 149). On meeting me and other queer men, she became increasingly interested, as I did, in Tezcatlipoca's associations with homoeroticism and gender diversity. Over the years we shared information we gathered about "Tezcat," as she liked to call him. I used some of this data in my books *Blossom of Bone* and the *Encyclopedia of Queer Myth*, for which Gloria wrote the Foreword. Given his associations with both same-sex eroticism on the one hand and shamanism, divination, and magic on the other—as recently validated in a very informative work, "None of the Above: Gender Ambiguity in Nahua Ideology," by Cecilia F. Klein—it is not hard to imagine how we arrived at the view of Tezcatlipoca as a symbolic embodiment of Queer persons practicing divinatory and magical arts. In the essay, Gloria once more evokes the image of the Queer person as border-crosser and as bridging worlds of flesh and spirit: "The mestizo faggot," she writes,

> is a borderlands person, not only crossing borders sexually but constantly traveling from one world to another...passing to the ecstatic...spirit

> world… […] Consider the word *mariposa*, "butterfly." It brings associations of soul, otherworldliness, the underworld,…metamorphosis (14; 2).

In a section of the essay she began working on in the 1980s, when AIDS was devastating gay communities and took the lives of friends of hers living on both coasts, Gloria, like many in the Bay Area during that period, came to view Queer people as *not essentially* but rather *potentially* as enacting the roles of priest, healer, and psychopomp, writing:

> In recent years, Chicano *jotos* have returned to their indigenous roots to search for ways of dealing with disease and death. It is there that they have found ancient survival techniques, teachings. Some, like Juan Pablo Gutierrez, have instituted the ceremony of the Day of the Dead to commemorate friends and lovers who have died of AIDS. Juan Pablo creates Day of the Dead altars ("Born Under the Sign" 17). […] If I were dying of AIDS, what words would I need to see me on my way, what rituals would speed me safely on?…Inspired by the reading of Aztec poems, I wrote:
>
> On your way, on your way
> Your flesh is the darkness of flowers
> You will die, but you will live on
> I want to see you thicken with life
> :
> You will be born in the house
> Of Tamoanchan
> On your way, on your way
> :
> And the dead shall take root in the sky ("Born Under the Sign" 18)

In this dirge, Gloria braided elements of various chants including praise-hymns to Tezcatlipoca and Xochiquetzal, whose paradise is Tamoanchan, which includes among its inhabitants the spirits of gender-diverse men who served as artists in life. I can imagine Gloria responding to those who argue that Aztlan is a fantasy (see Gaspar de Alba, "There's No Place," 103-4), "Maybe so. Maybe not. *But Tamoanchan does.*"

I realize that the portrait I'm sketching of Gloria may be distasteful to some academics. I hope, however, that we can begin to move beyond the anti-spiritual, anti-esoteric morass that often obstructs scholars within academic institutions so that we may undertake explorations of the work of Gloria, and other writers as well, in light of these esoteric systems. Her work might, for instance, be studied in light of Baudelaire's poem "Correspondences" and the so-called theory of correspondences or doctrine of sympathies, with which Gloria was intimately familiar. In this light, Inés Hernández-Ávila's beautiful and wise essay "Tierra Tremenda: The Earth's Agony and Ecstasy in the Work of Gloria Anzaldúa" suggests what such an exploration might look like. I'm reminded of a necklace that David and I made for Gloria; it was made of *milagros* we collected in San Antonio and Austin representing symbols in *Borderlands*. If further studies exploring esoteric systems in *Borderlands* and her other writings are *not* undertaken, I fear that Gloria's work will never be fully appreciated for the wealth of wisdom that is encoded within it.

I will never forget reading AnaLouise Keating's *Women Reading, Women Writing*; *Finally!* I said to David, *someone has grasped the spiritual heart of Gloria's work!* Chicana and Latina artists have long embraced the sacred dimension of life, as Laura Pérez amply demonstrates in her beautiful book, *Chicana Art*, as have Chicana and Latina writers of poetry and fiction including Sandra Cisneros, Ana Castillo, and Alicia Gaspar de Alba. Pérez understands *Borderlands* as Gloria meant it to be understood, as a work of art imbued with sacred presence or divine force (31-32). In recent years, scholars including Erika Aigner-Varoz, Alicia Arrizón, Jane Caputi, Theresa Delgadillo, Irene Lara, Lara Medina, Patricia Elise Nelson, Andrea Parra, Domino Renee Pérez, Emma Pérez, Jacquelyn N. Zita, and others have—in contrast to Gloria's detractors—been awakening to, and honoring, the spiritual dimension of *Borderlands* and of Gloria's life and work as a whole, despite the academic risk they take in doing so. Davíd Carrasco and Roberto Lint Sagarena, in "The Religious Vision of Gloria Anzaldúa," write:

> Many scholars and writers have focused on ethnic, gendered, and political elements of the space she describes. But we believe that the heart of her portrayal of the borderlands is articulated, and must be understood, as a religious vision. …[*L*]*a frontera*, her borderlands is a *shamanic space* where a different quality of knowledge is achieved through ecstatic trance states… (224)

"I make my offerings of incense and cracked corn, light my candle," Gloria relates; "On December 2nd…I clean my altars, light my Coatlopeuh candle, burn sage and copal, take [a ceremonial bath, and] sweep my house" (*Borderlands* 67; 88).

Wendy Doniger, professor at the University of Chicago Divinity School, in her introduction to the Hindu erotico-spiritual manual *Kamasutra*, writes:

> The very style in which most of the text is composed, aphoristic prose passages, or *sutras*, has associations with…religion….A *sutra* is literally a thread (cognate with the English words "sew" and "suture"), on which pages…and thoughts are strung like beads…to form a…string of meanings. The text is so intensely condensed, so starkly cryptic, that the task of understanding it frequently seems more like deciphering than translating. A *sutra*…requires the reader to understand what is being connected with what…[It] cries out for the help of a commentary to unpack it, just as the cryptic nature of the early religious texts…required the help of a guru. […] (xv)
>
> …The scholars that [guide us through the *Kamasutra*]…are called *acharyas*, the word for a spiritual guide. (xvi)

*Borderlands*, reminiscent of a *colcha de retazos*, a patchwork quilt, or a *paella*, includes, like many sacred texts, narratives of divine beings; an epic history of a people, focusing on their oppression and vision of liberation; a set of ethics; rituals, prayers, and praise-hymns. Thus, in my view, it qualifies as a *sutra*. Unaware of Doniger's comparison of a *sutra* to a string of beads, Gloria describes *Borderlands* as

> ...a hybridization of metaphor[s]...full of variations...contradictions... [existing in a] universe where all phenomena are interrelated and imbued with spirit. This almost finished product seems an assemblage, a beaded work with several leitmotifs and with a central core, now disappearing in a crazy dance. (66)

In this light, Burton L. Mack describes the deployment of Israelite history by proto-Christians as more often than not "ad hoc, experimental, and tentative" and as having more to do with "mythmaking" and constructing an "epic" than with the sort of factual accuracy one might expect from a historian (71, 73). "[E]arly Christians," he relates, "were...involved in a new religious movement that had to construct its mythology with borrowed ingredients. ...Their use of scriptures was playful, spotty, and naïve" (283).

In a similar vein, John Dominic Crossan, co-founder of the Jesus Seminar and an internationally acclaimed religious scholar, observes in *The Birth of Christianity*,

> [W]ords and deeds of Jesus were updated [by persons living after his departure] to speak to new situations and problems, new communities and crises. They were adopted, they were adapted, they were invented, they were created. (524)

It is in this light, I believe, that we begin to recognize *Borderlands* for what it is, what Gloria meant it to be: a *sutra*. In the terms of the Chicana/o movement, as expressed by Amalia Mesa-Bains in "Domesticana: The Sensibility of Chicana Rasquache, " *Borderlands* is a product of *rasquachismo*, in which

> the irreverent and spontaneous are employed to make the most from the least... one has a stance that is both defiant and inventive. Aesthetic expression comes from discards, fragments, even recycled everyday materials... The capacity to hold life together with bits of string, old coffee cans, and broken mirrors in a dazzling gesture of aesthetic bravado is at the heart of *rasquachismo.* (*Latinola.com*)

*Borderlands* is NOT an anthropology textbook. It is NOT a history textbook. It is NOT a sociology textbook. It is a work of art and a sacred text. It is imbued with sacred force. It is also a guidebook.

Just as she could have chosen to remain in the closet rather than to enact her bisexuality, Gloria could have chosen not to speak or write about Coatlicue, but it is doubtful whether or not she could not have chosen against encounters with Coatlicue, Coyolxauhqui, Yemayá, Oyá, or the other divinities who claimed her. She knew that forced Christianization had not succeeded, no matter how much it had been determined to do so, in committing deicide, as N. Scott Momaday refers to the killing of Indigenous gods. *Even though they might sometimes adopt new names and wear masks and different robes, she knew that the gods didn't die just because their worship was banned.* "Like the ancients," she wrote in *Borderlands*, "I worship the rain god and the maize goddess, but unlike my father, I have recovered their names" (90).

Gloria loved a Christmas card that David and I gave her in the early 1980s which, on the outside, listed "Santa Marta, Santa Rosa, Santa Elena," and so on, and when you opened it, a very jolly crone smiled out at you, under which appeared the name, "Santa Claus." Sadly, Gloria will most probably never be sainted. At least not by the Catholic Church. Her relationship with it was far too complex. While she loved the Church's way of ritualizing with chant and statuary and candles and incense, and she sincerely venerated la Virgen, Santa Teresa, and Sor Juana, by the end of her life, she had, like Mary Daly, moved well beyond the border of post-Catholic identification. Still, she rarely passed a Church without lighting a candle to Guadalupe. Her life was one of intense spiritual study, good works, love for all sentient beings, and deep faith in the Divine. Although a deeply passionate person, she was, for all intents and purposes, an ascetic, a hermit. Like Frida, she merits sanctification, but perhaps within a new Church or temple of *Spiritual Mestizaje*. Trashing Gloria and others whose ancestors have suffered forced Christianization for *seeking to deconstruct syncretism* in order to illuminate a fully conscious *Spiritual Mestizaje* that acknowledges both the Virgin and Tonantzin but which does not do so at the expense of erasing the horrific violence that led to the Virgin's displacement of the Goddess constitutes a further act of violence: *that of blaming the raped one, La Chingada, for trying to recover her virginity.*

*As for "Santa Nepantla," well*—and Gloria would reprimand me here, as, whenever I would say "well," she would roll her eyes and look at me and say, *"What did I tell you! A well is a hole in the ground!"* and years later would add, *"except when it's a cenote!"*—Nepantla commenced as an amplified and profoundly inspirited conceptualization of the Borderlands but by our last conversations had become much more multidimensional. As she explained it to me, Nepantla is not a Beckett-like, absurdist emptiness. It is the ground of being, the Implicate Order, that which has not yet manifested, that which has manifested but has been cast out by the hegemonic powers, holding within it all ancient pasts, all potential futures, all parallel universes, resembling but not identical to, Ometeotl, the Library of Babel, the Garden of Forking Paths, the telepathic ocean of the original Soviet film of *Solaris*, and a TAZ (or, Temporary Autonomous Zone). Ultimately, however, Nepantla must remain ineffable, as, once solidly defined, it is no longer Nepantla. Nepantla, like perfume or incense, cannot, must not be frozen.

*"Santa Nepantla."* If Michel Foucault, Fidel Castro, and Harvey Milk can be called "saints,"[1] then I have no trouble in calling Gloria one. Like Catholic saints, she healed many deep wounds, experienced miraculous events, and became, for all intents and purposes, a martyr to the sacred bridge that brought together women of color and many others to join in spiritual activism. Of course, Gloria would never in a million years have accepted the honorific of "saint," unless, perhaps, "Santa Nepantla" were applied to her *comadres* and all those coming together to enact a complex spirituality determined to heal and transform humanity while simultaneously honoring sentient beings, the earth, and the cosmos. To all those coming together who seek to know what lies beyond the fence.

Unlike her detractors, Gloria knew that La Diosa lives. She dwells, they dwell, in that ineffable place called Nepantla. *And it is as real as you are. Ashé. So mote it be. Gods and spirits, go in peace.* As Gloria would say, "*Ándale*!"

## Notes

1 See Halperin, "Saint Foucault"; by way of inference, see Orozco, and Bolívar Aróstegui, *Cuba Santa*; and, see Lentz, "Harvey Milk of San Francisco" (painting).

## Works Cited and Consulted


Anzaldúa, Gloria E. *Borderlands/La Frontera: The New Mestiza*. San Francisco, CA: Spinsters/Aunt Lute, 1987. Print.

-----. "now let us shift… the path of conocimiento… inner work, public acts." *This Bridge We Call Home: Radical Visions for Transformation*. Eds. Gloria E. Anzaldúa and AnaLouise Keating. New York, NY: Routledge, 2002. 540-578. Print.

-----. "Geography of Selves: Re-Imagining Identities: Nos/otras (Us/others), Las Nepantleras and the New Tribalism." 2003. MS.

-----. "Light in the Dark: Rewriting Identity, Spirituality, Reality." 2003. MS.

-----. "*Noche y su Nidada*/ Night and her Nest." N.d. MS.

Anzaldúa, Gloria E., Debbie Blake, and Carmen Abrego. "Doing Gigs: Speaking, Writing, and Change." 1994. *Interviews/Entrevistas*. Ed. AnaLouise Keating, 211-233. New York: Routledge, 2000. Print.

Anzaldúa, Gloria E., and Ana Louise Keating. "Last Words? Spirit Journeys." 1998-1999. *Interviews/Entrevistas*. Ed. AnaLouise Keating, 281-291. New York: Routledge, 2000. Print.

Anzaldúa, Gloria E., and Linda Smuckler. "Doing Gigs: Speaking, Writing, and Change." 1982. *Interviews/Entrevistas*. Ed. AnaLouise Keating, 17-70. New York: Routledge, 2000. Print.

Baca, Damián. *Mestiz@ Scripts, Digital Migrations, and the Territories of Writing*. New York, NY: Palgrave Macmillan, 2008. Print.

Beltran, Cristina. "Patrolling Borders: Hybrids, Hierarchies, and the Challenge of Mestizaje." *Political Research Quarterly* 57 (2004): 595-607. Print.

Bohm, David. *Wholeness and the Implicate Order*. London: Ark, Routledge, 1988. Print.

Bost, Suzanne. "Gloria Anzaldúa's Mestiza Pain: Sacrifice, Chicana Embodiment, and Feminist Politics." *Aztlán* 30 (2005): 5-34. Print.

Brant, Beth, ed. *A Gathering of Spirit: A Collection by North American Indian Women*. Ithaca, NY: Firebrand Books, 1988. Print.

Calabrese, Joseph D., II. "Reflexivity and Symbolism in the Navajo Peyote Meeting." *Ethos*. 22 (1994): 494-527. Print.

Carrasco, Davíd, and Roberto Lint Sagarena. "The Religious Vision of Gloria Anzaldúa: *Borderlands/La Frontera* as a Shamanic Space." *Mexican American religions: Spirituality, Activism, and Culture*. Eds. Gastón Espinosa and Mario T. García. Durham: Duke University Press, 2008. 223-41. Print.

Contreras, Sheila Marie. *Blood lines: Myth, Indigenism, and Chicana/o Literature*. Austin: University of Texas Press, 2008. Print.

Crossan, John Dominic. *The Birth of Christianity: Discovering what Happened in the Years Immediately After the Execution of Jesus*. San Francisco: Harper, 1998. Print.

Daly, Mary. *Pure Lust*. San Francisco: Harper, 1984. Print.

Doniger, Wendy. "Introduction." *Kamasutra: A New, Complete English Translation of the Sanskrit Text*. Trans. and ed. Wendy Doniger and Sudhir Kakar. Oxford: Oxford University Press, 2002. Print.

-----. *The Essential Kama Sutra*. Rec. Boulder: Sounds True, 2003. "Side 1A." Audiocassette.

Franco, Jean. "The Return of Coatlicue: Mexican Nationalism and the Aztec Past." *Journal of Latin American Cultural Studies* 13 (2004): 205-219. Print.

Gaspar de Alba, Alicia. "There's no Place Like Aztlán: Embodied Aesthetics in Chicana Art." *The New Centennial Review* 4 (2004): 103-140. Print.

Gollnick, Brian. "History on Edge: Josefina Saldaña's Revolutionary Imagination." *A Contracorriente* 1 (2004.): 107-120. Print.

González-López, Gloria. "Epistemologies of the Wound: Anzaldúan Theories and Sociological Research on Incest in Mexican Society." *Human Architecture: Journal of the Sociology of Self-*

*Knowledge* 4 (2006.): 17-24. Print.

Halperin, David M. *Saint Foucault: Towards a Gay Hagiography*. New York: Oxford University Press, 1997. Print.

Hay, Harry. *Radically Gay: Gay Liberation in the Words of its Founder*. Ed. Will Roscoe. Boston: Beacon Press, 1996. Print.

Hernández-Ávila, Inés. "Tierra Tremenda: The Earth's Agony and Ecstasy in the Work of Gloria Anzaldúa." *EntreMundos/AmongWorlds: New perspectives on Gloria Anzaldúa*. Ed. AnaLouise Keating. New York: Palgrave Macmillan, 2005. 233-240. Print.

Hernández-Ávila, Inés, and Gloria Anzaldúa. "Quincentennial: From Victimhood to Active Resistance." 1991. *Interviews/Entrevistas*. Ed. AnaLouise Keating. New York: Routledge, 2000. 177-194. Print.

Hernández-Ávila, Inés, and Domino Pérez. "Speaking Across the Divide." *Studies in American Indian Literatures* 2nd ser. 15 (2003.): 7-22. Print.

Klein, Cecilia F. "None of the Above: Gender Ambiguity in Nahua Ideology." *Gender in pre-Hispanic America*. Eds. Cecilia F. Klein and Jeffrey Quilter. Washington, DC: Dumbarton Oaks, 2001. 183-253. Print.

"Hollywood: Reel Rasquache." *LatinoLA.com*. LatinoLA, March 23, 2004. Web. 3 May 2009.

Lentz, Robert. "Harvey Milk of San Francisco." 1987. Painting. *Trinity Stores: Icons and Art*. Web. 1 May 2009.

Levine, Amala. "Champion of the Spirit: Anzaldúa's Critique of Rationalist Epistemology. In *EntreMundos/AmongWorlds: New perspectives on Gloria Anzaldúa*. Ed. AnaLouise Keating. New York: Palgrave Macmillan, 2005. 171-184. Print.

Mack, Burton L. *Who Wrote the New Testament?: The Making of the Christian Myth*. San Francisco: Harper, 1995. Print.

Markman, Roberta, and Peter T. Markman. *Masks of the Spirit: Image and Metaphor in Mesoamerica*. Berkeley: University of California Press, 1989. Print.

Michaelsen, Scott, and David E. Johnson. "Border Secrets: An Introduction." *Border Theory: The Limits of Cultural Politics*. Eds. Scott Michaelsen and David E. Johnson. Minneapolis: University of Minnesota Press, 1997. 1-39. Print.

Orozco, Román, and Natalia Bolívar Aróstegui. *Cuba santa; Comunistas, santeros y cristianos en la isla de Fidel Castro*. Madrid: El País Aguilar, 1998. Print.

Parra, Andrea. *Ecotheologies of Liberation: Chicana Reconstructions of Nature and Spirituality*. Diss. Columbia University, 2003.

Pérez, Domino Renee. *There was a Woman: La Llorona from Folklore to Popular Culture*. Austin: University of Texas Press, 2008. Print.

Pérez, Laura E. *Chicana Art: The Politics of Spiritual and Aesthetic Altarities*. Durham: Duke University Press, 2007. Print.

Pérez-Torres, Rafael. *Mestizaje: Critical Uses of Race in Chicano Culture*. Minneapolis: University of Minnesota Press, 2006. Print.

Sáenz, Benjamin Alire. "In the Borderlands of Chicano Identity, There are Only Fragments." *Border theory: The Limits of Cultural Politics*. Eds. Scott Michaelsen and David E. Johnson. Minneapolis: University of Minnesota Press, 1997. 68-96. Print.

Saldaña-Portillo, Maria Josefina. *The Revolutionary Imagination in the Americas and the Age of Development*. Durham: Duke University Press, 2003. Print.

Shurin, Aaron. "Exorcism of the Straight/Man/Demon." *Angels of the Lyre: A Gay Poetry Anthology*. Ed. Winston Leyland. San Francisco: Panjandrum/Gay Sunshine, 1975. 193-194. Print.

Whitman, Walt. *Leaves of Grass*. New York: Signet, New American Library, 1958.

Wright, Melissa. "Maquiladora Mestizas and a Feminist Border Politics: Revisiting Anzaldúa." *Hypatia* 13 (1998): 114-131. Print.

Zita, Jacquelyn N. "Anzaldúan Body." *Body Talk: Philosophical Reflections on Sex and Gender*. New York: Columbia University Press, 1998. 165-183. Print.

*Frutos del Río Bravo*
By IRMA CAROLINA RUBIO

# 2

# NEPANTLA SPIRITUALITY: NEGOTIATING FLUID IDENTITIES, FAITHS, AND PRACTICES[1]

*LARA MEDINA*

*I was born and live in that in-between space, Nepantla, the borderlands.*

—*Gloria Anzaldúa, "Border* Arte*"*

In this writing, I offer a name for the spirituality that I see many Chicanas practicing, myself included.[2] It is a spirituality that draws from multiple faith and spiritual traditions, one that reflects our historical, cultural, and biological *mestizaje*. Gloria Anzaldúa profoundly influenced my thinking about Chicana spirituality. Most of us were raised Catholic, some of us as Protestant, and much fewer of us with Indigenous spiritual knowledge. Many of us have left institutional Christianity and have reclaimed the knowledge and values of our ancestral Indigenous cultures. Yet, many of us also retain aspects of Christianity, the parts that are life giving and have cultural significance in our lives. We do this while at the same time we embrace the Indigenous path, and/or perhaps Buddhist teachings and practices, and/or have our relationships with the Orishas of Ifa or Santería.[3] We might even combine and create our own rituals and *ceremonias* drawing from the rich knowledge of all that has helped us. As we have understood the complexity of our diversity, we have given ourselves permission to be enriched by spiritual diversity. As Dr. Randy Conner shared in the 2009 opening plenary, this was Gloria Anzaldúa's path as well. Her knowledge of ancient Mesoamerican sacred forces was enriched by her involvement and studies with "Eastern philosophies, esoteric philosophy, magical technology, yoga, and transcendental meditation," to name just a few of the paths she traveled. It is so important for us to know the depth of the spiritual *cenote* from which she drew.[4] It is also important for us to name what we are doing, lest others name if for us under labels like "New Age spirituality," or merely "picking and choosing," implying a lack of consciousness or even recklessness; mere consumers of the American spiritual marketplace. Some of us have chosen the term "hybrid spirituality." While I respect highly the work of *colegas* who have chosen this term, for me hybrid spirituality implies a more mechanical process, a technical term that silences the heart and the mind, or *cara y corazón*, that we bring to this process of spiritual growth.

Other *colegas* choose "*mestiza* spirituality," but as Anzaldúa wrote after *Borderlands*, "Beware of *el romance del mestizaje... Puede ser una ficción*."[5] The concept of *mestizaje*, although useful to emphasize the racial/ethnic mixture of Chicanas, can easily diminish the presence of the Indigenous, the African, and even the Asian within our mixtures and the conditions under which they have struggled to survive within the *mestizaje*. Due to the influence of Anzaldúa on my thinking about spirituality, I offer the term "*nepantla* spirituality" to name what it is that many of us are doing. *Nepantla*, a Nahuatl term meaning "in the middle" or "the middle place," is usually attached to nouns. For example, *tlalli* means land and *tlalnepantla* means middle of the earth.[6] To be "in *nepantla*" implies to be at the center point.

By using a Nahuatl term to name our spirituality we are challenged first to engage with an Indigenous language and second, most importantly, to embrace the Indigenous epistemology that underlies what it means to be "in the middle." Third, members of other cultures are required to learn the meaning of the term and by extension interact with our Indigenous values and our Indigenous and racially mixed histories. The historical experience of being in the middle, in the center, and the worldview that results, must be understood when one uses the term *nepantla*.

In 1987, with the publication of *Borderlands/La Frontera,* Anzaldúa prophesied that the indigenous mother was truly emerging from the darkness "to fight for her own skin and a piece of ground to stand on, a ground from which to view the world--a perspective, a homeground where she can plumb the rich ancestral roots into her own ample *mestiza* heart" (23). At that time, the question posed by Anzaldúa reflected my own question as a student of Christian theology, "How could I reconcile the two, the pagan and the Christian?" (38). I came to the conclusion that the reconciling must take place in the depth of one's being rather than a mere acceptance of a syncretic symbol system or a *mestiza* identity formed from the best of two or more cultures. True reconciliation between the Indigenous and the Christian requires the privileging of the mother culture, the Indigenous, until the two can co-exist in mutuality and harmony and the Indigenous is fully respected and no longer silenced.

The first victims of colonization, our Indigenous ancestors, found themselves in *nepantla.* The use of *nepantla* was recorded by the Dominican friar, Diego Durán, in the 16th century in *Historia de las Inidias de Nueva España y Islas de Tierra Firme.* Durán quotes a conversation he had with an indigenous elder:

> Once I questioned an Indian regarding certain things, particularly why he had gone dragging himself about, gathering monies, with bad nights and worse days, and having gathered so much money through so much trouble he put on a wedding and invited the entire town and spent everything. Thus reprimanding him for the evil thing he had done, he answered me: Father, do not be frightened because we are still *nepantla,* and since I understood what he meant to say by that phrase and metaphor, which means to be in the middle, I insisted that he tell me in what middle it was in which they found themselves. He told me that since they were still not well rooted in the faith, I should not be surprised that they were still neutral, that they neither answered to one faith or the other or, better said, that they believed in God and at the same time keep their ancient customs and demonic rites. And this is what he meant by his abominable excuse that they still remained in the middle and were neutral. (268)

Durán's apparent lack of regard or understanding of indigenous communal responsibility, communal obligations, and communal celebrations marking rites of passage clearly blurred his interaction with the native elder. Within indigenous epistemology, community participation symbolizes the strength of a community and is proof of one's belonging in a community.[7] Rather, the friar found this behavior to be an "evil thing" and condemned the actions. Furthermore, the possibility of their believing in the Christian God <u>and</u> maintaining their ancient customs repulsed the missionary.

According to the renowned Mesoamericanist, Miguel León-Portilla, the response of the "elder Indian" exemplified "the trauma of nepantlism." He elaborates:

> The violent attacks against the indigenous religion and traditions, the death of the gods, and the difficulty in accepting the new teachings as true had already affected the people deeply and had brought about, as a consequence, the appearance of nepantlism. The concept of nepantlism, "to remain in the middle," one of *the greatest dangers* of culture contact ruled by the desire to impose change, retains its full significance, applicable to any meaningful understanding of similar situations. (10)

León-Portilla's often quoted interpretation of the exchange of words between the friar and the "wise old native" presumes indecisiveness and confusion on the elder's part. The elder's use of the term *nepantla* is assumed to mean confusion and conflict, the result of imposed change. Clearly, the native peoples experienced extreme psychological, physical, and spiritual violation, and subsequently found themselves caught or bound between worlds leading to inner and outer turmoil. But the elder himself stated they were neutral, implying their unwillingness to take sides in the religious conquest. As a matter of survival, they would choose both religions. And as he told the friar, "Do not be frightened."

With all due respect to León-Porilla, I would like to suggest a different interpretation of the elder's response, an interpretation that broadens the concept of *Nepantla* and illuminates the multifacetedness of "being in the middle." It is not possible that the elder was referring to his survival strategy of remaining in the middle, by describing how his people could incorporate Christianity into their native worldview, but also could hold onto their traditional beliefs and practices? Was not the elder strategically maneuvering the fissures, boundaries, and borders of his changed world by claiming the middle space, the center space, the space of meaning-making where his people's religious and cultural agency could construct new ways or simply provide space for both religions to co-exist side by side? In other words, for the elder, the pagan and the Christian could co-exist in harmony, in a middle space, a neutral space where one does not have power over the other. Perhaps what appeared to be a state of confusion and ambiguity to the friar, and to León-Portilla, was the manner in which the elder attempted to hold onto his dignity and the ways of his ancestors. The elder consciously chose the middle space, the center, as his worldview was large enough to encompass multiple manifestations of the divine. For his own native cultural experience had taught him to incorporate the knowledge of sacred forces held by neighboring cultures and those that had preceded his own.[8] From this perspective, *nepantla*, the middle place, presumes agency, not confusion.

My interpretation of *nepantla* in this manner does not suggest that there is only harmony or peaceful co-existence in the middle space. Rather, there is duality within *nepantla*, consisting of a transparent side where there is clarity, creativity, and self-determination, and a shadow side, where diversity confuses and creates disorientation. I see *nepantla* as a multifaceted psychic and spiritual space composed of complementary opposites: obscurity and clarity. Such duality is a constant within indigenous Mesoamerican understandings of the universe (Marcos). As duality or complementary opposites exist in all things, *neplanta* itself is comprised of the shadow side or the bewildering state of uncertainty, and the transparent side or the state of clarity and meaning making.

According to Mexican anthropologist Sylvia Marcos, "the duality implicit in Mesoamerican cosmology was constantly in flux and never fixed or static… movement gave its impulse to everything… everything flowed between opposite poles" (30). And as Anzaldúa advised us, "rigidity means death" particularly for border people, people who live with constant movement, constant fluidity.

So if fluidity remains a constant, "the critical point of balance has to be found"

(Marcos 30). For our Mesoamerican ancestors, maintaining balance/equilibrium in all things, including oneself, was the moral responsibility of all individuals. Without balanced individuals, the community could not exist in harmony. Achieving balance required not "negating the opposite but rather by advancing towards it and embracing it, in an attempt to find the ever-shifting center of balance" (Marcos 31). Thus, the confusion of *nepantla* must be embraced and worked through in order to reach the balanced state of clarity on the opposite pole. The elder and his people chose to move toward the opposite pole, toward Christianity and embrace it in order to survive and regain balance in their changing world. And its opposite, the native worldview, was/is held onto in order to sustain balance.

Anzaldúa understood the duality of *nepantla*. In *Borderlands* she refers to "mental and emotional states of perplexity...psychic restlessness...an Aztec word meaning torn between ways" (78). In later work, she refers to *nepantla* as the site of transformation, "the dark cave of creativity...one that brings a new state of understanding" ("Border *Arte*" 113).

*Nepantla* is not to be confused with syncretism that refers to the blending of diverse beliefs and practices into new and distinct forms. The term "syncretism" is often used to describe Latin American religions resulting from the European imposition of Christianity upon native religions. But the term "syncretism" silences complex historical contexts, power relations, and the psychological distress in which syncretic traditions evolved. Syncretism is useful when it reveals the agency and ingenuity of the indigenous to transform Christianity for their benefit. For example, a crucifix made of cornhusks joins the sacrifice of Christ with the sacredness of maize and "the cosmo-magical powers stemming from the earth" (Carrasco 76).

In *nepantla*, the pre-Christian Indigenous traditions and syncretic Christianity co-exist, side by side, in mutual harmony and respect. In *nepantla*, there is room for all. *Nepantla* provides a place where the Indigenous elders and their descendants can survive, rest, and prosper. In the transparency of *nepantla*, there are no power struggles regarding who holds "the truth."

## NEPANTLA SPIRITUALITY IN PEDAGOGY

In my teaching about Chicanos/as and religion, I encounter many students who are spiritually searching. Many express interest in learning about their Indigenous roots, knowledge that has been denied them in the Western educational system. Most have never openly challenged Christian doctrine. The class intends to provide the opportunity to question religious "truths" so that through the process of critical thinking about religion, healing from the psychic wounds of spiritual colonization can occur. My emphasis on Indigenous epistemology challenges the majority to confront their internalized biases against non-Christian and non-Western worldviews. For Chicanos/as who are products of cultural *mestizaje* reconciling the differences and discovering the similarities between Christian and Indigenous traditions offers healing. Healing in this context is about bringing forth self-knowledge and historical consciousness so that one may claim religious agency, or the ability to determine for oneself what is morally and ethically just, and what enables communication with spiritual sources. For the young women in the class, discussions about moral authority over one's body constitutes a central part of the healing process.

Many students reveal their parents concern that in college they will leave their Christian upbringing behind and turn to Indigenous ways or forget about spirituality altogether. To help the students bridge their worlds, I introduce the concept of *nepantla* spirituality, spirituality at the biological and cultural crossroads where diverse elements converge, at times in tension and at other times in cohesion.

As in any relationship, co-existence is not always easy, but once the tensions of *nepantla* are understood and confronted, and the native-Self is recovered and continuously healed, *nepantla* or the middle space becomes a psychological, spiritual, and political space that Latinos/as transform as a site of meaning-making and healing. Rather than limited by confusion or ambiguity, we act as subjects in deciding how diverse religious and cultural forces can or cannot work together. Like the native elder of the 16$^{th}$ century, we creatively maneuver the fissures, boundaries, and borders and consciously make choices about what aspects of diverse worldviews nurture the complexity of our spiritual and biological *mestizaje*, and what for us enables communication with spiritual sources. Within nepantla, Chicanas/os and other Latinos, can have the wisdom of the Indigenous and the Christian, and more.

As one student states,

> I feel more at peace with myself now, there is nothing wrong with me trying to practice indigenismo…I don't see myself as only Catholic…I don't want to leave Catholicism but, I have always felt a strong connection to the earth, to herbs, and especially to the ocean, I now feel at peace being in the middle, being in *nepantla*. (Interview with Celia Ramos. May 2004)

Or as another student wrote,

> *Nepantla spirituality* is a useful concept because many people feel that the Catholicism alone will not satisfy their spiritual needs. *Nepantla* is the common ground, where both Indigenous and Christian religions can meet.

In conclusion, to be *en nepantla* is to exist on the border, on the boundaries of cultures and social structures, where life is in constant motion, in constant fluidity. To be *en Nepantla* also means to be in the center of things, to exist in the middle place where all things meet and come together. *Nepantla,* the center place, can be a place of balance, a place of equilibrium, or as discussed earlier, a place of chaos and confusion. Border people, *las mestizas y los mestizos* constantly live *en nepantla*. We can never leave the middle space as that is where we were created and where we live, in "the contact zone" (Carrasco 78). As Anzaldúa stated, "As you make your way through life, *nepantla* itself becomes the place you live in most of the time-home" ("now let us shift" 548). How we choose to occupy our home is crucial. *Nepantla* spirituality offers a choice, a choice to be inclusive.

**Notes**

1 A longer version of this paper appears in *Rethinking Latino(a) Religion and Identity*, Miguel A. De La Torre and Gastón Espinosa, eds. Cleveland: Pilgrim Press, 2006, 248-266.

2 I define spirituality as the multiple ways in which persons nurture balanced relationships with themselves, others, the world, and their creator.

3 There are many other spiritual traditions that Chicanas have embraced.

4 Cenote is a Nahuatl term meaning a deep sacred well of water.

5 Beware of romanticizing mestizaje…it could be fictional. Author's translation. Anzaldúa, Gloria. "Border Arte." 111. Anzaldúa offered the term and theory of a "new mestiza consciousness."

6 Personal conversation with Fermin Herrera, professor of Nahuatl in Chicana/o studies at California State University, Northridge and author of *Nahuatl-English, English-Nahuatl, Hippocrene Books Concise Dictionary*, 2004. Nahuatl was the language of the Nahuas, the largest indigenous ethnic/cultural group in the central valley of Mexico in the 1500s. Nahuatl is a living language spoken in central Mexico and parts of the Southwest of the United States.

7 Examples of communal responsibility in helping to make celebrations a success can be seen in contemporary Indigenous and mestizo communities. The communal participation is proof of one's belonging to the community. One example occurs in the film, *Blossoms of Fire*. Oakland: Intrepidas Productions, 2000.

8 For example, the Mexica had incorporated the sacredness of Quezalcóatl, the feathered serpent, into their spirituality as they passed through Teotihuacan on their migration south. See Davíd Carrasco, *Religions of Mesoamerica: Cosmovision and Ceremonial Centers*. San Francisco: Harper & Row, 1990, 40-45.

**Works Cited**

Anzaldúa, Gloria. *Borderlands/La Frontera: The New Mestiza*. San Francisco: Aunt Lute Books, 1987.

-----. "Border Arte: Nepantla, El Lugar De La Frontera." *La Frontera/La Border; Art About the Mexico/U.S. Border Experience*. San Diego: Centro Cultural de la Raza and Museum of

Contemporary Art San Diego, 1993. Print.

-----. "Now let us shift...the path of conocimiento... inner work, public act." *This Bridge We Call Home.* Eds. Gloria Anzaldúa and AnaLouise Keating. New York: Routledge, 2002. Print.

Carrasco, David. "Jaguar Christians in the Contact Zone." *Enigmatic Powers: Syncretism with African and Indigenous Peoples' Religions among Latinos.* Eds. Anthony M. Stevens-Arroyo and Andres I. Pérez y Mena. New York: Bildner Center for Western Hemisphere Studies, 1995. Print.

-----. *Religions of Mesoamerica: cosmovision and ceremonial centers.* San Francisco: Harper & Row, 1990. Print.

Durán, Diego. *Historia de las Indias de Nueva España y Islas de Tierra Firme.* Trans. Doris Heyden. Norman: University of Oklahoma Press, 1994. Print.

León-Portilla, Miguel. *Endangered Cultures.* Dallas: Southern Methodist University Press, 1990.

Marcos, Sylvia. "The Sacred Earth." *Concilium: Third World Theology.* Ed. Leonardo Boff and Virgilio Elizondo 5.261 (1995). 27-37. Print.

Medina, Lara. "Nepantla Spirituality: Negotiating Multiple Religious Identities among U. S. Latinas." *Rethinking Latino(a) Religion and Identity.* Eds. Miguel De La Torre and Gastón Espinosa. Cleveland: Pilgrim Press, 2006. Print.

Ramos, Celia. Personal Interview. May 2004.

*Niña Mariposa*
Andrea Velásquez Collection
By LILIANA WILSON

# 3

# CAMINANDO CON GLORIA: WALKING AS EXPERIENCE, THOUGHT, AND ACTION

*SUZANNE BOST*

I always assumed I'd meet Gloria Anzaldúa, but I never did. If I had suspected she was going to die in 2004, I would have made a pilgrimage. I was waiting to develop clarity in my ideas about her work, but now I'm quite certain she would have rejected clarity as an endpoint. When I learned that she walked and talked with students along the ocean near Santa Cruz, I nearly cried. I would have loved that walking.

I walk to think, especially when I'm writing something new. When I couldn't decide what to propose for this conference ("El Mundo Zurdo"), I took my baby out in sub-freezing Chicago temperatures to walk through my ideas. Walking gives rhythm to one's thinking. Most importantly, it literally links a body to the environment. Walking is transformative—if only to the extent that it presents one with new sights, new experiences, and new sensations as one moves through the world. It is therefore totally appropriate that many of us spent the first day of the conference in pilgrimage. At the cemetery in Hargill, we walked together in procession, finding a communal rhythm with former strangers, fellow academics, writers, Anzaldúa's friends and family. That shared movement was, in many ways, more powerful than our individual tributes, our movements shaped by each other, our vision filtered by the backs of those before us. Prickly burrs embedded themselves in my sandals at the cemetery, and several of us found ourselves standing in the middle of an ant hill, both disruptive and disrupted. When we walked across the border into Nuevo Progreso that afternoon, we reinforced our joint commitment to the power of border-crossing, though each in his or her own distinct corporeal fashion, with his or her distinct personal history and legal documents. I boarded the bus tired, slightly sunburned, and fell asleep amongst new friends.

Since I've always walked (except for six months on crutches in college and the first few weeks after my son was born), walking might have seemed too obvious, too omnipresent to have particular significance for a conference paper, if it weren't for three modes of thinking in my life today: yoga practice, disability studies, and new developments in feminist science studies. First, yoga: by making breath the most important part of a successful practice, traditional yoga inverts the ways in which contemporary sports value the most visible corporeal achievements (the highest jump or the hardest hit). The breath, like the rhythm of walking, is the subtle, constant, unifying aspect as the body moves through different poses. It lets in the outside air and lets out the in. It is how the self functions. Yoga, moreover, refuses the split between mind, body, and spirit, assuming that moving the body mobilizes mind and spirit, too. Encouraging my body into a particular posture involves remembering previous times I've made that movement, faith in my body's ability to move that way again, and, often, an emotional response to the limits and the marvels of what a body can do. So why didn't I choose yoga as the framework for this paper? Because, as much as I like to persuade myself that there is something communal and relational about it, yoga is largely an internal, individual, and self-controlled practice. Though I might invoke the energy of the universe, I can (and often do) practice it with my eyes and mouth closed, safe on my mat. Walking, by contrast, creates unpredictable encounters with the world outside. It requires that we witness changes around us and that we move in accordance with these changes. While yoga is silent (or, at its loudest, accompanied by audible breath or chanting), walking is accompanied by unpredictable noise—barking dogs, passing buses, conversation with a friend. Walking is dialogue.

Secondly, walking is an experience of differing abilities. I am influenced by "second wave" disability studies scholars who have shifted the focus from the exceptional embodiments of people with disabilities to surrounding social and material structures that facilitate or limit movement. Rather than concentrating on identity politics, critics like Lennard Davis, Celeste Langan, and Tobin Siebers examine the ways in which all bodies are enabled or disabled by socially-constructed environments: the placement of chairs and light-switches; the design of sidewalks, city buses, and doorways; or the ways in which signs communicate their messages. In this way, walking is not the measure of an individual walker's ability or disability but a meeting of that particular body, the natural world, and the cultural assumptions that groom the world for human uses. Walking is an occasion for testing how the world enables or disables, for checking out the functionality of legs, wheels, curb cuts, crosswalks, animal guides, crossing guards, trees, and streetlights. Walking highlights changes in our body as well as changes in the territory we move through. Though she was not disabled in the conventional sense of the term, Anzaldúa's diabetes shifted her ways of moving. In a 1999 interview with AnaLouise Keating she explains, "I get dizzy and mentally foggy when I'm having a hypo. I lose my equilibrium and fall. Gastrointestinal reflex has me throwing up and having diarrhea…." (*Interviews* 289). I imagine the intersecting fluctuations of diabetes with the fluctuations of the surrounding world would make walking an adventure in adaptability.

The third mode of thought that puts walking into focus for me is exemplified by Karen Barad's essay "Posthumanist Performativity: Toward an Understanding of how Matter Comes to Matter" (originally published in *Signs* in 2003), which provides a difficult but transformative theory for understanding what happens when bodies meet worlds. Barad reconfigures the material world as a process of "intra-action" between elements (human and non-human, organic and man-made): "It is through specific agential intra-actions that the boundaries and properties of the 'components' of phenomena become determinate and that particular embodied concepts become meaningful" (133). That is, things get their shapes and their meanings from intra-action with each other. Barad chooses the term "intra-action," as opposed to interaction, to highlight the mutually-productive relationship between components that are not separate entities with fixed boundaries; rather, they exist in dynamic relation with other components. The "posthumanism" in this essay is not a rejection of humanist values but, rather, a refusal to put humans at the center of any model of the universe, an understanding that humans are not the only agents in the world. The language of "components," "things," and "apparatuses" that she uses to effect this shift is sterile but also exhaustively inclusive.

> Reality is not composed of things-in-themselves or things-behind-phenomena, but of "things"-in-phenomena. The world *is* intra-activity in its differential mattering. It is through specific intra-actions that a differential sense of being is enacted in the ongoing ebb and flow of agency. That is, it is through specific intra-actions that phenomena come to matter—in both senses of the word. The world is a dynamic process of intra-activity in the ongoing reconfiguring of locally determinate causal structures…. (135)

The radical possibility (as well as responsibility) presented by this vision is the materializing effects of our intra-actions. As I walk, not only am I reconfiguring my own body, I am also reconfiguring everything my body meets. In light of disability studies, in particular, this possibility can be politically empowering. Human body, curb design, and assistive devices take their shapes from each other. (Though concrete and metal might seem to resist the strength of flesh, human bodies can assert their agency in many other ways.)

Walking highlights the intra-action between body, environment, and social structures. It is an experience of how bodies and their limits meet the world and its limits. In this way, it parallels thinking: ideas are produced by engagement with the limits and delights of the world. Both my movement and my thoughts are shaped by the material conditions I move through. I am aware of the way my foot moves over a patch of deep grass; I notice that I am not the only animal who moves more quickly in the cold. Likewise, my corporeal (and emotional) particularities—my throbbing right knee, my imbalanced hearing, my elation at the first signs of Spring—alter my consciousness of the world. My ideas develop from these intra-actions. Unlike standing still, walking initiates changes to the body and its physical backdrop. It produces encounters rather than waiting passively for an idea to catch one unawares.

I believe that walking is central to Anzaldúa's worldview. In the opening chapter of *Borderlands*, she normalizes and decriminalizes the "illegal" crossing of Mexicans into the United States by viewing it as an extension of the Aztecs' legacy of migration and a return to the homeland, Aztlán. Chicana/os have "a tradition of migration, a tradition of long walks," she asserts (11). Though migrations are often conducted on foot, to call these border-crossings "long walks" is subtly provocative. "Long walks" refers to the journeys without the destination. The phrase implies discovery and leisure, in opposition to the familiar images of migrants frantically trying to cross rivers and deserts, risking their lives to get *al otro lado*. Emphasizing the process of walking points out the encounters along the way, not only with the border and *la migra* but also with the desert or the river, itself. In this way, "long walks" highlights the dialogue between human and environment rather than reducing the journey to its juridical aspect (the moment of leaving one nation and entering another). Migration must thus be seen as a story rather than a criminal act. This comparison also radicalizes our understanding of walking. Comparing long walks to border-crossing highlights the friction involved in all walks: the minor borders we cross between places, over property lines, across cracks in the sidewalk. All walking, in some manner, involves intra-action, meeting personal or environmental barriers and shifting perspectives. We are all *atravesados* in the borderlands produced by walking, out-of-place, outsiders in front of another's house, alert to unfamiliar terrain, queerly away from home.

In this light, I take the "camino" of Anzaldúa's theory of "el camino del conocimiento" literally. Her essay "now let us shift" takes us through this journey of shifting consciousness. The first paragraph describes a reciprocal relationship between the self and nature:

> As you walk across Lighthouse Field a glistening black ribbon undulates in the grass, crossing your path from right to left. You swallow air, your primal senses flare open. From the middle of your forehead, a reptilian eye blinks, surveys the terrain. This visual intuitive sense, like the intellect of heart and gut, reveals a discourse of signs, images, feelings, words, that, once decoded, carry the power to startle you out of tunnel vision and habitual patterns of thought.... Often nature provokes un "aja," or "conocimiento," one that guides your feet along the path, gives you el ánimo to dedicate yourself to transforming perceptions of reality, and thus the conditions of life. (540)

Human, animal, and environment meet in this passage in a way that resembles Barad's posthumanist intra-action. The "you" in this passage is inseparable from the animal and the environment, and all three mutually shape each other. As the "you" crosses the field, a snake crosses her path, presenting a physical, psychological, and spiritual barrier to her walking. The serpent is sacred to Anzaldúa—a symbol of instinct, sexuality, creativity, and femininity (*Borderlands* 35)—and, in this passage, it quickly shifts from being a separate entity on the grass to reappearing as the third eye in her forehead, making visible a "discourse of signs" to read in the "terrain." Though an encounter with nature might seem to have provoked the "aja" in this passage, the serpent is equally a part of the viewer, and it is the "you" who will transform "perceptions of reality, and thus the conditions of life." To argue that transforming "perceptions of reality" transforms "the conditions of life," as Anzaldúa does here, breaks down the hierarchical separation between human and environment. Perception and the conditions of life are causally related. Decoding and perception are not the property of a seer who stands outside or before nature but, rather, seeing is part of a physical exchange between the nature that gives insight and the seeing that transforms the world in which the seer sees. Human, animal, and environment are all agents of this process.

Three pages after this passage, Anzaldúa outlines the seven stages of "the journey," "the path of conocimiento," beginning with the image of walking through an earthquake (another sort of "aja" produced by a meeting of body and, this time, urban nature):

> You're strolling downtown. Suddenly, the sidewalk buckles and rises before you. Bricks fly through the air. Your thigh muscles tense to run, but shock holds you in check. Dust rains down all around you, dimming your sight, clogging your nostrils, coating your throat. In front of you the second story of a building caves into the ground. Just as suddenly the earth stops trembling. ("now let us shift" 543)

The pause between aftershocks gives the people on the ground an opportunity to observe, first, a hand protruding from the rubble and, then, the woman attached to the hand, her face gashed, her arm broken, her skirt riding up to reveal a plump thigh. The second person narrator of the essay fights "the urge to pull her skirt down, protect her from all eyes" (543). Is she fighting identification with the "victim" or simply resisting the urge to hide the injured woman from public sight? The earthquake has opened up questions about the relationship between bodies and nature, and between one body and another, by lifting the sidewalk and the woman's skirt together.

I believe this ambivalence about the wounded body is a precursor to the revelation of Anzaldúa's diabetes diagnosis in the third part of the essay, which is also explored through walking, this time crossing a "trestle bridge":

> You listen to your footsteps echoing on the timber, the reality of having a disease that could cost you your feet… your eyes… your creativity… the life of the writer you've worked so hard to build… life itself… finally penetrates, arresting you in the middle del puente (bridge). (550)

Diabetes seems to have alienated the speaker from her self, to the degree that she hears her footsteps rather than feeling them. Her feet become separable from her self-perception since she knows the disease might lead to amputation. Yet out-of-body experiences are not uncommon in Anzaldúa's work, and they usually lead to great insight—like her repeated use of bridges as powerful places of divergent perception, friction, and (sometimes painful) in-between-ness. The fact that her movements are "arrested" on the bridge invokes the demonization of disease and disability, which renders those who experience these conditions outcasts. The bridge "arrests" the speaker like the diagnosis, forcing her to remain in a suspended state of *nepantla*, caught between worlds, or to walk into a new reality. "now let us shift" ultimately embraces conditions deemed pathological by the dominant society (including diabetes, wounds, and depression) as triggers that lead one to feel and to think beyond the numb stasis of the status quo:

> Depression is useful—it signals that you need to make changes in your life, it challenges your tendency to withdraw, it reminds you to take action. To reclaim body consciousness tienes que moverte, go for walks, salir a conocer el mundo, engage with the world. (553)

Rather than withdrawing or remaining in the uncomfortable position of "arrest," the speaker "reclaims" not just her body but her body's consciousness, her body's mind and perception, by moving through the world. "Knowing" the world through walking helps the body to know itself again. As the essay proceeds, "you" is decreasingly alienated from her illness: as "your body's illness has taken residence in all your thoughts," "you" is "catapulted" into the various stages of the "camino del conocimiento." The taboo knowledge produced in outcast positions "catapults" "you" from previously held assumptions into a new reality, one better suited to the movements and perceptions of a diabetic. Walking creates possibilities for trauma and transformation.

> These shifts in consciousness are not just metaphorical; they have real, physical effects: As you learn from the different stages you pass through, your reactions to past events change. You re-member your experiences in a new arrangement. Your responses to the challenges of daily life also adjust.... Instead of walking your habitual routes you forge new ones. The changes affect your biology. The cells in your brain shift and, in turn, create new pathways, rewiring your brain. (556)

Consciousness causes a material re-ordering of experience, a "re-membering" of the limbs of memory. It is true that memories transform the mechanical workings of the brain, creating neural pathways or allowing others to atrophy. In Anzaldúa's description, these neural pathways have their parallel in the outside world: the new routes that one walks help to forge new routes in the brain. In her essay, "Landscape, Memory, and Forgetting," Catriona Mortimer-Sandilands celebrates this parallel between the mind and the world. As she watches her mother's mind alter with the effect of Alzheimer's disease, she embraces the kinetic memory that her mother's body retains through walking and questions why we value abstract recollection more than the journeys her mother is able to "recall" while moving through them:

> It is no longer (if it was ever) a question of challenging the detachment of mind from body, thinking from perception, or reason from nature; on this view, it is a question of asking *how* particular modes of thought are located in embodied experience, of *how* both symbolic reflection and sensuous perception are phenomenally organized in particular techno-historical relationships between human bodies and others. (270)

As a trigger for our memories, the world itself is a storage depot for our memories, and, thus, an extension of the most intimate part of ourselves. This attachment poses a reciprocal ethical arrangement: we must examine the "techno-historical relationships" formed by our intra-actions. Let us not extend our bodies into the world or allow the world to form our thoughts in a way that is destructive.

What Barad's theory of posthumanist intra-action and Anzaldúa's accounts of walking seem to demand is a heightened awareness of the subtle ways in which our existence engages other matter. The perceptions we form in dialogue with the world shape our movements and the material traces our movements leave around us. Our being is dialogic; set in motion, it is transformative. This conclusion supports some of Anzaldúa's most optimistic assertions, such as the following:

> In struggling with adversity and noting your reactions to it you observe how thoughts direct perceptions of reality. You realize that personal/collective reality is created (often unconsciously) and that you're the artist scripting the new story of this house/self/identity/essay under construction. You realize it's the process that's valuable and not the end product, not the new you, as that will change often throughout your life.

("now let us shift" 562)

This passage claims adversity as an enabling dialogue. In the process of reconceptualization that adversity requires, the artist is able to re-script her self and reality in much the same way that she scripts a story or an essay. This passage also prioritizes process over selfhood, which sidesteps any privileging of identity positions, any attempt to be exclusive or to claim supremacy, since any "you" is temporary.

This conclusion is not, however, utopian. It rests on the assumption that our bodies and our identities are permeable, subject to transformation by everything we encounter, and these transformations might be painful and destructive as well as pleasurable and productive. But this very permeability, I would argue, is the site of our agency, the place where we reach beyond our individual selves and skins and the place where we take in intellectual, emotional, and physical nourishment.[1] It makes sense that we would have to relinquish a bit of our safety in order to imprint the world around us, and I much prefer this model of agency to the self-defensive and self-aggrandizing mode that underlies militarism and competitive capitalism. What I think I've found, by choosing Anzaldúa as my walking partner in this essay, is a tangible model for how it is that we really can (and already do) change the world, with every step we take.

**Notes**

1. In my new book, *Encarnación: Illness and Body Politics in Chicana Feminist Literature*, I link this model of permeability to Anzaldúa's theory of mestiza consciousness: both involve openness, fluidity, and constant encounters with difference.

**Works Cited**

Anzaldúa, Gloria E. *Borderlands/La Frontera: The New Mestiza*. San Francisco: Aunt Lute, 1987. Print.

------. *Interviews/Entrevistas*. Ed. AnaLouise Keating. New York: Routledge, 2000. Print.

------. "now let us shift... the path of conocimiento... inner work, public acts." *This Bridge We Call Home: Radical Visions for Transformation*. Eds. Gloria Anzaldúa and AnaLouise Keating. New York: Routledge, 2002. Print.

Barad, Karen. "Posthumanist Performativity: Toward an Understanding of how Matter Comes to Matter." *Material Feminisms*. Ed. Stacy Alaimo and Susan Hekman. Bloomington: Indiana UP, 2008. Print.

Bost, Suzanne. *Encarnación: Illness and Body Politics in Chicana Feminist Literature*. Bronx: Fordham UP, forthcoming. Print.

Davis, Lennard. *Bending over Backwards: Disability, Dismodernism and Other Difficult Positions*. New York: New York UP, 2002. Print.

Langan, Celeste. "Mobility Disability." *Public Culture* 13.3 (2001): 459-84. Print.

Mortimer-Sandilands, Catriona. "Landscape, Memory, and Forgetting." *Material Feminisms*. Ed. Stacy Alaimo and Susan Hekman. Bloomington: Indiana UP, 2008. Print.

Siebers, Tobin. "Disability as Masquerade." *Literature and Medicine* 23.1 (Spring 2004): 1-22.

------. "Disability in Theory: From Social Constructionism to the New Realism of the Body." *American Literary History* 13.4 (Winter 2001): 737-54. Print.

------. "Disability Studies and the Future of Identity Politics." *Identity Politics Reconsidered*. Ed. Linda Martín Alcoff, et al. New York: Palgrave, 2006. Print.

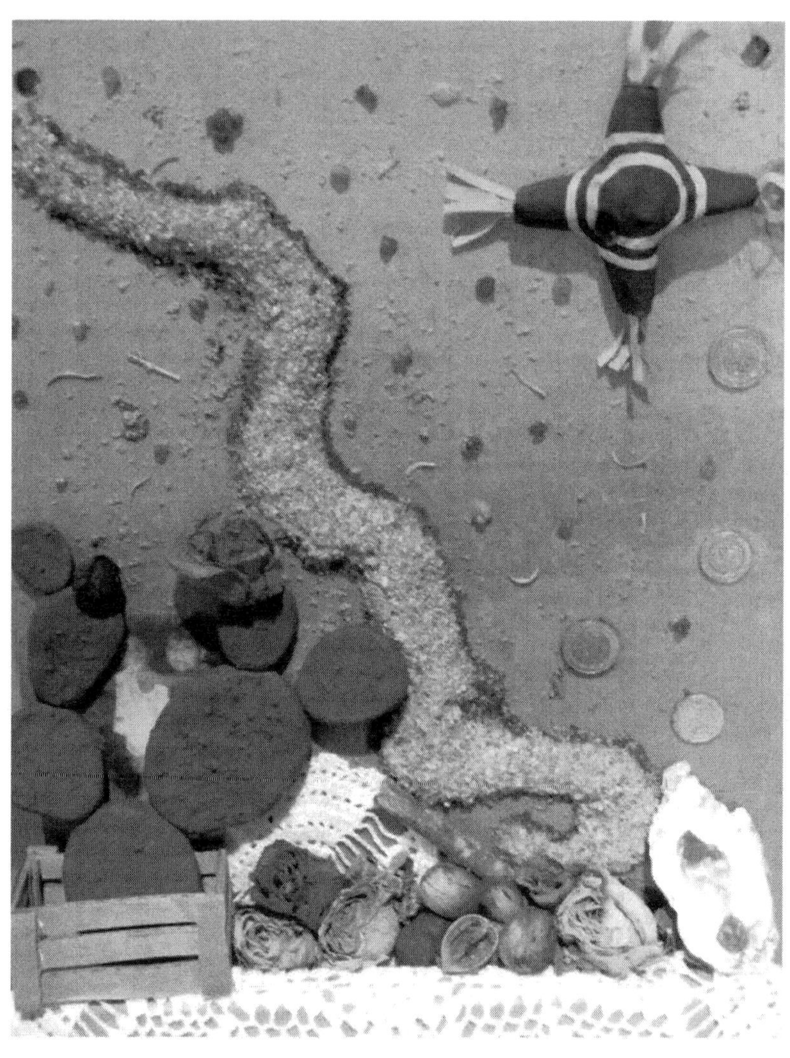

*Una herida abierta*
María Isabel Rico Collection
By FABIOLA OCHOA TORRALBA

# 4

# THE AGONY OF INADEQUACY

*PATRICIA PEDROZA*

My entry into the academic teaching of Women's Studies in the U.S. came relatively late in life. I spent nearly sixteen years as a non-governmental feminist worker in Mexico with two important pioneer feminist organizations. I grew up as feminist in a highly charged political feminist Mexican environment. While completing my M.A. in the Art of Teaching, I became a women's studies teacher in a liberal arts college in New England.

From the moment I faced my first classes about feminist perspectives I knew I was talking about something that did not fit my students and colleagues. To students, it was hard to accept being challenged by a female Mexican, and several times I was asked if I was legal as an instructor, and how I entered the United States. To colleagues, I became just invisible. I became accustomed to expressing my opinions and not getting any answers, just cold smiles. Despite experiencing a state of inadequacy, I have been rewarded with excellent teaching evaluations. However, my political identity has suffered dramatic changes by navigating disparities and acculturation processes which, after my Anzaldúan education, I can name as a process of crossing borders and a permanent agony of inadequacy. Acculturation as a process of becoming familiar with "being able to negotiate, adopt, and value" dominant mainstream culture, may take different and diverse strategies (Cervantes and Felix-Ortiz 337). For my purpose in this paper, acculturation is a process that is part of crossing borders within a permanent, dynamic, and dialectic journey.

From Anzaldúa we have learned what it means to develop a new mestiza consciousness as one of the aspects of borderland identities (*Borderlands/La Frontera: The New Mestiza).* The multiplicity of crossing borders includes that after crossing, we discover we are not welcome on the other side. Thus, we may take some time to reflect on the process by learning the meaning of being the crosser. After the crossing, the way of navigating what we have encountered on the other side becomes a process of permanent inadequacy. Anzaldúa describes this as an agony where adopting strategies of acculturation may be for some bordercrossers *una tabla de salvación*. However, if one does not want to take the first available *tabla de salvación* the agony of inadequacy may be a creative path to navigate within a culture where one does not fit or belong.

I define myself as an Anzaldúan feminist and I position myself as a woman who is not interested in *aculturarme*—or in engaging an acculturation process. My position is Anzaldúan because it requires applying *la facultad* as a skill of being able to see surfaces, and being able to have the courage to engage all aspects of living within a culture that I cannot recognize, where I am not welcomed. Thus, *inadecuadez*—inadequacy as an Anzaldúan state of consciousness is a self-position from which I navigate what situates me as a foreigner. I make a decision to follow Anzaldúa's invitation to have the courage to live outside societal norms that make me feel *inadecuada* and at the same time give me the freedom to "*no darle cuentas a nadie*" (*Borderlands* 43).

Inadequacy as process starts at the moment of discovering that the borderland is a daily territory and crossing borders is part of creating (un)natural bridges, and (un)safe places. Inadequacy is a way of living. It is a path I have decided to follow, because after all, most of the time, my ideas, dreams, fantasies, beliefs, practices, and experiences have been *inadecuadas*. It is a path I have decided to walk and take as a guide to center my curiosity, inquiry, power, creativity, transformation, and political commitment. It is a path I follow after *la maestra de maestras*, my theoretical mother Gloria Anzaldúa.

Anzaldúa reflects the agony of inadequacy[1] that we colonized people experience in different situations. How we may internalize rage, persecutory feelings, and judgmental ideas against us in order to escape the threat of shame when an agony or fear distract us from our political awareness. It is here that she develops the Coatlicue state (*Borderlands/La Frontera)* defined as the courage to see ourselves in these human conditions, to generate the power of self-transformation. Anzaldúa's key essay "now let us shift… the path of conocimiento… inner work, public acts" is the synthesis of the steps I have adopted and follow as Chicana Sutra[2] because it is the journey I learned from her. Anzaldúa transmitted to us/ me an intellectual legacy: "we are ready for change...leaving huellas—footprints, footsteps—for others to follow.... Sí se puede, que así sea, so be it, estamos listas, vámonos ("Now let us shift" 540).

I follow Anzaldúa's guide for self-transformation because I consider that any intention to create social change needs to start with our personal transformation. Anzaldúa invites us to create our own selfs and to have the courage to challenge the status quo. "The path of *conocimiento*" that Anzaldúa draws, is the *conocimiento* taken from "the meaning cognoscera, a Latin verb meaning 'to know' and it is the Spanish word for 'knowledge' and skill." Anzaldúa calls "this *conocimiento* that aspect of consciousness urging us to act on the knowledge gained" ("now let us shift" 541). Each individual can be touched by nature which provokes an "aha" (or I finally got it!) —or "*conocimiento.*" We have the situations that place us in front of the opportunity to dedicate ourselves to "transforming perceptions of reality" ("Now let us shift" 549). The reality of collapsing and transforming traditional binary systems (body/mind, female/male, white/color, heterosexual/ homosexual, etc.) immerses us as a global society in obsolete labeling ("Now let us shift" 546). However, oppressive powers still use such binaries to "single out and negate those who are 'different' because of color, language, notions of reality," and citizenship ("Now let us shift" 541). Anzaldúa affirms that identity is a filtering screen limiting our awareness to a fraction of reality. This *distorsionada y fragmentada* identity is provisional and depends on a specific perspective. Thus a big *verdad, donde la verdad es que la verdad no existe* becomes a smoking mirror where such big reality goes beyond my/our personal perceptions. Nevertheless, the opportunity to experience fragments of this reality/*verdad* offers a chance to see a broken reality, a broken verdad, *la verdad quebrada*, where what is important is not the broken pieces, but what we/I do with them, *es decir, no importa romper el esquema, lo importante es qué hacemos con los cachos rotos*. This is the claim I add, because I must examine the paradigm that results from my personal perception with my *facultad* to "open my eyes, ears, beliefs and physical senses" so that I can approach those broken *pedazos*/pieces (*Borderlands* 60).

The (un)safe place where I exercise power, the power of inadequacy, is located in academia, in the halls and classrooms of U.S. universities. As a Mexican *inadecuada* faculty of color working in a white Anglo environment, *el conocimiento Anzaldúano* as a performative task, requires the decision to engage a commitment of a permanent reflective process where inadequacy is the center. The Inadequacy paradigm requires a permanent confrontation with the feelings of not fitting in, but engages at the same time, the *alivio* of *ser inadecuada*.

Within inadequacy, there is a moment of "click, aha, got it" – which Anzaldúa teaches us, but the interesting step is to observe what happens with or what we do with this aha moment. Knowing and feeling my inadequacy, saber *que soy inadecuada y conocer o experimentar cómo soy la inadecuada*, are two different actions and processes that require at least two visions of *conocimiento* as a knowing process. Now, I know that I know, *sé que lo sé*. I know what it means to experience inadequacy. *Ahora sé que conozco la* inadequacy, and as *una Anzaldúana, ya no hay marcha atrás, sé lo que conozco, conozco lo que sé*, I know what I know, I know what I experience. It is a stage of *conocimiento* that sounds easy to say, because most people would agree that we know something because we experience it. But to know and to feel the agony of inadequacy requires being aware of the processes of conocimientos in multiple, spiral-like stages. We walk and grow up in spirals, *donde a veces ya no sabes si estás arriba o estás en el centro, o abajo,* a spiral that moves like the wisdom of the serpent.

Anzaldúa describes seven stages of transforming conocimiento. This is my interpretation of her essay, which I rewrite here, borrowing her words as a Sutra. I use the first person, assuming this is the process that I experience when I want to be transformed and I want to engage in a decolonizing process of change.

1. Rupture, fragmentation

As I move from past presuppositions and frames of reference, letting go of former positions, I will be like an orphan, abandoned by all that is familiar. I will be *inadecuada,* exposed, naked, disoriented, wounded, uncertain, confused, and conflicted. As *inadecuada* I live *en la orilla* – a razor-sharp edge that fragments me ("Now let us shift" 547).

*Yo quebré* my sense of being Mexican and became an orphan. I decided to engage in a self-exile in order to heal and start breathing again. This shame and inadequacy are over me, I can blame only myself. I don't have a history where my parents or family needed to cross the border; I decided to cross it by myself knowing that the other side would never welcome me. Nevertheless, I had the skills to navigate the rejection; I have been trained on that journey as an *inadecuada*. What could be different? *Inadecuada aquí, inadecuada allá.*

2. Nepantla…torn between ways

> De pequeña fui a la escuela, a donde aprendí a leer,
> fui una nena normal,
> soñaba ser mexicana,
> soñaba serlo de verdad,
> me encontré que en el mercado no existía esta nacionalidad.

Leaving home cast me adrift in the liminal space between home and school. While home, family, and ethnic culture tugged me back to the tribe, the world that I experienced at school was assimilated, homogenized, whitewashed ("Now let us shift" 548). I face divisions of class, nationality, and ethnicity within my culture. I am in Nepantla where everything comes into conflict. I am living between cultures and I am living *como inadecuada.* I see everything from two or more perspectives simultaneously and this renders these cultures as transparent. My inadequacy, finally, is transparent to me, and as *cristalina agua, calma mi sed* and gives joy *to my esipíritu.*

3. The Coatlicue State

I cannot change my reality of inadequacy, and I do not know if I want to change it, but I observe my attitude toward it. Inadequacy feels as depression but it signals that I need to make changes in my life, it challenges my tendency to withdraw and it reminds me to take action. To reclaim inadequacy consciousness *tengo que moverme*—I need to move on; *salir a conocer el mundo,* engage the world in order to face it with its contradictions and conflicts ("Now let us shift" 553). I am still grieving an original trauma of domestic and sexual violence, I am still *enojada* with my own *machista* culture, and I am *enojada* with colonization in my life, on both sides of the border, *aquí y allá.* But *aquí y allá* I am proud, I am a descendent of the world's oldest races (*así me lo enseñó y escribió la maestra de maestras, mi maestra Gloria) de la raza mestiza, le duela a quien a le duela, le moleste a quien le moleste* ("Now let us shift" 550). I am a daughter of Coatlicue. I reverse the dichotomy of mind/body. I engage the integration of death and life. I reclaim spiritual consciousness and the integration of all forces and my inadequacy.

4. The call, *el compromiso*… the crossing and conversion

To transform myself I need the help of a community, and the help of written and spoken words ("Now let us shift" 557). Help from those who have crossed before me. Help from those who have written before me. I want to follow them through the opening of doors and borders, to hold their hands while crossing them. I ask that Chicanas, queers, artists, feminists, and spiritual healers help me. I want to cross the bridge (boundary between the world I just left and the one ahead). *Conocimiento* consists of crossings ("Now let us shift" 557). Changes and crossings are not comfortable. Mental constructions were imposed on me; because they are all made up, I can create a new *different, inadecuada* consciousness ("Now let us shift" 558).

5. Putting Coyolxauhqui together...new personal collective stories

I have a reflexive awareness after examining the old self's stance on life/death, individual/collective consciousness. I shift structures and references reversing the polarities, erasing the slash between them. I make meaning from my experiences to look through an archetypal psycho-myth-spiritual lens ("Now let us shift" 561). Led by the Coyolxauhqui in a new composition, my story is *la búsqueda del conocimiento*--looking for new knowledge, inadequacy knowledge. Coyolxauhqui represents how to connect and use the information gained, with intelligence, imagination, and grace to solve my problems and to create intercultural communities ("Now let us shift" 563). *Yo, la inadecuada aprendo a jugar con mis cachos de inadecuadez.*

6. The blow-up... a clash of realities

The refusal to think about race is a white privilege ("Now let us shift" 564).

The refusal to think about language is a colonial privilege.

The refusal to think about multiplicities is a privilege of the *imperio*. As bilingual I am open to multilingual communication.

As an intellectual, I am forced to take sides, forced to negotiate others and another identity crisis. I will be called disloyal if I don't write in Spanish and walk with Mexicanas. I will be labeled *Malinchista* if I prefer life in the U.S. rather than in Mexico. If I don't walk with Latinas, I am forced to take sides again. My bridge buckles under the weight of these feminist *modos* ("Now let us shift" 565). In gatherings where I feel powerless I connect with my condition of *neplantera* and connect the irreconcilable parts *para que todo el mundo sea* the same town, the same people, the same pueblo, *el mundo zurdo* ("Now let us shift" 519).

7. Shifting realities...acting out the vision or spiritual activism and the agony of inadequacy

I want to move from militarized zones, *guerras de narcos, asesinos de mujeres en*

*Ciudad Juárez* in Mexico to roundtables conversations, dialogues and *justicia, justicia, justicia, ¿te queda claro? JUSTICIA.* I want to continue learning from Anzaldúa from her words of re(con)ceiving the other, because the other—Anglo—does not welcome me, but the other—Mexican—wants to kill me and traffic with me, with my body. I am not asking for a miracle. I want to use my intelligence to cross alive and *conectar*/connect across colors, *poderes machos y corruptos* to negotiate racial contradictions, survive the stresses and traumas of daily life. I want to develop a combined vision of spiritual inadequacy and a new political practice with *conocimiento* that shares a sense of affinity with all things that advocate mobilizing, organizing, sharing information, knowledge, insights, and resources with other groups.

I realize that home is this bridge, the in-between place of *nepantla* and constant transition, a space where change happens, and inadequacy is the estate of being and changing; and change requires inadequacy (557).

This document then, includes every step of transformation described by Anzaldúa. It attempts to create the foundation of an individual epistemology based on inadequacy as a method. Here, I want to develop it as a personal journey, beginning in a classroom setting, which later extends as a pedagogical tool in order to generate critical thinking and social transformation. I must begin by honoring Anzaldúa. This is my first step and my first *huella*. The journey of this specific pedagogical research has just started and at the center is the Anzaldúan philosophy, which I engage as a sutra to remember that we are the dialogue between ourselves and *el espíritu del mundo* that is waiting for change each day. If we have the courage to change ourselves, as Anzaldúa has stated, we change the world. Finally, it does not matter where one is born or where one dies, and how many borders we cross; what is critical is where we fight for social justice for everyone in each corner of the planet that each human being calls home.

*Honor a la maestra, gracias madrina Gloria,* I keep *la creatividad de lucha* and continue your example because academia and the world must be transformed.

**Notes**

1 For deep discussion see Chela Sandoval, "Mestizaje as Method: Feminists-of-Color Challenge the Canon" in *Living Chicana Theory,* ed. Carla Trujillo, 352-370 (Berkeley: Third Woman Press, 1998).

2 " Santa Nepantla: A Borderland Sutra" was the title by Randy Conner as Plenary Speaker at The International Conference on the Life and Work of Gloria Anzaldua on May 16-17 UTSA San Antonio Texas. I took his idea to me as a Chicana Sutra.

**Works Cited**


Anzaldúa, Gloria E. "Now let us shift…the path of conocimiento…innerworks, public acts." *This Bridge We Call Home.* Eds. Gloria E. Anzaldùa and AnaLouise Keating. New York: Routledge, 2002. 540-578. Print.

Anzaldúa, Gloria. *Borderlands/La Frontera: The New Mestiza.* San Francisco: Aunt Lute Books, 1999. Print.

Cervantes, Richard C., and Maria Felix-Ortiz. "Substance Abuse Among Chicanos and Other Mexican Groups." *The Handbook of Chicana/o Psychology and Mental Health.* Eds. Roberto J. Velásquez, Leticia M.Arellano, and Brian W. McNeill. New York: Lawrence Erlbaum Associates-Taylor & Francis Group, 2004. 325- 352. Print.

Trujillo, Carla, ed. *Living Chicana Theory.* Berkeley: Third Woman Press, 1998. Print.

Velasquez, Roberto J., Leticia M. Arellano, and Brian W. McNeill, eds. *The Handbook of Chicana/o Psychology and Mental Health.* New York: Lawrence Erlbaum Associates Taylor & Francis Group, 2004. Print.

*Stepping Out*
By LAHIB JADDO

# 5

# CROSSING THE PALESTINE/ISRAEL BORDER WITH GLORIA ANZALDÚA: SOVEREIGNTY, TRANSNATIONALISM, AND THE ART OF STAYING PUT[1]

*SMADAR LAVIE*

This essay tells the story of Fatma—a veiled, old Palestinian woman from `Akka, my ultra-orthodox Yemeni granny, and myself. Fatma and I met at three points in our lives. The first was in 1992 when I was a professor coming to research the new phenomenon of Palestinian feminist NGOs in the State of Israel. One NGO referred me to Fatma, who was the model agential Palestinian working-class secular feminist informant. In 2001 I met Fatma's ghost, conjured up by Fatma's daughter as an Islamist small business owner. In 2006, I encountered Fatma for the third time when the Knesset (Israeli Parliament) displayed photos of her and my grandmother on its walls. This exhibit tried to spice up existing photos of female *Ashkenazi* ("European Jewish," Hebrew) Zionist leaders by adding in photos of *Mizrahi* ("Oriental, non-European Jewish," Hebrew) and Palestinian-Israeli neighborhood women activists.

Gloria Anzaldúa, an auto-ethnographer of her own culture, writes that the border is an open wound "where the Third World grates against the First and bleeds. And before a scab forms it hemorrhages again, the lifeblood of two worlds merging to form a third country—a border culture" (2-3). She proposes that this "third country'" is a location where South/South feminist coalitions are possible without the mediation of U.S.-European feminism.

In this essay, I argue that in the case of Euro-Israel, the volatile gender/race/nation South/South coalition among subaltern Arabs is forced upon Mizrahi women, as well as Palestinian women with Israeli citizenship like Fatma. These women do not want to be in this "third country," dispossessed of their lands, languages and cultures. They are stuck. For them, Anzaldúa's border's imagistic ambiguity is not liberating, but rather claimed by the Ashkenazi Zionist hegemony as yet another frontier to conquer. For Anzaldúa, South-South feminist coalitions are often discursive constructs, but in Palestine/Israel, they are involuntary time-spaces that are lived somatically.[2]

For Anzaldúa, the borderzone between transnational hyphens connotes fluidity, and movement across boundaries. This essay further argues that the Mizrahi and Palestinian-Israeli hyphens are what allow subaltern non-European women in the State of Israel to radically stay put. Staying put thus becomes a source of empowerment, a means of dancing a delicate dance on the hyphen while concurrently rejecting it, in the hopes that life becomes easier if one is able to enter the Ashkenazi mainstream "center of culture of power within the state" (Donnan 70).

When life's upheavals forced me to unexpectedly move back to Israel and become my own informant, I realized that staying put is not representational, but somatic, and therefore difficult to theorize beyond the bounds of the lived. Why and how was I forced to revise the anthropological process of inquiry as I lived, professionally and personally dispossessed by the State of Israel? How did my own daily experiences with the State of Israel become a source of insight for intra-Jewish racism? Through focusing on my meetings with Fatma, I question the feminist ethnographic renditions of "discourse" and "transnationalism" by examining the limits that feminist postcolonial methodology and theory encounter when they attempt to describe the lived horrors of borderzone traumas.[3]

This essay thus challenges the modes of textualization of the gendered ethnographic experience, and calls into question not only the older "reflexive" style of feminist ethnographies, but also the new genres of feminist ethnography that call for, yet problematize, the ethnographer's commitment to bear public witness to suffering. It presents modes to dehegemonize the methodology and practice of anthropological fieldwork and ethnographic writing. It thus offers means to undo the power relations inscribed in the standard anthropological process of inquiry, and to create accessible texts. These texts can be read both across disciplines and by the general public, linking academe, the public sphere, and feminist activism. Nevertheless, writing up the somatic is intricately elusive, even though somatic pains cut to the bone. When I finished writing this paper, I realized it is an arabesque—an attempt to capture unspeakable torture through the intricate recapitulation of the horrifically lived.

## I. MEETING FATMA

One sweltering August day in 1992, Kamla,[4] a Palestinian feminist activist from `Akka ("Acre", Arabic), an ancient harbor city on the northern Mediterranean shore of Israel/Palestine,[5] sent me to meet a Palestinian-Israeli woman whom we shall call "Fatma." Kamla told me: "She is a feminist anthropologist's dream. She is old and lives in the old walled town. She really is an indigenous informant. But she was the first woman around here to kick her battering husband out of the house, and go to work. She mopped floors at the local school."

I was hesitant to contact Fatma. When I hear about "really indigenous informants," I recoil. I remember the paternalism embedded in the production of academic knowledge, and the imperialist history of my discipline. "Really indigenous informant" means taking a surreal journey through time and space, simultaneously back and forth between the atavistic indigeniety of Fatma and the postcolonial subjectivity of Kamla, interlocuted through the language of theory from which I am to conjure up a publishable academic text. But I am drawn into playing my part in a theatricalized *vie quotidienne* fieldwork coevalness. In 1992 this meant an immediate chummy friendship between alleged equals—one from haughty academe, the other from a slum.

`Akka was not always a slum. It was a Palestinian walled town until the 1948 *Nakba* ("Catastrophe," Arabic),[6] when the new Zionist regime expelled most but not all of its residents. The regime resettled immigrant Jews there, but only non-Ashkenazi ones, from North Africa and other Arab and non-Arab countries. The remaining Palestinian Arabs and the new Arab-Jews and other Mizrahim lived side by side. Thus `Akka became one of the few mixed Israeli-Palestinian towns in the new State of Israel. The regime built cinderblock housing projects for Jews only, outside the town wall, but without essential public services to sustain them. When Mizrahi families had enough money, they sold their apartments at an inflated price to Palestinian-Israelis eager to move in, to escape the overcrowded conditions in the old city. Both populations suffered underemployment, underfunded schools, and local crime due to the police department's deliberate neglect of the area except for surveillance of the Palestinians on national grounds.

Unlike the Palestinians, the Mizrahim do not belong to their own nation struggling for sovereignty. On the contrary, they are the majority of Israeli citizens,[7] even though—like the hyphenated Palestinian citizens of Israel—they are treated as a deracinated ethnic minority. Therefore, although Israel is forced to negotiate with the Palestinians as equals, it does not have to offer this level of recognition to the Mizrahim. The negotiations with the Palestinian Authority, however, never depart from the realm of "discourse," while on the ground the Zionist architects of this peace continue to annex Palestinian lands, siphon off Palestinian water, blow up Palestinian homes, and destroy any possibility of civic and family life through hundreds of roadblocks.

Israeli human rights NGOs, Ashkenazi Left and Zionist by default, now acknowledge that there is racism against the Palestinians, but they will not admit to the racism Ashkenazim inflict on Mizrahim because, in the Jewish state, all Jews are to be equal. Palestinians continue to speak and write and dream in Arabic. This mother tongue was cut off from Mizrahim, though when they speak Hebrew with even the slightest traces of Arabic, the language of the enemy, it immediately connotes the Mizrahi low class.[8] The Ashkenazi Zionist regime and its Ur-Design tactics of divide and conquer pitted Mizrahim and Palestinians against one another. Throughout Israel, however, these two groups constitute 70% of the population. The regime settled Mizrahi immigrants in `Akka, brainwashing them that anything Arab, like where they had just come from, was inferior.

When I met Fatma in 1992, the First *Intifada* ("Uprising," Arabic) was winding down, while Israel was clandestinely maneuvering to sign the Oslo peace accords to position itself as the regional superpower in the Post-Cold-War globalized "New Middle East." One outcome of this "New Middle East" was privatized and greatly reduced social spending. The Palestinian citizens of Israel were the first to feel the slashes in welfare benefits. To fill the gap, some Palestinian-Israelis, under the regime's strict and continuing surveillance, wrote grant proposals to international foundations, and were able to establish their own NGOs.[9] I had made the trip from Tel Aviv to `Akka hoping to publish a scholarly scoop on the new phenomenon of Palestinian NGOs working to replace State welfare benefits. But Kamla's workday was so hectic she had no time to tape-record an intense intellectual dialogue with me, as we had done before. So I called Fatma.

When Fatma heard I was an anthropologist, she immediately invited me over. As the evening breeze wafted in from the Mediterranean, we went out and sat on stools on the balcony. I gazed down at the narrow alleys of old `Akka, and saw them full of wining-and-dining Israeli and foreign tourists. Oh, no, I did it again! Smadar! Snap out of that Zionist imperialist nostalgia! You know that both Ashkenazi and Mizrahi Jews love that Israelized Palestinian cuisine. And they escape their modernistic urban cement blocks by weekend touring of crumbling Palestinian sites. But the Ashkenazi Left bohemian revelers eye dilapidated Arab houses keenly, ready to pounce on what they know will soon be the next real estate boom ripe for gentrification. The State prohibits the original inhabitants from doing routine maintenance. By 2007, Palestinian property values had skyrocketed, and only American or French Right-wing Zionists, or post-Soviet oligarchs, could afford to make the fine investment of owning a Bible-times vacation home.

Meanwhile, back on the balcony, Fatma was pointing her finger: "There's the heroin dealer again. He gives out free samples so kids will get hooked, and then they work for him. They shoot up over in that house the regime boarded up when the family moved to the Projects. This other guy specializes in the hash and opium he gets from the IDF in Lebanon. The new biggest seller is Persian coke [crack cocaine]. It's cheap, even though it comes from Tel Aviv."

"The Nakba split us up. I want you to meet my family." She retrieved her well-worn photo albums from the massive buffet, showing off pictures of her older brother in Beirut, her cousin in Damascus, her middle brother in Toronto. Fatma went on like this, covering the globe with relatives: Venezuela, Doha, London. Closing the last album abruptly, she said, "People come, people go, people always moving around. I'd rather have them come here to me than go visit them, even though it's hip to travel. You know, the most radical act these days is to stay put."

## II. SCREEN-TESTING FATMA

In 1992, I settled down to my "ethnographic authority," writing a disjointed stream of field notes to let the concept termed "Fatma" audition for a star performance role in my scholarly show. Which theory, which setting and costume, would best frame Fatma's lived reality on the big screen of poststructural-deconstructionist-postcolonial cognition?

Is Fatma forced into agentless rhizomatic nomadism—a Deleuze and Guattari slide down a slippery slope through smooth surfaces? Or is the rhizome her survival tactic against the war machine of capitalism? Is the Palestinian forced nomadism a viable alternative to structures of Euro-American dominance and hegemony?

Her category is Third World women. But Mohanty says this category objectifies Third World women so that U.S.-Anglo feminist scholarship can redeem them through textual benevolence. If we let Fatma follow in Alarcón's Chicana-feminist "tracks of the native woman," who walks through multiple migrations and dislocations, then conquest and colonization would splinter Fatma into sets of deracinated and gendered ethnic identities, through which she would struggle for her own subjectification and juridical rights to resist. Unlike D&G's anti-historical model, the Alarcón model allows Fatma her cultural, historical and political specificity, as a departure point that facilitates a critical consciousness. But the dream of return to Palestine has not "been broken down by conquest and colonization," and Palestine is real, unlike the mythical Aztlán ("Tracks of the Native Woman" 250).

Or, following James Clifford, has Fatma transcended her `Akka roots by means of the multiple airplane routes that unite her large extended family network? How could she? So many people can't save enough cash to move their household. In 1992, when I was trying to fit Fatma into some theory, the shuttling of goods and people had caught the researchers' eyes—roots transforming into rhizomes. The new generation of cultural studies scholars transcended the modernist tropology of world systems and leaped into flows and fluxes, but I decided rhizomes were inadequate, and good old roots were unfashionable.

Maybe Fatma speaks in Gilligan's and Abu-Lughod's different voice. Well, she didn't speak to me with timid hints of pain shrouded in shame, and didn't distill and abstract her pain into poetic language, either. She said straight to my face that her husband battered her for many years.

So, is Fatma herself the Differend? Is she the Lyotardian signification of a conflict without possibility of resolution? She could have gone to a shelter for battered women, run of course by Ashkenazi feminists, but she wouldn't give them another opportunity to attack Arab patriarchy. Like the Differend, she is always acting in pursuit of justice, yet in vain, because she refuses to be drawn into the juridical language of her dominator.

How about casting Fatma as a freedom fighter struggling for a homeland? If I shouted that with the anger it deserves, the journal's first reader would toss it on the slush pile as a piece of Neanderthal essentialism. And my grant funds wouldn't cover a long enough stay in `Akka for me to co-author Fatma's memoire with her, Rigoberta Menchú style.

Has Palestine been transformed into just a language game, so it no longer contains its own legitimation?[10] Could it be a contract between players who ignore the rules of the game? Really, Fatma has no time for all this. She struggles just to survive the day.

Am I starting to over-romanticize Fatma with all these theoretical auditions? If so, why not try the anthropological legacy of anti-colonial peasant resistance studies, where resistance is an explosion in the colonizer's face? Most Palestinians before the Nakba were peasants. But even before 1948, `Akka was an ordinary town. So there's no peasant resistance. Is she performing the implosive Fanonian black-skin/white-mask hybrid resistance instead?

Does Fatma "keep on moving," as Gilroy would have it (*The Black Atlantic* 16; *Small Acts* 120-45)? Do her "diasporic circuits" make her Amiri Baraka's "changing same" (Gilroy 86; Jones 180-211)? What is Fatma's "same"? Is Fatma "an expression of culture…at its most unselfconscious," as Baraka describes it (Jones 180)? Is that one self the historical collectivity of pre-partition Palestine, the map countless diaspora Palestinians wear as neck pendants? Is that "one self" "the same"? Is "the changing" her family's non-linear system of multiple diasporisities? Does her radical act of staying put have "dynamic potency" ("Route Work" 23)?

How could it be that I have run out of theoretical costumes for Fatma? Theory must have models Fatma could fit into. But back in 1992—just before Cultural Studies turned into an empire itself—I was getting suspicious of such theories even as I practiced them. To feel better about what I then thought was my sense of belonging to radical academe, I ticked off a chart for what was Out, and what was the new In:

| OUT | IN |
|---|---|
| Area Studies | Ethnic Studies<br>Cultural Studies |
| Latin American Studies | Chicano/a Studies |
| African Studies | African-American Studies |
| Southeast Asian Studies | Asian-American Studies |
| SOAS[11] | Black British Studies |
| Etudes Maghrebiennes[12] | Francophone Studies |

| OUT | IN |
|---|---|
| The Cold War | The Sixties |
| The Reagan Era | The Multicultural Nineties |
| Objectified, neutral representation<br>White by default | Politicized, gendered/racialized positions<br>Postcolonial studies |
| Self and Other | Multiple-subject positions (governments never heard of it) |
| Invisible Whiteness studying homogenized, colored alterities, (though White here is not a phenotype, but a subject position acquired at an elite university) | A Chicana studying Chicanas, or a queer studying queers (still, their departments are in the elite university—but what if they are among the browned-skinned gringos?) |

But then it got unruly. Middle East Studies. Arab-American Studies?[13] This concept didn't exist until 9/11. Jewish Studies—that's European Judaism. So, Sephardic Studies. Arab-Jewish Studies? No-o-o, that's Folklore. And now, in 2009, I ask, what about Israel Studies? The discipline that appeared overnight on campuses all over the US after the al-Aqsa Intifada in 2000? Is Israel Studies a subset of Area Studies? Or part of Non-U.S.-European Ethnic Studies? In any case, its carefully vetted faculty are often Ashkenazi Zionists.

As I was thinking through all the "theoretical alternatives," I had a "Eureka!" moment: What if the study of Culture itself was another "changing same," used to decolonize the humanities and social sciences?

But the colonialist infrastructure of the study of Culture has persisted underground, even though the pyrotechnics of sophisticated theoretical jargon makes it hard to see. According to Ribiero and Escobar, World Anthropologies Network Collective, the data kept coming from neo/post-colonial situations, whether in the Third World or in "Third Worlded" Western metropolises, and although much of the manual labor was outsourced, most of the theory has been articulated in Western metropolitan universities and then exported back to the Third World.

## III. THE OMINOUS HYPHENS: PALESTINIAN-ISRAELI AND ARAB-JEW

In 1987, Chicana lesbian feminist Gloria Anzaldúa published *Borderlands/La Frontera.* Determined to textualize the North's historical dominance over dark women, she articulated, from the ground up and the inside out, her thinking about her life far outside the "Northern conventions of research, writing and thinking about the world" (Gledhill). Nevertheless, in less than a decade her book gained canonical dominance in the halls of academe. As I was reading it in 1990, I was formulating my research about the Israeli-Arab borderlands, and thinking about the liberating possibilities of South-South coalitions of knowledge and activism between Mizrahim and Palestinians.

Back in 1992, Fatma and I were located on different levels of the hierarchy of oppression. As a University of California professor, I was obviously far more privileged than she, although I was too embarrassed to let her know that even as I spoke with her, I too was a battered woman. I was still married to my abuser and lived in denial. But anyway, how could an American university anthropologist ask for shelter from the Third World informant she is supposed to atavize?

Yet even then we shared the borderlands in our part of the world, Fatma as a Palestinian-Israeli, and I as a Mizrahi. Only after I became a welfare mother in 2001 did I really understand the potential of Anzaldúa's Borderlands concept to embody the hyphen. In February 1999, my 9-year-old son was transferred to the sole custody of his father. If I had not fled with him to my family in Israel, he would have managed to kill himself.[14] But the support system of my extended family had been shattered long ago when the Zionist state's welfare authorities forced the Mizrahim to have compact nuclear families like the Ashkenazim without the intergenerational wealth to sustain them. Because I refused to limit my academic freedom to the Zionist-"post" Zionist confines, I was barred from gainful employment in Israel's universities. And for almost eight years Israel legally barred me from leaving the country for work elsewhere, where my color and politics do not matter. I was all alone, and became entangled in the thicket of Israel's phantasmagorical, relentlessly abrasive welfare bureaucracy.[15] I endured chronic stress from the endless round of desperate encounters with lower-level

Mizrahi bureaucrats subservient to the Ashkenazi who hired them. With the skyscrapers of the "White City" of modern Tel Aviv in the background, I became just another mother in the welfare lines of the "Black City" of South Tel Aviv.[16]

I met other Jewish mothers—not only Mizrahim like myself, or some post-Soviet immigrants from the Asian parts of the former USSR. I also met the Fatmas of Jaffa, annexed as the Palestinian part of South Tel Aviv. This time the Fatmas and I were in the same line. I wondered: Have I become another Fatma, so elusive to theory? After their production-line jobs were outsourced to Jordan, Egypt, or South Africa, both the Mizrahi and the Palestinian-Israeli women stood together, no bickering, so droopy and sweaty, in the long food line of Operation Open Heart. From the far-flung ghettos, they would travel every Thursday to a stuffy parking basement on the doleful outskirts of any major Israeli city's industrial zone, just to be able to feed their families with donated leftover food. I didn't give a damn then about different language games, or the liberation of Palestine... I just wanted food for Shabbat. As I interacted with them, every once in a while the original Fatma would flicker in my mind. But it was way more important to me to make sure my electricity was back on after I scurried around to find money to pay the bill—we lived on candlelight until then. Or to find money to get the water running again in my place—when we couldn't pay, we had to haul buckets of water from the neighbor's apartment. When she was broke, we reciprocated.

In time, the mothers in the welfare lines became friendly with each other. We shared the sudden panic at a knock on the door that might be the police, or an unauthorized search by the welfare detectives, or the welfare officers of the family court, coming at dawn to remove the children, for their own good, to the regime's forced boarding school system, since the family had failed to make ends meet and was therefore unfit to parent. Weaker after each round with the labyrinthine bureaucracy, many just gave up, knowing it is hopeless to try to claim whatever supposed rights the law gives them. It took me three years to gradually realize that, with these women, I was living the South/South sisterhood, though it had been forced on us. While in the lines, the Mizrahi women, who said good Arabs are dead Arabs, nevertheless developed situational friendships with the Palestinian-Israeli women, who on their part, continued to refer to the Mizrahi woman as Jewish, indicating they did not distinguish between Ashkenazi and Mizrahi Jews.

Meanwhile, the al-Aqsa Intifada raged. The random curfews, house searches, arrests, and random openings and closings at hundreds of checkpoints result in lost work opportunities, lost medical appointments, lost family ties, lost civic life, lost demolished houses, lost fetuses. Finally, the apartheid wall.

Why is it that South-South coalitions, as potent as they are, or could be, cannot travel beyond discourse, so that Mizrahim and Palestinians as the majoritarian population implode Ashkenazi Zionism from within the State of Israel? Is it because the spectacularly successful Ur-Design has a stranglehold on the situation? It sure does keep the two subaltern populations hostile to and prejudiced against each other.

While transnational hyphens connote fluidity and movement across boundaries, Fatma's and my borderland hyphens allowed us to radically stay put. But neither Western academe nor government, each with its own linear discourse, would permit Fatma and me to use our hyphens. I cannot be a Mizrahi, an existence entailing being a hyphenated Arab-Jew. Fatma cannot be a Palestinian-Israeli. To the Israeli regime, Fatma is an Arab. Period. She cannot be a Palestinian, because that would force Israel to recognize the ruins of Palestine underneath it. I am a Jew with extra rights in the Zionist Jewish State. For the progressive academic community in the West, I am the dominating Israeli, while she is the oppressed Palestinian.

Amidst the angry pleading and yelling in the food line around me, my mind wandered back to academic habits, in a dissociated state of escape. I fantasized that if I ever got out of this line, and back into academe, I would write it all up. What theories could I use so that I myself would get quoted? Even the theories of embodiment seemed to misrepresent somatic reality, by having no way to test the theories against the actual experiences—the deepest cuts to the bones. The closest I could get was Gloria Anzaldúa, whose somatism seemed beyond theory, because she was writing from her open wound. In 1992, when I read

*Borderlands* to keep up with scholarly trends, I understood her only on the level of mimetic representation, but it was a perfect fit for my data, and perhaps even for the problem of Fatma. Now I felt it, in my own non-mimetic hunger and humiliation. I went up north to visit Fatma in 2001. Her daughter said that in 1994, after one of her sons died from a heroin overdose, she died of a broken heart.

## IV. ANZALDÚA'S GHOST

Sunday 16 May 2004, the news arrived in an email from Norma Alarcón:

> Dear All:
>
> With great sorrow I pass on the news of Gloria Anzaldúa's death Her family is taking her back home to Texas. She was finishing a book for Routledge. She is a great loss to us. A woman of great spirit—the Chicanita from Texas, as she said of herself.

My hands froze on the laptop. I was hallucinating conversations between whatever was left of my "facultad"—the agency entailed in "the capacity to see in surface phenomena the meaning of deeper realities"—and Anzaldúa's "shadow beast"—the woman of color's power to struggle against the "intimate terrorist" of patriarchal late capitalism that converts her fearless creativity into compliance (Anzaldúa 60; 20). One 2005 summer Thursday morning, near fainting in the foodline, I saw Anzaldúa's ghostly face.

GLORIA: A border culture…a shock country, a closed country, a warzone… my home… (2; 3; 11).[17]

SMADAR: Gloria, I've taught it so much in class. In all the welfare lines, the Palestinian-Israelis and the Mizrahim grate against that Ur-Design, and bleed. But the Ur-Design is so sophisticated. No specific laws, but caught in the relentless bureaucracy, everyone knows their place. Palestinian women see their children's blood spilled. Mizrahi women are the sleepwalking wounded, entranced by the drumbeat of the miraculous ingathering of the diasporas. Their wounds—so deep. Invisible blood. Aren't all these welfare lines just our joint third country? Or maybe Fatma's `Akka is. Or—this Thursday line is, until we split up and go back to our segregated ghettos and 'hoods.

GLORIA: Facultad—we don't fully engage our agency ... what we need to do is gather our strength and fight for control (21).

SMADAR: Mizrahi and Palestinian women terrorize each other. Palestinian women know why they hurt. Sharing Nakba memories with the younger ones in the lines. The Mizrahi women—no one in the line to teach them their history. How can they realize that without the Nakba, they would not have been drawn in from their non-Yiddish speaking homelands to become the Mizrahi diaspora in the Ashkenazi 'villa in the jungle?'[18]

GLORIA: The Global South. One big borderland in constant transition (31). Our people. Transgressors. Aliens. Chicanos. Indians. Blacks (3). The White elite wants us—people of the South—behind separate tribal walls. To pick us off one by one. To keep us prejudiced against each other. Stunned and apart (86). We speak an orphan tongue. We speak with tongues of fire (58).

SMADAR: Southside Tel Aviv. Borderlands. Dangerous. The National Security Bureau—a sleek highrise. Number 870, a single mom, finally cracks, shrieking curses at the State in Moroccan Arabic—a tongue of fire. A Mizrahi woman bureaucrat jabs the buzzer. A big blond Russian guard clubs the mother. She falls face down, gloms onto the floor. Stays put. She can't afford to lose her place in the line. He snaps the cuffs on her wrists above her head, grabs the chains between her hands, and drags her away, screaming in her orphan tongue. Each of us suddenly inside her own wall. Petrified. Each thinking—it could have been me. No transitions here. The line keeps moving. We're all stuck.

## V. THE UR-DESIGN: THE WALL AND THE MAW

In addition to the many walls erected within Israel to block Mizrahim and the Palestinian citizens of Israel from housing, education, let alone coalitions, Israel has almost completed a massive apartheid wall demarcating the border it has claimed for itself on the lands of Palestine. The Eurocenter craves borders because they invite its civilizing mission of taming them by absorbing them into its maw and transforming them into frontiers. Most of the workers building the wall are Palestinians or Mizrahim. Around the wall, Israel operates a vicious border machine, with patrols, electric fences, roadblocks, and further land confiscations. The borderland between the pre-1967 Israel and the 21st-century Palestine behind the Israeli apartheid walls of the West Bank and Gaza is destined to become the *maquiladora* of the Middle East. For the Fatmas, and also for working-class Mizrahi women, the border is becoming a prison house. Out of every dollar the West has invested in the Palestinian Authority economy, 35 cents have ended up with Israeli industrial conglomerates. The political economy of the US-designed New Middle East will be assembled by the nimble fingers of these women, who have no choice but to do whatever they can to make a living. Their unatavized regional specificity is not compromised by their transnational labor. And the worse their economic situation gets, the more they are drawn to orthodox or fundamentalist religion.

## IV. THE QUILT AS TIME-BOMB

In February 2005, I got an email from a researcher working for the Committee on the Status of Women at the Knesset, the Israeli national legislature. He asked if I knew of old Mizrahi and Palestinian-Israeli women activists who died and never made it to the rosters of Israel's official Ashkenazi history and/or schoolbooks. The Committee plan for its 2005 International Women's Day session was to display photos of them, among photos of hegemonic Ashkenazi-Zionist women, as a quilt of photos hung on a Knesset wall, with a catalogue of short bios. I called the researcher and found he was looking for the "indigenous informant" he could atavize into a visual text, to create an artificial coevalness between the charismatic women from skid row and those of the Ashkenazi-Zionist elite. I suggested the researcher hang my granny's photo on the wall and get in touch with Fatma's family.

The Knesset exhibit was meant to transmute "race" to "poverty," so that the Knesset's racinated ideology and practice in the formation and maintenance of the Ur-design of an apartheid nation-state would continue to remain invisible. In the lines about Fatma from the exhibit's catalogue, the fact that she was a Palestinian, let alone an Arab, is conspicuously absent. In this project the committee meant to actually enact its outback colonialist anthropology in Israel's border sites.

Yet, by being very enthusiastic about participating in the exhibit, Fatma's family—and the families of the other Palestinian-Israeli and Mizrahi women in the collage—displayed the common phantasmagorical aspiration of Israel's deracinated populations to live and work in the Israeli power centers. Depoliticized as the exhibit catalogue was, I could still find traces of Mizrahi and Palestinian historical specificity as I read it against the Zionist grain: the Arabic last names, and the women's dark complexions or their modestly kerchiefed heads. These features inadvertently third-worlded the Israeli Ashkenazi-Zionist center simply by being displayed within it. Gloria Anzaldúa taught me that the border is an "open wound" (2-3). But none of the border's South/South coalition members—Mizrahim or Palestinian—want to be in this "third country" emerging out of their painful dispossession of lands, languages and cultures. Its imagistic ambiguity is not liberating, but rather is used by the Zionist hegemony, as in the case of the exhibit, or the Operation Open Heart food lines. And despite all this, the border's imagistic ambiguity invites the projections and misreadings which enable Fatma's experiences in the borderlands to be displayed in Israel's Ashkenazi-Zionist centers of power. Fatma, and even I, are thus able to leave landmines dormant all over Israel. Perhaps one day, the gender/race/nation fissures in the Zionist narrative will no longer be containable. They will blow up when the South/South coalition is among Arab feminists—Muslim, Christian and Jewish—a coalition of hope, to reabsorb Mizrahim into the area in which they have become exiles from within and without.

The main speaker celebrating the Knesset's 2005 International Woman's Day was Major General Moshe Boogie Ye`elon, Israel's Army chief of staff. He praised the contribution of women to the Israeli military. So much for the borderization of the Knesset by Fatma, my granny, or myself. Here came the colonialist frontiersman striding up to the podium, even as Fatma's traditionally-garbed sons and daughters in the audience tried hard to muffle their spontaneous hiss. Giant images of Fatma and a handful of other Palestinian-Israeli and Mizrahi women grinned from the wall. The General, seated as he was, had to look right at them. Right on, Fatma: "These days, the most radical act is to stay put."

Each theory has its own flash of life. First unthinkability. Then exciting praise for its new set, or provocative net, of abstractions that sound like floating signifiers without much data. Then its long process of becoming obsolete. Nowadays, in the U.S., borderzone theory is out—9/11 cut the border festivities of theoreticians, artists, etc. We're now all doing Islam, rights, NGOs, and sovereignty. The rest of the world is soon to follow, given the U.S.-European theoretical hegemony of the Humanities and the Social Sciences. But if not even Gloria Anzaldúa's borderzone managed to contain Fatma, the veiled feminist on the Knesset wall, who can guarantee that the new theories of Islamist feminism can do better? And what is left for me, as an ethnographer?

Forever the anthropologist, I photographed the event and scribbled notes.

**Notes**

1 This article started as an Atlanta, GA, 1994 paper with the title "Sovereignty, Transnationalism, and the Art of Staying Put: Crossing the Palestine/Israel Border with Gloria Anzaldua" (Lavie 1994) presented at the Annual Meetings of the American Anthropological Association, in the invited Panel, 'Intersections: Minority Discourse/Area Studies/Cultural Studies,' organized by Lisa Yoneyama. Fieldwork and research were conducted during 1990-1994 and funded by the Wenner Gren Foundation, the University of California Humanities Research Institute at Irvine and the University of California, Davis faculty development grant. Further fieldwork was conducted between 1999-2007, supported by an inadequate single mother welfare and housing allowance or augmentation of minimum wage provided by Israel's Bureau of National Security (paralleling the Social Security programs for the poor in other countries). I am deeply indebted to Suad Joseph, who in 1993 shared with me a conversation she had with poet Jerry Snyder, about the art of staying put in postmodernist times. Without it, the data I used for this paper in 1994 would have probably been buried in my fieldnotes until this very day. My conversation with Suad led to a "eureka moment" from which this paper flowered forth. As this paper transformed into its present state, Norma Alarcón generously provided helpful

comments and insights about the centrality of Gloria Anzaldúa to my own research. My thanks also to Haim Hazan and Esther Hertzog, who made me translate the activists bridges I built between Chicana and Mizrahi feminisms into scholarlese. Ilise Ben-Shoushan Cohen, Angana Chattergi, Richard Shapiro and the participants of the departmental seminar of the California Institute for Integral Studies challenged me to further revise the piece. Ilise's gracious hospitality helped shape this paper into its final form. Jim and Penny Bowen generously shared with me their home and farm as I gathered up courage to write up the critique of my 1990s hipster theory trash. Jim's encyclopedic knowledge, impressive Palestine with Provenance data bank, and many Skype chats were invaluable to the referencing process. My deepest gratitude to my Mzeini family in Dahab for their support and understanding—roof, food, company, care and love—as I revised and revised, groping for calmer words to write up the demons of my recent 'Israeli' past.

2 Donnan (2005:98) terms this somatic borederzone lived experiences "the materiality of place." His thorough longterm work on the North Ireland border Protestants as majoritarian communities is critical of deconstructionist, "post" colonial theories of diasporas, borders, and migrations, and inspires my analysis of Mizrahim. In this piece I refer to one of his recent works, which I have found the most useful axis to my analysis of Mizrahim. Thanks to Donnan's body of work, I find the parallels between Mizrahim and Northern Ireland border Protestants striking. Similarly it is interesting to compare the Mizrahi-Palestinian rift on its historical striations of memories to that of the working class Protestants and Catholics in Northern Ireland. Unsurprisingly, Donnan's earlier fieldwork has been in the Arab and Muslim Worlds.

3 Julie Peteet's landmark "Problematizing a Palestinian Diaspora" (2007) provides a review of diaspora theories, the reasons for their becoming an academic fashion, and the possibility for their critical engagement with the Nakba and the Palestinian displacement.

4 All names of persons mentioned in this article have been changed.

5 Rebecca L. Torstrick's *The Limit of Co-Existence: Identity Politics in Israel* (2000) is the most comprehensive ethnography of `Akka, and a ground-breaking analysis of Mizrahi-Palestinian relations in the State of Israel.

6 The Nakba was the 1948 Ashkenazi-Zionist expulsion of almost all the Palestinian population of Palestine due to the founding of the State of Israel.

7 Through careful analysis of Israeli census figures Ducker (2005) exposes the myth that the former Soviet Union immigrants to Israel increased the number of Ashkenazi Jews. She shows that even though the main purpose of Israel's leaders in initiating this mass migration was to

increase the number of European Jews in Israel, they failed to take into account the Central Asian Jews of non-Yiddish speaking origins in the former Soviet republics.

8 Aside from accent discrimination, Mizrahim are often discriminated against for their darker skin colors and last names (unless they Hebrew-ize them). Cf. Yedi'ot Aharonot 2002, Nevo and Ronen 2000.

9 I do not have the exact number of Palestinian-Israeli civil society NGOs in 1992. I was sent to Kamla's NGO because it was one of the firsts. Yet in 2002, 56 NGOs were registered with Ittijah, the Union of Arab Community Based Organizations in Israel.

10 Palestine's national poet laureate, Mahmoud Darwish, contemplates this idea in his epic *Mural* (1999), written about his near-death experience.

11 SOAS stands for the venerable School of Oriental and African Studies in London that dates back to the times of high colonialism.

12 *Etudes Maghrebiennes* is the periodical where anthropologists and other scholars in the Humanities and Social Sciences writing in French published their studies of North Africa.

13 When I wrote this fieldnote, Arab American Studies was not an academic field of inquiry. How ironic it is to note that the field of Arab American studies solidified after the 9/11 events.

14 With major depression around the divorce, my son had started falling apart in 1995.

The Israeli courts strictly observe the Hague Convention on the Civil Aspects of International Child Abduction, even disregarding the allowable exceptions in it that specify the rare conditions allowing the abducted child to stay in the country where he or she has been brought. The return rate of children abducted to Israel from the United States is much higher than in other countries who are signatories to the convention (cf. Bruch 1988/89; 2000 a, b; 2003; Schuz 2004). When our trial began, we had to submit both our Israeli and American passports to the court. International law recommends that a child abduction trial at all levels of courts should last no longer than one year, to provide a swift remedy in the best interest of the child (Schuz 2002; 2004). But in our case it took two years to decide, because the court chose not to ignore the evidence we presented.

In a precedent-setting 2001 decision, the Israeli Supreme Court cleared me of any child abduction charges (Israel's Supreme Court Verdict 5253/00; cf. also Schuz 2008). Because of the delay, I was not able to honor the terms of my University of California job, so I resigned. Recognizing the Israeli court decision, the US State Department instructed me to go to the Tel

Aviv US Consulate and get a new valid American passport. I did so, but it was too late—I had already resigned my job, and in any case, as an Israeli citizen I had to have my Israeli passport to leave or enter Israel.

Under international custody law, after a minor lives in a country for two years, the domicile of the minor changes to that country (Schuz 2001; 2004). Now that we had been living in Israel for two years, and the Hague matter was behind us, I should have been granted automatic custody, so that I could be the legal parent of my child. So in order to get my Israeli passport back, I now had to ask the Israeli family court for Israeli custody of my son. For almost six more years, the Tel Aviv family court refused to make a decision to grant the custody orders, so that I would have been able to appeal (Bruch 2003). I was stuck.

15 Anthropologist and feminist activist Esther Hertzog has dedicated her life to exposing the atrocities committed by Israel's Welfare Authorities against women, mothers and children, and has assisted hundreds of women as they got entrapped in the lethal thicket of Israel's welfare bureaucracy. She has published many op-ed public anthropology columns in Israel's high circulation dailies on Israel's surreal welfare authorities. In her role as the convener of Israel's Women's Parliament she organized several sessions on the topic as well.

16 An eloquent analysis of the division of Tel Aviv into a "White City" and a "Black City" is provided in Rotbard.

17 As I was writing this part of the article in summer 2008 I went back to Anzaldúa's book and found the relevant pages in the book that correspond to my hallucinations of Anzaldúa in summer 2005.

18 Israel's former chief of staff and defence minister Ehud Barak has defined Israel as a European villa in the Arab jungle (see, for example, http://www.hagada.org.il/hagada/html/modules.php?name=Newsandfile=articleandsid=5602) This definition corresponds exactly with the vision Theodor Hertzl, the progenitor of modern Zionism had for the Jewish state (Hertzl 1986).

**Works Cited**

Abarjel, Reuven and Lavie, Smadar. "A Year into the Lebanon-Gaza War: A Mizrahi Guide to the Perplexed, and the One State Vision." *Sedek*: *A Hebrew Nakba Periodical* 1.2 (2008): 71-79. Print.

Abdo, Nahla, and Lentin, Ronit, eds. *Women and the Politics of Military Confrontation*. New York: Berghahn Books, 2002. Print.

Abu Lughod, Lila. *Writing Women's Worlds*. Berkeley: University of California Press, 1993. Print.

Alarcón, Norma. "Chicana Feminism: In the Tracks of the Native Woman." *Cultural Studies* 4 (1990): 248–56. Print.

-----. "Anzaldúa's Frontera: Inscribing Gynetics." *Displacement, Diaspora, and Geographies of Identity*. Eds. S. Lavie and T. Swedenburg. Duke University Press, 1996. 41–53. Print.

Alcalay, Ammiel. *After Jews and Arabs: Remaking Levantine Culture*. Minneapolis: University of Minnesota Press, 1993. Print.

Alexander, Jacqui M. *Pedagogies of Crossing*. Duke University Press, 2005. Print.

Anzaldúa, Gloria. *Borderlands/La Frontera: Mestiza*. San Francisco: Aunt Lute Books, 1987. Print.

Aretxaga, Begona. *Shattering Silence: Women, Nationalism, and Political Subjectivity in Northern Ireland*. Princeton: Princeton University Press, 1997. Print.

Beinin, Joel. "The Demise of the Oslo Process." *MERIP.* Middle East Report Online, 26 March 1999. Web. 24 March 2010.

Ben Porat, Guy. *Global Liberalism: Peace and Conflict in Israel/Palestine and Northern Ireland*. New York: Syracuse University Press, 2006. Print.

Berger, Joseph. "Israeli Executives Urge Moderation on Netanyahu." *The New York Times*. 8 June 1996. Web. 24 March 2010.

Bichler, Shimson and Nitzan, Jonathan. *From War Profits to Peace Dividends: The Global Political Economy of Israel*. Jerusalem: Carmel, 2001. Print.

Bitton, Simone, dir. *Wall*. Lifesize Entertainment, 2004. Film.

Bruch, Carol. "Religious Law, Secular Practices, and Children's Human Rights in Child Abduction Cases Under the Hague Child Abduction Convention." *NYU Journal of International Law and Policy* 33.49 (2000). Print.

-----. "The Hague Child Abduction Convention: Past Accomplishments, Future Challenges." *European Journal of Law Reform* 97 (1998/1999): 101-117. Print.

-----. "Temporary or Contingent Changes in Location under the Hague Child Abduction Convention" *Gedächtnisschrift Alexander Lüderitz*. Ed. H. Schack. 43 (2000). Print.

-----. *An Expert Opinion Concerning the Effective International Implementation of the November 17, 2003 Israeli Custody Decision, which was Entered Following the Conclusion of Hague Proceedings that Denied the Return of Shaheen Lavie Rouse to California*. 5 December 2003. MS.

Chetrit, Sami Shalom. *The Mizrahi Struggle 1948–2003: Between Oppression and Emancipation*. Tel Aviv: `Am-Oved, 2004. Print.

Clifford, James. "On Ethnographic Authority." *Representations* 1 (1983): 118–46. Print.

-----. *Routes: Travel and Translation in the Late Twentieth Century*. Boston: Harvard University Press, 1997. Print.

Darwish, Mahmoud. *Mural*. 1999. Trans. Muhammad Hamza Ghanaim. Tel Aviv: Andalus, 2006. Print.

Das, Veena, et al., eds. *Remaking a World: Violence, Social Suffering, and Recovery*. Berkeley: University of California Press, 2001. Print.

Deleuze, Gilles, and Guattari, Felix. *Nomadology: The War Machine*. Trans. Brian Massumi. New York: Semiotext(e), 1986. Print.

Donnan, Hastings. "Material Identities: fixing Ethnicity in the Irish Borderlands." *Identities: Global Studies in Culture and Power* 12 (2005): 69-105. Print.

Ducker, Clare Louise. "Jews, Arabs, and Arab Jews: The Politics of Identity and Reproduction in Israel." The Hague, Netherlands: Institute of Social Studies, 2005. Print.

Ebron, Paulla, and Lowenhaupt Tsing, Anna. "In Dialogue? Reading Across Minority Discourses." *Women Writing Culture*. Eds. Ruth Behar and Deborah A. Gordon. University of California Press, 1995. 390–411. Print.

Fabian, Johannes. *Time and the Other: How Anthropology Makes Its Object*. New York: Columbia University Press, 1983. Print.

Fanon, Franz. *Black Skin, White Masks*. New York: Grove, 1976. Print.

Gilat, Israel Zvi. "On the Legal Failure Structured in the Diagnosis of the Child's Best Interest through the Welfare System." *Moznei Mishpat—Nataniya Academic College Law Review* 5 (2006): 403-88. Print.

Gilligan, Carol. *In a Different Voice*. Cambridge: Harvard University Press, 1982. Print.

Gilroy, Paul. *The Black Atlantic*. Cambridge: Harvard University Press, 1993. Print.

-----. *Small Acts*. London: Serpent's Tail, 1993. Print.

-----. "Route Work: The Black Atlantic and the Politics of Exile." *The Postcolonial Question: Common Skies, Divided Horizons*. Eds. Iain Chambers and Lidia Curti. London: Routledge, 1996. 17-99. Print.

Gledhill, John. "Reinventing Anthropology, Anew." *Anthropology News* Oct. 2005. Print.

Hajjar, Lisa. *Courting Conflict: The Israeli Military Court System in the West Bank and Gaza*. Berkeley, University of California Press 2005. Print.

Halper, Jeff. *An Israeli in Palestine*. London: Pluto, 2008. Print.

Hasson, Yael. *Three Decades of Privatization*. Tel Aviv: Adva Center Publications, 2006. Print.

Hertzog, Esther. "Who Benefits from the Welfare State?" *Teoria uBikoret* 9 (1996): 81-101. Print.

Herzl, Theodor. *The Jewish State*. 1896. New York: American Zionist Emergency Council, 1946. Print.

Jones, Leroi [Amiri Baraka]. *Black Music*. New York: Apollo Press, 1968. Print.

Katz, Yitzhak. *Privatization*. Tel Aviv: Pecker Publishers, 1997. Print.

Kearney, Michael. *Reconceptualizing the Peasantry: Anthropology in Global Perspective*. Boulder: Westview Press, 1996. Print.

Keshet, Yahudit. *Checkpoint Watch: Testimonies from Occupied Palestine*. London: Zed Books, 2006. Print.

Lavie, Smadar, and Ted Swedenburg. "Between and Among the Boundaries of Culture: Bridging Text and Lived Experience in the Third Timespace." *Cultural Studies* 10 (1996): 154-79. Print.

Lavie, Smadar, A. Hajj, and, Forest Rouse. "Notes on the Fantastic Journey of the Hajj, His Anthropologist, and Her American Passport." *American Ethnologist* 20 (1993): 363-84. Print.

-----. "Area Studies, Transnationalism, and the Art of Staying Put." *Proceedings of the Annual Meetings of the American Anthropological Association: Panel 'Intersections: Minority Discourse/ Area Studies/Cultural Studies.'* Organizer Lisa Yoneyama, 1994. Print.

Liberman, Guy. "Romance with Neve Tzedek." *Haaretz—Marker Weekly*. 21 March 2008. Print.

Lyotard, Jean-Francois. *The Postmodern Condition*. Minneapolis: University of Minnesota Press, 1979. Print.

-----. "The Differend, the referent, and the Proper name." *Diacritics* 14 (1984): 4-14. Print.

Mahmood, Saba. *Politics of Piety: The Islamic Revival and the Feminist Subject*. Princeton: Princeton University Press, 2005. Print.

Mansergh, Nicolas. "The Prelude to Partition: Concepts and Aims in Ireland and India." In *Nationalism and Independence: Selected Irish Papers*. Cork: Cork University Press, 1997. 32-63. Print.

Menchú, Rigoberta. *I… Rigoberta Menchú*. Writer Elisabeth Burgos-Debray. London: Verso, 1984. Print.

Mohanty, Chandra Talpade. "Under Western Eyes: Feminist Scholarship and Colonial Discourse." *Third World Women and the Politics of Feminism*. Eds. C.T. Mohanty, A. Russo, and L. Torres. Bloomington: University of Indiana Press, 1991. 51-90. Print.

Nagar, Richa. "Footloose Resesarchers, 'Traveling' Theories, and the Politics of Transnational Feminist Praxis." *Gender, Place and Culture* 9 (2002):179-2002. Print.

-----. "Collaboration Across Borders: Moving Beyond Positionality." *Singaphore Journal of Tropical Geography* 24 (2003): 356-372. Print.

Nagar, Richa, and Saraswati Raju. "Women, NGOs and the Contradictions of Empowerment and Disempowerment: A Conversation." *Antipode: A Radical Journal of Geography* 35 (2003):

1-13. Print.

Nagar, Richa, and Eric Sheppard. "From East-West to North-South." *Antipode: A Radical Journal of Geography* 36 (2004): 557-563. Print.

Penslar, Derek J. "Broadcast Orientalism." *Orientalism and the Jews*. Eds. Ivan Davidson Kalmar and Derek Jonathan Penslar. Waltham: Brandeis University Press, 2004. 182-200. Print.

Ribeiro, Gustavo Lins and Escobar, Arturo. *World Anthropologies: Disciplinary Transformations Within Systems of Power*. Oxford: Berg, 2006. Print.

Ronen, Moshe and Nevo, Amos. 'When They Invited Yossi Kasirrer for an Interview—I wept', *Yedi`ot Aharonot*. "24 Hours" section, pp. 2–3 (in Hebrew), April, 24 2000.

Rosaldo, Renato. *Culture and Truth: The Remaking of Social Analysis*. Boston: Beacon Press, 1989. Print.

Rosenfeld, Henry. *They Were Peasants*. Tel Aviv: HaKibbutz HaMeu'had, 1964. Print.

Rotbard, Sharon. *White City, Black City*. Tel Aviv: Babel Publishing, 2005. Print.

Sabbagh, Suha, ed. *Palestinian Women of Gaza and the West Bank*. Bloomington, Indiana University Press, 1998. Print.

Sandoval, Chela. *Methodology of the Oppressed*. Minneapolis: University of Minnesota Press, 2000. Print.

Schuz, Rhona. "Policy considerations in Determining the Habitual residence of a Child and the Relevance of Context." *Journal of Transnational Law and Policy* 11 (2001): 2-61. Print.

-----. "The Hague Child Abduction Convention and Children's Rights." *Transnational Law and Contemporary Problems*, 393 (2002). Print.

-----. "Rights of Abducted Children: Does the Hague Convention Law (the Return of Abducted Children) 1991 Dovetail with the Children's Rights Doctrine?" *Mehkarei Mishpat* 20 (2004). Print.

-----. "In search of a settled interpretation of Article 12(2) of the Hague Child Abduction Convention." *Child and Family Law Quarterly* 20 (2008): 64-80. Print.

Scott, James. *Weapons of the Weak: Everyday Forms of Peasant Resistance.* New Heaven: Yale University Press, 1985. Print.

Shohat, Ella. "Sephardim in Israel: Zionism from the Point of View of its Jewish Victims." *Social Text* 19-20 (1988): 1-35. Print.

Shubeli, Rafi. "It Is Not the Occupation that Corrupts." *Mizad Shen* I.14/15: 38-41, 2006. Print.

Torstrick, Rebecca L. *The Limits of Coexistence: Identity Politics in Israel.* Ann Arbor: University of Michigan Press, 2000. Print.

Warshawski, M., et al. "The New Middle East: Textiles as Fable." *Mitzad Shen* I.7: 16-23, 1997. Print.

Wolf, Eric. *Peasant Wars in the Twentieth Century.* New York: Harper Collins Press, 1970. Print.

World Anthropologies Network Collective. "Establishing Dialogue among International Anthropological Communities." *Anthropology News* Nov. 2005. Print.

"The Cadets told the Yemeni Couch: No Parking for Blacks." *Yedi'ot Aharonot.* 21 July, 2002, sec. A: 17. Print.

Yuval-Davis, Nira. *Gender and Nation.* London: Sage, 1997. Print.

Yuval-Davis, Nira, and Floya Anthias. *Racialized Boundaries.* London: Routledge, 1992. Print.

# PART 2

POETRY

## DE LA MEMORIA DEL VIENTO

*EDNA OCHOA*

*A la memoria de mis hermanas de Ciudad Juárez:*
*¡Ni una muerta más!*

¿Cuál silencio se murió de más silencio?
Shhhhhhhhhhhhhhhhhhhhhhhhhhhhhhhh
que voy desbaratándome
Entre los calcinados pedruscos
mi mano habla mi pie sin su zapato habla
Un pedazo de plástico se mueve y el ojo
alcanza un rayo de sol sin que el párpado musite
Sólo queda el sueño de mi madre
flotando en mis arterias

Un periódico da volteretas y el aire acalora
la tinta de la modorra de los que dicen ya casi ya
Estamos trabajando Avanza la investigación
Prontitito aclararemos eso, eso de las muertas

¿Cuál silencio se murió de más silencio?
Enrarezco sin saber
Desmembradas en las hendiduras del aire
las letras de justicia revolotean mudas

En las roturas de lo que aun fui
el fósforo de mis huesos alumbra un carrusel
caramelos las vocales lápices
el cuaderno donde mi madre puso mi nombre
la dulzura de sus manos trenzándome el cabello
Sí porque yo antes me llamaba
Era.

# FROM THE MEMORY OF THE WIND

*EDNA OCHOA*

*TRANSLATION BY RITA E. URQUIJO-RUIZ AND NORMA ALARCÓN*

*To the memory of my sisters from Ciudad Juárez*
*Not one more death!*

Which silence died from more silence?
Shhhhhhhhhhhhhhhhhhhhhhhhhhhhhhhh
I'm coming undone
Between the burnt sharp stones
my hand speaks, my bare foot speaks
A piece of plastic moves and the eye
catches a sun ray without blinking,
Only my mother's dream is left
floating in my arteries

A newspaper swirls away and the air suffocates
The ink from the drowsy ones who say almost there
we are already working, the investigation advances
Very quickly we'll clear up the dead women's cases

Which silence died from more silence?
I shudder without knowing

Dismembered in the air's fissures
Justice flutters around silently

In the remains of what I used to be
The phosphorous from my bones lights up a merry-go-round
Candies, vowels, pencils
the notebook where my mother wrote my name
the sweetness of her hands braiding my hair
Yes, because I used to have a name
I existed once

# MásCara

*RITA E. URQUIJO-RUIZ*

Sentada frente al espejo
me transformo:
desprendo milímetro a milímetro
mi máscara de fuerte
mi máscara de valiente
mi máscara sonriente,
empezando por la frente, la doblo
hacia abajo entre mis diez dedos;
se van desprendiendo
las dos cejas,
los párpados cerrados,
el tabique de la nariz, la punta,
la mejilla derecha, y a mitad de ésta,
la izquierda,
mi labio superior,
seguido por el otro
para terminar con la barbilla.
Quedan debajo:
una mueca triste;
mi cara: bistec crudo, palpitante.
Cualquier viento aterciopelado

al menor contacto,
podría tajarla dejando escapar
un hilito de líquido viscoso,
rosado, rojizo, rojo.
Pero con cada rasguño llega una cicatriz
y de costra en costra
formará otra cara
que aunque nueva,
aprenderá a ser fuerte,
a expresar una sonrisa arraigada,
profunda, verdadera.
Quedaré sin máscara,
quedaré con más cara.

# MASKS

*RITA E. URQUIJO-RUIZ*

In front of the mirror
I'm transforming:
I slowly peel away
My mask of strength
My mask of courage
My smiling mask.
Starting with my forehead, I fold it
downward between my ten fingers
My two eyebrows,
My closed eyelids,
The bridge of my nose, the tip,
My right cheek, and half way,
my left one;
My top lip,
Followed by the bottom one
are pulled away.
Underneath:
A sad smirk,
my face: raw, throbbing flesh
The softest wind
With its velvety touch

May cut it, exposing
a thin thread of viscous liquid,
pinkish, redish, red.
Each scratch, a new scar,
and scab by scab
a new face
Learning to be strong,
With a deeply rooted,
Smile.
Without a  mask,
My new face,
My new soul.

# PART 3

## CROSSING BORDERS: LEGACIES OF GLORIA ANZALDÚA

*Don't Tie me Down/No me amarres los pies*
By GRACE BARRAZA-VEGA

# 6

# GLORIA ANZALDÚA: CONSTRUCTING A THIRD WAY: ON HEGEMONY, COUNTER-HEGEMONY AND DISCURSIVE POWER RELATIONS

*ROMANA RADLWIMMER*

I am white. I was not born, but made to be white. The color of my skin, just like my gender precast cultural condition, provides me with "privileges" comfortable—too comfortable—to overlook. Gloria places a mirror before my face and asks me to listen in. Once more, I dismiss the tempting safe thought that I am every woman.

Anzaldúa's theory, a constant act of resistance, uses the imposed tools to subvert hegemony, rewriting semantics, constructing alternatives, claiming space for liberation. Reflecting on the discursive power relations Anzaldúa inscribes, some essential questions arise. How do counter-hegemonic notions defy hegemonic traditions? To what extent does hegemony try to silence counter-forces? More specifically asked: How does Anzaldúa's counter-hegemonic discourse confront hegemony? Which role does the concurrent over-, under- and misrepresentation of Anzaldúa's works in the mainstream play in hegemony's effort to regain control? In search of answers, I would like to show how Gloria Anzaldúa creates an exceptional "third way" to dismantle hegemony—a "third way" through which she rises up above subtle censorship, overexposure and misinterpretation.

Contemporary border critics have successfully applied and further developed the initially Gramscian[1] concept of "hegemony"; still, I encounter "hegemony" like Medusa's heads appearing in many forms and faces, even more so because it incorporates phenomena which are themselves multi-faceted and not to be reduced to one representation. The term seems to need further specification. Reading hegemony as "Western," "white," "U.S.-American and European" theory models (centering on their own specific needs and conditions, repudiating other forms of expression) elucidates power relations, but also implies what Spivak calls "the much publicized critique of the sovereign subject" which "actually inaugurates a Subject" (271). Aware of this discursive controversy and its consequences, I choose to work on my and the reader's "tolerance for contradictions/tolerance for ambiguity"[2], and "inaugurate the subject" not in the sense of traditional philosophy, but by proposing a differentiated perspective on dominant forces.

The term "hegemony" includes theory and practice *models* (colonialism, nationalism, patriarchy, capitalism, etc.), as well as paternalist, patriarchal, racist, homophobic, modernist, exclusive *structures* with its *elements* and *mechanisms*. Movements with the subliminal label "counter-hegemonic" (like Feminism/s, Queer or Postcolonial theory, etc.) are not per se immune against hegemonic elements. Women-of-color have contributed to visualize such eventual (or strategically embedded) irregularities: only in the last decades, it has become commonplace to criticize hegemonic elements within the supposedly counter-hegemonic discourse of feminism. Women identifying themselves as being "othered" within patriarchal reality, while at the same time ignoring "the other of the other" in a racist context, have especially been questioned by an Anzaldúan school of thought.[3]

> To call a text or methodology under discussion in a classroom or conference "racist," or to call a white person on her or his Racism, is to let loose a stink bomb. Like a tenacious weed, Racism crops up

> everywhere—it has a stranglehold on everyone. ("Haciendo caras" xix)

Anzaldúa is aware of the ongoing silencing of women of color in the mainstream and replies to it not only on a discursive level, but also as an editor, providing space for "women who do not consider themselves writers, or at least not yet" (xvii).

Many critics have agreed on the innovative power of Anzaldúa's works. Her re-invention of the theoretical form, language and content "stands clear against disciplinary and linguistic boundaries" and functions as counter-hegemonic discourse linguistically and philosophically (Contreras 116). She consciously sets up theory against the European tradition of textuality: holistic, subjective, fragmented instead of partial, objective, totalitarian. Holistic, meaning "to engage the reader's total person" subjective as not being distanced, fragmented as considering multiple angles ("Haciendo caras" xviii).

> I wanted a book which would teach ourselves and whites to read in nonwhite narrative traditions-traditions which, in the very act of writing, we try to recoup and to invent.... Contrary to the norm, [the book] does not address itself *primarily* to whites, but invites them to "listen in" to women-of-color... (xviii)

Anzaldúa develops theory for those whose voices have been systematically excluded from power. Creating a new terminology, she refers to her philosophical concepts with Nahuatl, Spanish, Spanglish vocabulary: *Nepantla, New mestiza, Women-of-color/Mujeres-de-color...* The languages in her texts constantly change; she employs Spanish as subversive element within Anglo hegemony, indigenous lexis as subversive element within Spanish hegemony and Spanish feminine endings as subversive element against patriarchal use of language, linguistically revealing the various layers of oppression. Valuing Chicana/o language, as well as oral and popular culture, hits against elitist myths of the purity of language and culture.

> Chicano Spanish is a border tongue which developed naturally. Change, *evolución, enriquecimiento de palabras nuevas por invención o adoptación*

> have created Chicano Spanish, *un Nuevo lenguaje*. Un lenguaje que corresponde a un modo de vivir. Chicano Spanish is not incorrect, it is a living language. (*Borderlands* 77)

Anzaldúa evokes non-European mythology and refashions it, which has received much acclaim in reception. She is "rewriting the myths, using the myths back against the oppressors" (*Interviews* 219). Oppositional to the inherent hegemonic structures. Nevertheless, this remodeling has been judged as "appropriating... Indian culture in order to create a new identity" which is "not so different from Englishmen appropriating 'classical' culture and history of the ancient Greeks" (Alire Sáenz 85). Such criticism underestimates the ideological significance of mythical and historical knowledge which hegemonic discourse has designed. Hegemony works with and on our collective memory. Out of the position of *mestiza* resistance, Anzaldúa knows that she "can't disown the white tradition" or any other tradition or culture "because they're all in me" (*Interviews* 254). By subverting hegemonic tools, Anzaldúa's texts take a firm stand against a signifying network dominated by hegemony and are enabling to react to myths that are undeniably part of our cultural memory.

> Theorists-of-color are in the process of trying to formulate "marginal" theories that are partially outside and partially inside the Western frame of reference (if that is possible), theories that overlap many "worlds". [...] In our *mestizaje* theories we create new categories for those of us left out or pushed out of the existing ones. We recover and examine non-Western aesthetics while critiquing Western aesthetics..." ("Haciendo caras" xxvi)

Anzaldúa's engagement, amongst others, has caused academia to open up for the unique presence of women-of-color's notions. At the same time, academia plays an ambiguous role propagating Anzaldúa. A systematic under-representation of Anzaldúa's works contradicts the inflationary profanation and depoliticization of Anzaldúan terminology in the mainstream, which has led to an over- and misrepresentation. If we take a closer look, the contradiction becomes logical. Hegemony tends to either negate and ban counter-forces or to subdue and incorporate them. Both strategies follow one same goal: to silence productive voices, voices unproductive within hegemony's needs. Anzaldúa's concepts of fragmented and queer identities have been leveled by an empty rhetoric of difference and diversity. The border "as a metaphor has become hollow" (Gómez-Peña, "Death on the Border," 9), and, after 9/11, "has become another form of censorship, and cultural exchange is now a nostalgic project of the late 20th century" (Gómez-Peña, "Death on the Border" 9; "Disclaimer"). Hegemony disguised as multiculturalism incorporates meaningful specific experience into senseless common sense, stating all equal (but some more equal). Anzaldúa refers to multiculturalism as a "euphemism for the imperializing and now defunct melting-pot" ("Haciendo caras" xxii).

The under-representation of Anzaldúa's works (achieved by exclusion, e. g., from anthologies) has been demonstrated[4], as well as a constant, even well-intended over-representation which Anzaldúa herself denounced as "repeatedly tokenizing ... stymieing our literary/political development ("Haciendo caras" xvi). However, my focus lies on the misrepresentation of Anzaldúa's theory within an academia that is imposing an excluding vision on culture. Analyzing 21st century cultural phenomena on an academic level centrally implies the debate on the "ubiquitous and much abused term" "postmodernism" as a theory position developed in European and US-American academia (Sánchez and Pita 492). Anzaldúa comments on the poststructuralist school of thought[5]:

> [T]he ideas are out there because we are all in more or less the same territory. We occupy the world of academy and of the late twentieth century. ... In reflecting on what we know and on our experiences we come up with these paradigms, concepts of what life is about, how interactions and power struggles work. Those theorists give it different terms than I do... (*Interviews* 267)

In this self-reference, Anzaldúa situates her work in a "post-" context. At the same time, the postmodernist embrace of her conceptualizations affects our perception of them. Her philosophy is not identical with the postmodernist turn in academia: although she clearly rejects modernist categories inventing new ones, the relationship between theory and practice, between ideals and concrete social matters is never completely interrupted or dissolved. I believe that as academics we are accountable for critically discussing the dialectic nature of postmodernism. On one hand, postmodernism as the critique of modernism, has broken up boundaries, limitations, nationalisms and has challenged patriarchy and homophobia. The most valuable and effective postmodernist representations form vanguards, counter-cultures and revolutions. On the other hand, its ideological paradigm of the annihilation of the subject and the negation of history understood as rational process and progress correlates politically with the debilitation of engagement and responsibilities. Id est, as Britto García points out, also the ideological representation of market economies.[6] The symbolic order of a global economic hegemony has far-reaching cultural implications. Distorting the imperative of tolerance and humanity, it has nourished the narrative of open borders with a new subtle meaning.

Examining from my so-called "Western European" point of view the mixed perceptions that exist in Europe about the political and economic opening (and closing) of our borders, I would like to recall the euphoria about the fall of the iron curtain, followed by a (officially neither celebrated nor joyfully remembered) disillusionment caused by structural problems such as how to successfully reunify the two "Germanys." I would also like to recall the hasty substitution of one economic system for the other, the incorporation and ongoing marginalization of Eastern Europeans as cheap labourers, perceived as "second class citizens" in Western Europe (still existing political, not geographical categories). I recall the issue the European Union has defining and opening/closing our borders to the Asian and African continents. "*En unas pocas centurias*," writes Anzaldúa, visionary, universalist, "the future will belong to the *mestiza*. Because the future depends… on the straddling of two or more cultures" (*Borderlands* 102). What does the European present look like? During one of the biggest European sports events, the European Soccer Championship 2008, at one point chances were the finale could be decided between Turkey and Russia, leaving either one of them as "European Soccer Champion." If the subject is not human beings but millions of Euro or Dollars, Eurocentrism allows those nations to "elevate" themselves to "Europeans," and (virtual) borders open easily. The frequently pronounced critique of the omnipotence of the market is a consequence of the way and form borders were opened (or not). For these reasons, I have carefully come to consider that postmodernist notions participate in the processes which form the conglomerate of "hegemonic discourse." Rosaura Sánchez and Beatrice Pita explicitly refer to postmodernism as "cultural dominant" or "cultural hegemony" precisely for it's tendency to incorporate resistant forces (Sánchez and Pita 493-4).

Postmodern theorists have found in Anzaldúa "a rich terrain of support for their own analyses of subjectivity" (Contreras 114). Contreras explains how these theorists disregard "Anzaldúa's treatment of indigeneity," which she calls a "return to origins" which does not "easily align with theories of hybridity and anti-nationalism" (115). Linda Martín Alcoff discusses how the prestige Anzaldúa obtained "as authentic voice of the multiply oppressed was often paradoxically used to provide epistemological foundation of anti-foundationalist postmodern theories," and how her texts served "to bolster some of the exclusionary and elitist fashions of the institution that made her marginal" (255-6). The iconoclast status coincides with a lack of serious intellectual engagement; Anzaldúa's works are therefore often misread and misrepresented as the "hopeful portrayal of the mestiza's social positionality," gifted with an "enhanced capacity for cultural translation and flexibility" and are in this way supporting "a current trend that celebrates hybridity as the political and theoretical antidote to essentialism" (Martín Alcoff 256). Anzaldúa's understanding of hybridity does not generate romanticized images, but is one of a difficult and precarious political situation:

> *Soy nopal de Castilla* like the spineless and therefore defenseless cactus that Mamagrande Ramona grew in back of her shed. I have no protection, so I cultivate needles, nettles, razor-sharp spikes to protect myself from others. [...] As a person, I, as a people, we Chicanos, blame ourselves, hate ourselves, terrorize ourselves. (*Borderlands* 67)

Anzaldúa subverts hegemony's tools by rewriting its semantics. Aware of the consequences, she calls for developing a language of one's own. She appeals to remember the Nahuatl concept to speak with the body and act with the soul, because

> [w]hen we, the objects, become the subjects, and look at and analyze our own experiences, a danger arises that we look through the master's gaze, speak through his tongue, use his methodology—in Audre Lorde's words, use the "master tools." ("Haciendo caras" xxiii)

Her affirmation of hybridity is part of her project to achieve coherence in order to "avoid incessant cultural collisions" and modifies the postmodern liquidation of history and subjectivity. Her texts work against the hype of incoherence. For Anzaldúa, "incoherence is neither inevitable nor acceptable," and "coherence will be achieved through conscious effort and political struggle"; that is why her "description and analysis of mestiza consciousness is not at all in line with the postmodern celebration of hybridity" (Martín Alcoff 257). She deconstructs, not as nihilistic statement, but only to construct anew.

> As a mestiza I have no country [...,] yet all countries are mine [...] As a lesbian I have no race [...] but I am all races [...] I am cultureless because as a feminist, I challenge the collective cultural/religious male-derived beliefs of Indo-Hispanics and Anglos; yet I am cultured because I am participating in the creation of yet another culture... (*Borderlands* 102-3)

The under-representation of Anzaldúa's texts on one side, as well as the over- and misrepresentation on the other can be interpreted as intent to devalue her intervention and as an ideologically motivated effort from the reactionary side to debilitate the dynamic effect of Anzaldúa's words. I take it as a sign of strength and commitment, rather than of debility of Anzaldúa's discourse, when Susan Stanford Friedman criticizes "the 'brown' and 'white' of Anzaldúa's borderlands as binary thinking" which is in her opinion "creating dead ends" (Stanford Friedman 39-40). Anzaldúa employs these terms based on and exposing a concrete social reality, but enriched by a metaphoric quality of the symbolic order she tries to alter and harmonize.

The way I read it, Anzaldúa in her sense of empowerment fragments in order to create, and is not participating in nihilist dynamics. Instead, she finds a unique third way in between essentialism and careless postmodernism, leaving room for actual social, cultural and spiritual development. When I was teaching literature to 21st century teenage immigrants, they encountered in Anzaldúa's healing notions of space for identification and self-esteem. Anzaldúa is meaningful, not only to an elite of scientists, and that is what she wants her texts to embody:

> Some feminist theorists-of-color write jargonistically and abstractly, in a hard-to access language that blocks communication, makes the general listener/reader feel bewildered and stupid. These theorists often mistakenly divide theory and lived experience and are more off-putting than many of the masters they ape. ("Haciendo caras" xxiii)

If the notions of difference, plurality and the "other" remain primarily abstractions, the postmodern perspective disqualifies them as inadequate and incomplete.[7] Anzaldúa truly deals with the actual processes by which diversity is socially and politically constructed and acts from a vanguard position. Dismantling and rearranging limiting political and cultural categories, inventing emancipating contributions to the conceptualization of post-identities, her work is not part of rigid ideas supporting traditionalisms, hegemony and the omnipotence of the market. Instead, it strongly advocates for progress and cultural liberation.

> I am possessed by a vision: that we Chicanas and Chicanos have taken back or uncovered our true faces, our dignity and self-respect… I seek to recover and reshape my spiritual identity... (*Borderlands* 109)

Gloria Anzaldúa writes against all forms of domination, against "a white frame of reference" and holds the mirror before our faces ("Haciendo caras" xxii). Her "third way" is all about healing, all about transformation. Hegemony has imposed ideas on discourse and actions on history for too long. Before acting, she calls us whites to "listen in": we have a long way to go. *La frontera* can help.

**Notes**

1 Antonio Gramsci, *Quaderni Del Cacere*. Ed. Valentino Gerratana. Torino: Guilio Eidauri editore, 1975.

2 Gloria Anzaldúa, *Borderlands/La Frontera: The New Mestiza*. San Francisco: Aunt Lute Books, 2007, 101. I use Anzaldúa's terminology to underline the dialectic nature of a central discussion in feminist theory, whose political and ideological impact has to dissolve the category of the subject as such.

3 Compare, e.g.: Chela Sandoval's "Feminism and Racism. A Report on the 1981 National Women's Studies Association Conference," in *Making Face, Making Soul. Haciendo Caras. Creative and Critical Persepctives by Feminists of Color*, ed. Gloria Anzaldúa. San Francisco: Aunt Lute Books, 1990. 55-71.

4 Compare e.g.: Debra A. Castillo, "Anzaldúa and Transnational American Studies," *Publications of the Modern Language Association of America* 121 (2006): 261.

5 She explicitly talks about Jacques Derrida, amongst others.

6 In this paragraph, I paraphrase and translate Luis Britto García, "La vitrina rota: Narrativa y crisis en la Venezuela contemporánea," in *Literatura venezolana hoy*. Historia nacional y presente urbano, ed. Karl Kohut. Madrid: Vervuert, 1999, 38.

7 Paraphrasing Raymond Rocco who refers to postmodern architecture. Raymond Rocco, "The Theoretical Construction of the 'Other' in Postmodernist Thought," in *The Chicana/o Cultural Studies Reader*, ed. Angie Chabram-Dernersesian. New York: Routledge, 2006, 409.

**Works Cited**

Alire Sáenz, Benjamin. "In the Borderlands of Chicano Identity, There Are Only Fragments." *Border Theory. The Limits of Cultural Politic.* Eds. Scott Michaelson and David E Johnson. Minneapolis: University of Minnesota Press, 1997. 68-96. Print.

Anzaldúa, Gloria. *Borderlands/La Frontera: The New Mestiza.* 3rd eds. San Francisco: Aunt Lute Books, 2007. Print.

-----. *Interviews/Entrevistas.* Ed. AnaLouise Keating. New York/London: Routledge, 2000. Print.

-----. "Haciendo caras, una entrada." Introduction. *Making Face, Making Soul. Haciendo Caras Creative and Critical Persepctives by Feminists of Color.* By Anzaldúa. Ed. Gloria Anzaldúa. San Francisco: Aunt Lute Books, 1990. xv-xxviii. Print.

Britto García, Luis. "La vitrina rota. Narrativa y crisis en la Venezuela contemporánea."

*Literatura venezolana hoy. Historia nacional y presente urbano.* Ed. Karl Kohut. Frankfurt a. M. / Madrid: Vervuert, 1999. 37-54. Print.

Debra A. Castillo, Debra A. "Anzaldúa and Transnational American Studies." *Publications of the Modern Language Association of America* 121 (2006): 260-265. Print.

Contreras, Sheila Marie. *Blood Lines: Myth, Indigenism, and Chicana/o Literature.* Austin: University of Texas Press, 2008. Print.

Gómez-Peña, Guillermo. "Death on the Border: A Eulogy to Border Art." *High Performance* 53 (1991): 8-9. Print.

Gómez-Peña, Guillermo. "Disclaimer: Notes on the death of the American artist." *In These Times.* In These Times, 19 May, 2006. Web. 10 Jan. 2009.

Gramsci, Antonio. *Quaderni Del Cacere.* Edizione critica dell'Instituto Gramsci. Ed. Valentino Gerratana. Torino: Guilio Eidauri editore, 1975. Print.

Martín Alcoff, Linda. "The Unassimilated Theorist." *Publications of the Modern Language Association of America* 121 (2006): 255-259. Print.

Rocco, Raymond. "The Theoretical Construction of the 'Other' in Postmodernist Thought: Latinos in the New Urban Political Economy." *The Chicana/o Cultural Studies Reader.* Ed. Angie Chabram-Dernersesian. New York: Routledge, 2006. 404-12. Print.

Sánchez, Rosaura, and Beatrice Pita. "Mapping Cultural/Political Debates in Latin American Studies." *The Chicana/o Cultural Studies Reader.* Ed. Angie Chabram-Dernersesian. New York: Routledge, 2006. 492-516. Print.

Sandoval, Chela. "Feminism and Racism. A Report on the 1981 National Women's Studies Association Conference." *Making Face, Making Soul. Haciendo Caras. Creative and Critical Persepctives by Feminists of Color.* Ed. Gloria Anzaldúa. San Francisco: Aunt Lute Books, 1990. 55-71. Print.

Spivak, Gayatri Chakravorty. "Can the Subaltern Speak?" *Marxism and the Interpretation of Culture.* Eds. Carry Nelson and Lawrence Grossberg. Urbana: University Press, 1988. 271-313. Print.

Stanford Friedman, Susan. *Mappings: Feminism and the Cultural Geographies of Encounter.* Princeton: Princeton University Press, 1998. Print.

*Norma Cantú*
Norma E. Cantú Collection
By RAQUEL VALLES-SENTÍES

7

# THE LEGACY OF GLORIA ANZALDÚA: FINDING A PLACE FOR WOMEN OF COLOR IN ACADEMIA

*MELISSA CASTILLO-GARSOW*

Although this was not always the case, Gloria Anzaldúa is a U.S. woman of color who has found a place in the academy and the English canon. As Debra Castillo describes in her article, "Chicana Feminist Criticism," "until astonishingly recently, Anglophone Chicana literature had been institutionally homeless, perceived as marginal, or second rate, thus not respected within English Department circles," yet critics have also "made Anzaldúa 'the representative' of 'the border'" (Baca 21). Yet, while Anzaldúa is a wonderful representative of Chicana literature and scholarship, despite the inclusion of her work in many university syllabi and editions such as the Norton anthology, I think she would agree that there are still many issues with the exclusion of our literature and theorizing in academia. As Cynthia Franklin points out in her article "Recollecting *This Bridge* in an Anti-Affirmative Action Era," published in *This Bridge We Call Home*, even the inclusion of "*Tlilli, Tlapalli:* The Path of the Red and Black Ink" in the Norton anthology instead of one of Anzaldúa's more activist pieces that challenges what constitutes literature and theory is problematic (418). Laura Harris adds,

> across the board, where efforts are made to diversify departments, curricula, and other academic structures, it is not the systemic foundation of the particular department, curriculum, or academic structure that itself is altered. Instead, existing conditions are augmented by adding token diversity… tokenism functions only to validate large-scale exclusion by providing a misleading veneer of diversity and transformation. (376)

Anzaldúa wrote,

> I got tired of hearing students say that *Bridge* was required in two or three of their women's studies courses; tired of being a resource for teachers and students who asked me what texts by women of color they should read or teach and where they could get these writings. I had grown frustrated that the same few women-of-color were asked to read or lecture in universities and classrooms, or to submit work to anthologies and quarterlies. Why weren't other women-of-color being asked? (*Haciendo Caras* xvi)

Similarly, while at Arizona State University, I found that I was unable to move forward in my study of Latino Literature at the graduate level within the English Department because any classes that included a Latino author were writers I had already read and discussed in another class, often more than once. Yet by revisiting Gloria Anzaldúa's groundbreaking works, *Borderlands /La Frontera: The New Mestiza, The Bridge Called my Back: Writings of Radical Women of Color* and *Making Face, Making Soul/Haciendo Caras: Creative and Critical Perspectives by Feminists of Color* using Chela Sandoval's "methodology of emancipation," new answers and strategies to the marginalization of Chicana theory in academia can be found—strategies that both take full advantage of the legacy left by a thinker of such wide-ranging reach.

In *Methodology of the Oppressed,* Chela Sandoval maps out a proposal theorizing for U.S. peoples of color who have long acted, spoken, and intellectualized "from the halls of academy where it has been intercepted and domesticated" (11). This "methodology of emancipation" functions "to develop the kinds of oppositional powers that are *analogous* to but at the same time *homeopathically resistant* to postmodern transnationalization, along with peoples who are skilled enough to wield those powers," she writes. "Like U.S. third world feminists, practitioners of this methodology act as interventionists, negotiators, assimilationists, radical transformers, separatists, and so on" (26). Chela Sandoval's "methodology of emancipation" is four fold:

1. To develop sign-reading skills, reading power everywhere and always.

2. To engage interventionary tactics that are designed to shift the powers that operate inside any sign system: The choices on the level of the sign are (a) to deconstruct, of (b) to meta-ideologize.

3. To willingly inhabit an eccentric consciousness that permits its practitioner to carry out any these techniques by moving within, between, or through meaning *differentially.*

4. To enact any of these principles with the purpose of equalizing power among interlocutors. This *democratizing aim* directs all other techniques toward the goal of egalitarian redistributions of sexed, gendered, raced, physiological, social, cultural, and/or economic powers (27).

By seaching out and analyzing each of these steps within Anzaldúa's work, new strategies can be found—strategies which may help expand the place of Latinos in the standard English canon, both within the areas of literature and theory.

In terms of the first method, in her lifetime, Anzaldúa developed a number of sign-reading skills that made her a powerful force in the academic world. Although, she uses familiar, dominant culture forms of theorizing, and she peppers her language with key words and phrases in her own Tex-Mex Spanish in order to be less academic in her style, Anzaldúa was an academic in profession and in mind. She was the first from her family to go to college, receiving a Bachelor of Arts degree from Pan American University in 1969 in English, art and education. She went on to earn a masters of arts degree in literature and education from the University of Texas at Austin in 1973 and up until her 2004 death was pursuing a Ph.D. in literature from the University of California at Santa Cruz. Anzaldúa taught creative writing, Chicana/o studies and Feminist studies at a number of institutions and received many honors such as the National Endowment for the Arts Fiction Award, American Book Award, and Sappho Award of Distinction (Reuman 1). Her academic inclinations, however, go back much earlier: "From the time when I was in elementary school I was this little kid that was carrying around Nietzsche, Kierkegaard, -so I had that kind of identity… now it's a very important part of my making a living because it's the academic community that hires me," she comments (Reuman 29).

Anzaldúa was also motivated to join the academic setting "to show up, the arrogant racist teachers who thought all Chicano children were dumb and dirty" (*The Bridge Called My Back* 166). She learned to read "academese" and maneuver in the white world in order to empower herself. In an interview with Andrea Lunsford, she relates how she was marked down both at the undergraduate and graduate levels by almost all of her professors for "code-switching" and not writing the 'status quo way' (19). Yet despite these difficulties, she learned the "foreign tongue—standard American English" and thrived. She also sees the importance and power of having done so:

> Some feminist theorists-of-color write jargonistically and abstractly, in a hard-to-access language that blocks communication, makes the general listener/reader feel bewildered and stupid. These theories often mistakenly divide theory and lived experience and are more off putting than many of the masters they ape….I too am seduced by academic language, its theoretical babble insinuates itself into my speech and is hard to weed out. At the same time I feel that there is a place for us to use specialized language addressed to a select, professional, vocational or scholarly group –doctors, carpenters and seamsters use language that only those in their particular work can understand. We should not give up these 'languages' just because they are not accessible to the general public. (*Haciendo Caras* 29)

By adding "academese" into her arsenal of voices (the voice of the dyke, the Chicana, the professor, first person, second person, third, vernacular, formal, six varieties of Spanish, English, etc.) to speak and write in, Anzaldúa is able to create an impact in various ways. She not only broadens her audience, but she is able to challenge both how people of color and the white academic world view dominant forms of theorizing. This is why her theories have been so influential. Many non-Chicana feminists, for example, have studied, analyzed and expanded on Anzaldúa's metaphor of the border as a clash between two cultures. For example, in "Metaphors of a Mestiza Consciousness: Anzaldúa's Borderlands/La Frontera," Aigner-Varoz views the borderland metaphor in a more universal context: "Because many of the metaphors and archetypes she cites are cross-cultural and inter-referential, Anzaldúa's text necessarily embraces and validates experiences of people from varied cultures, races, classes, and sexual orientations" (47).

Nevertheless, while Anzaldúa takes no offense from her ideas being used by others (in an interview with Ann E. Reuman, she stated that "it validates me as a writer that people can take my images or ideas and work them out in their own way and write their own theories and their own books") this is not the point of her metaphor nor her central preoccupation. In the same interview she comments that, "the people that I most want to affect is my home ethnic community, my family" (Reuman 4). In this way she also refuses to be dichotomized in yet another way, as an academic or as a creative writer. "Who, me confused? Ambivalent? Not so. Only your labels split me" (*This Bridge Called My Back* 205).

Through this understanding of the academic world, Anzaldúa is able to code-switch both linguistically and in her use of different registers in rhetorically effective ways. Her uses of both "*mestiza* rhetoric" and revisionist history are just two of the ways that she engages in what Sandoval terms "interventionary tactics that are designed to shift the powers that operate inside any sign system." Clearly language is a key component of this rhetorical strategy to define, describe and empower her Chicana identity. In "How to Tame a Wild Tongue," she writes, "Ethnic identity is twin skin to linguistic identity—I am my language. Until I can take pride in my language, I cannot take pride in myself" (98). Anzaldúa's most obvious, and most commented upon linguistic choice is her mix of both

Spanish and English in her essays, as she points out in her preface to *Borderlands/ La Frontera: The New Mestiza* :

> The switching of "codes" in this book from English to Castilian Spanish to the North Mexican dialect to Tex-Mex- to a sprinkling of Nahuatl to a mixture of all these, reflects my language, a new language—the language of the Borderlands. There, at the juncture of cultures, languages cross-pollinate and are revitalized; they die and are born. Presently this infant language, this bastard language, Chicano Spanish, is not approved by any society. But we Chicanos no longer feel that we need to beg entrance, that we need always to make the first overture—to translate to Anglos, Mexicans and Latinos, apology blurting out of our mouths with every step. Today we ask to be met halfway. (22)

Yet this is not the only "code-switching" that Anzaldúa employs and it is not the only place where she asks to be met halfway. Although Anzaldúa regularly uses slangy, informal Spanish, she does it in a way that does not diminish the academic validity of her work. She is clearly a scholar. Not only are her ideas and evidence complex, well-constructed and well-supported, but through her language she also demonstrates the scholarly nature of these essays. She may write "*chingado*" in one sentence, only to be followed by high diction such as "dominant paradigms," "pseudo-liberal," "doppelganger" or "metamorphoses" alchemically. Most importantly, this is clearly a conscious act. Anzaldúa comments:

> If I had made *Borderlands* too inaccessible to you by putting in to many Chicano terms, too many Spanish words, or if I had been more fragmented in the text than I am right now, you would have been very frustrated. So there are certain traditions in all the different genres—like autobiography, fiction, poetry, theory, criticism—and certain standards that you have to follow… My whole struggle is to change the disciplines, to change the genres, to change how people look at a poem, at a theory or at children's books. So I have to struggle between how many of these rules I can break and how I still can have readers read the book without

getting frustrated... They do have to somehow like and approve what I am writing and accept it. (*Borderlands* 233)

Thus, while she incorporates academic language to include some readers she also chooses to include fiction and poetry to alter their experience of theory. "Instead of coming in through with the intellectual concept, you come in through the back door with the feeling, the emotion, the experience," she said (Lunsford 50). Although she acknowledges that fiction is harder to theorize in, it is also a genre that is accessible to her community as well. Anzaldúa's work, then, is to both keep traditional academic approaches in mind without being limited by them. By negotiating how much of white culture, theory and academic tradition to employ and how much to resist, she opens up a path where formerly marginalized scholars can both be themselves and be relevant. As Anzaldúa points out, many of these more western methods are incredibly valuable. "I like the English language, for example, and there is a lot of Anglo ideology that I like as well. But not all of it fits with our experiences and culture roots" (*Borderlands* 234). According to Baca, "By merging Western and Mesoamerican practices of writing, Anzaldúa is no longer obliged to accept the Western philosophy of a grammar, of linguistic control and 'taming the wild tongue' and mind, as universal components of writing instruction. Mestiza consciousness potentially reveals a new politics of teaching that no longer privileges speaking, writing, and thinking within a single language controlled by conventions of scholarly prose" (29). Mestiza rhetoric thus revals the conditions of subjugated peoples across the United States while highlighting the significance of cultural studies today.

Similarly, Anzaldúa's method of revisionist history offers a powerful critique of dominant stories of assimilation, colony and the border, which are still needed. In her most famous work, *Borderlands/La Frontera: The New Mestiza* Anzaldúa articulated both the internal and external conflict of the Chicana, by describing a radical Chicana history on the border using a form of visual writing the author calls "autohistoria-teoría." Her sources are a mix of history texts, Mexican popular music, poetry, anthropology, psychological studies, novels, Mexican sayings and her own personal experiences. For example, mixed in with incredibly vivid images of the border such as:

Across the border in Mexico
stark silhouette of houses gutted by waves,
cliffs crumbling into the sea
silver waves marbled with spume
gashing a hole under the border fence. (23)

are sentences that read like history texts. "In 1000 B.C., descendants of the original Cochise people migrated into what is now Mexico and Central American and became the direct ancestors of many of the Mexican people" (26). This is a unique approach to writing history: a new way to *contra historias*: "A moving personal narrative about her Grandmother's dispossession occupies the same discursive space as a dry recitation of historical fact, while lyrics from a *corrido* about 'the lost land' butt up against a poetic rendition of an ethnocentric Anglo historian's vision of U.S. dominion over Mexico," writes Sonia Saldívar-Hull in the introduction to the 2nd edition of *Borderlands* (3).

Similarly the incorporation of historical figures ranging from Mexican philosopher José Vasconcelos to a wide variety of pre-Columbian deities to Mexican icons rewrites history. Baca writes, "Anzaldua's declaration of Mesoamerican deities and traditions enacts a transformation of rhetorical performance from a Greco-Roman Western practice to a site of Mestiz@ resistance" (18). This creation of a "new" knowledge and history is again, a strategic practice. As Castillo points out, Anzaldúa's work is not an empirical, historical or sociological study of life on the U.S.-Mexican border. It omits, for example, any concrete reference to the Mexican side of border, despite evoking its presence metaphorically. She doesn't mention Tijuana or Juárez and her primary indigenous imagery comes from the Aztecs (who inhabited south central Mexico), not from a Northern Mexico/Southwestern US indigenous nation where the borderland is located. Thus Anzaldúa is not working from a third world perspective but in fact working to revise both Western rhetoric and Chicano nationalism which originally incorporated these images, creating "new" memories. According to Saldívar-Hull, "Using a new genre she calls *autohistoria,* Anzaldúa presents history as a serpentine cycle rather than a linear narrative. The *historia* she tells is a story in which indigenous icons, traditions, and rituals replace post-Cortesian Catholic customs. Anzaldúa reconfigures Chicana affinities with the Catholic *Virgen de Guadalupe* and offers an alternative image: *Coatlicue,* the Aztec divine mother" (2).

This switch from cuento to historia, from an academic voice to an angry outsider's is again another way in which Anzaldúa both broadens her audience and challenges them.

> [What] I was trying to do by code-switching was to inject some of my history and some of my identity into this text that White people were going to read or Black people were going to read or Native American people were going to read. I was trying to make them stop and think. Code-switching jerks readers out of their world and makes each think 'Oh, this is my world, this is another world, this is her world where she does this, where it's possible to say words in Spanish. (Lunsford 59)

It is Sandoval's third step (to willingly inhabit an eccentric consciousness that permits its practitioner to carry out any of these techniques by moving within, between, or through meaning *differentially)* that reveals one of Anzaldúa's biggest challenges to the academia. Despite the scholarly nature of many of her essays, Anzaldúa refuses to become a prisoner to western rationality. As collaborator AnaLouise Keating notes, "Given the academy's over emphasis on rational thought, coupled with the mind/body oppositional dualisms pervading western cultures, this resistance to exploring the spiritual dimensions of Anzaldúa's work is not surprising" (Entre mundos 242). Nevertheless as "Anzaldúa's spiritual-activist perspective shapes her theory of transformative writing, or what I call her *shaman aesthetics*" it should not be ignored in any discussion of her theory.

For example in her essay, "Entering Into the Serpent," the poem, "Ella tiene su tono," describes the supernatural power derived from serpents. This connection to her animal counterpart is a powerful image but also a meditation on Anzaldúa's personal spirituality derived from an indigenous background. She also incorporates Catholic representations such as Guadalupe into her symbolism, creating a unique and powerful blend that rivals western rationality.

"Like many Indians and Mexicans, I did not deem my psychic experiences real," she writes, "I denied their occurrences and let my inner senses atrophy. I allowed white rationality to tell me that the existence of the 'other world' was mere pagan superstition. I accepted their reality, the 'official' reality of the rational, reasonable mode which is connected with external reality, the upper world, and is considered the most developed consciousness—the consciousness of duality" (*Borderlands* 58-9). In this other consciousness rationality exists but it also incorporates dreams, imagination, soul and spirituality at the same time. While a Western brain may split these two sides, Anzaldúa develops *"la facultad"* to inhabit both at the same time. It is "the capacity to see in surface phenomena the meaning of deeper realities, to see the deep structure below the surface" (*Borderlands* 60). Here, Anzaldúa's concern is not necessarily the creation of a standard academic argument, but instead a more artistic, spiritual and metaphorical expression of herself and her culture. She, like the Indians, "did not split the artistic from the functional" (*Borderlands* 88).

This is what Anzaldúa describes as "The Coatlicue State." For Anzaldúa, the Aztec goddess Coatlicue represents, simultaneously and depending on the person, "duality in life, a synthesis of duality, and a third perspective—something more than mere duality or a synthesis of duality" (*Borderlands* 68). By exploring her Chicana identity using both western conventions and a "mosaic pattern (Aztec-like)" Anzaldúa both resists labels and creates new ones. It is in this state, which Anzaldúa expands into "Nepantla" or an in-between state, in which a unique perspective emerges. It is a threshold where the boundaries of culture, academia, and genre break down creating a new form of expression, thought, and cultural theory. Anzaldúa describes it as follows: "Those of us who live skirting otros mundos, other groups, in this in-between state I call Nepantla have a unique perspective. We notice the breaches in feminism, the rifts in Raza studies, the breaks in our disciplines, the splits in this country. These cracks show the flaws in our cultures, the faults in our pictures of reality. The perspective from the cracks gives us different ways of defining self, of defining group identity" (*Women Reading* 1). As a self-described "Chicana tejana feminist-dyke-patlache poet, fiction writer and cultural theorist" (*Women Reading* 1) she is able to serve as a "Nepantlera" or mediator between what might seem like incompatible worlds, for example spirituality and rational thought. This is why so many find Anzaldúa's writing so powerful, even after her death or decades after *Borderlands* was written.

It is this mestiza consciousness that completes Sandoval's "methodology of emancipation." As the final integration of all the complexities of the borderlands the mestiza consciousness is a "*democratizing aim* that directs all other techniques toward the goal of egalitarian redistributions of sexed, gendered, raced, physiological, social, cultural, and/or economic powers" (Sandoval 27). Anzaldúa describes this democracy in *Borderland's* final essay "*La concencia de la mestiza:* Toward a New Consciousness." "*La mestiza* constantly has to shift out of habitual formations; from convergent thinking, analytic reasoning that tends to use rationality to move toward a single goal (a Western mode), to divergent thinking, characterized by movement away from set patterns and goals and towards a more whole perspective, one that includes rather than excludes" (101). Anzaldúa's work is made up of fragments, colorful pieces of a puzzle that individually may not go together, but together form a distinct identity and perspective. Just as she calls for Chicanas to accept all aspects of their heritage and identity, her writing refuses to dichotomize her presentation of self, allowing for contradictions. She is male and female, White and Black, *Mexicana* and *indígena*, a new being: "that has no names/ that she has many names/ that she doesn't know her names" (65). She says as a queer, she has no culture, yet at the same time she has so much. Thus, she inhabits Sandoval's idea of a new kind of social movement that is "differential."

When AnaLouise Keating was first collecting submissions for what would become Anzaldúa's final anthology, *This Bridge We Call Home*, she questioned the place of the work within the academy. "Bridge has been repeatedly praised for its oppositional stance to the academy, for its use of nontheoretical language, for its challenge to high theory. How could so many people respond to our call for papers which so clearly links our new book with *This Bridge Called My Back* with such theoretical pieces?," she asked (13). Shortly after she realized, "You can't make simplistic assumptions about who does and does not use theory. Maybe academic theory is not necessarily/automatically 'white'" (14).

Anzaldúa's legacy shows us not only that academic theory does not necessarily need to be white but also the absolute necessity of academic theory that falls outside the standard western rational modes of discourse. Anzaldúa writes: "Because we are not allowed to enter discourse, because we are often disqualified and excluded from it, because what passes for theory these days is forbidden territory for us, it is *vital* that we occupy theorizing space, that we not allow whitemen and women solely to occupy it. By bringing in our own approaches and methodologies, we transform that theorizing space" (*This Bridge Called My Back* xxv). Yet before we can transform the theorizing space we must familiarize ourselves to the current situation, Anzaldúa argues. "I think that before you can make any changes in composition studies, philosophy, or whatever it is, you have to have a certain awareness of the territory; you have to be familiar with it and you have to be able to maneuver in it before you can say, 'Here's an alternative model for this particular field, for its norms, for it rules and regulations, for its laws' (Lunsford 40). Anzaldúa's participation in both scholarly and more creative pursuits, her various ways of code switching, her Nepantlism is so striking because of her ability to both be of the canon and vigorously battle against it. "But it is not enough to have our books published," Anzaldúa warned. "We must also actively engage in establishing the criteria and standards by which our work can be viewed" (*This Bridge Called My Back* 163).

Thus on Anzaldúa's encouragement I add my own "theory of the flesh" and fuse my personal experience in this essay. I never expected to fall in love with literature. Then I read Gloria Anzaldúa in a Latino literature class at NYU. I was shocked by her mixture of poetry and academic scholarship, her beautiful prose filled with Spanish slang and borderland images. I had never read anything that spoke to me in that way. She understood and articulated the experience of Chicanas who are not only situated between cultures, but also face the oppression of their Mexican counterparts. This writing empowered, grounded, and clarified a cultural identity I had been struggling with for two decades. In Gloria Anzaldúa I found not only literature but literary criticism and its ability to provoke thought, debate, and even change. This fall I will start my masters at Fordham University in English Literature with a concentration in creative writing. I too refused to be dichotomized. As exciting as this is for me, what has been consuming my mind recently is my TAship and the wonderful opportunity to take a first step towards my goal of training English literature students to be global thinkers—people who see American literature not just as a group of white and African American writers—but as a richly inclusive range of writers, including Latino/as, Asian Americans and Native Americans. Growing up with two languages and in multiple cultures, I was afforded the privilege of what W.E.B. Dubois first conceptualized as "double consciousness." This is a privilege that many Departments of English historically have not provided students. And yet, given the recent election of Barack Obama, in part due to Latino voters, this is a reality we can no longer afford to neglect. It was the Zapatistas who envisioned "a world in which many worlds will co-exist." That is also my hope for English literature studies and why Anzaldúa's legacy in academia is so crucial. I wish to be a part of a continued effort to understand the multiple meanings of America in all their complexity. It would be my privilege to find bridges and greater links between the canon and newly canonized texts and at the same time express this complexity through the topics I chose to write about, which are neither "Latino" or "white" or "female" but the blend that I grew up with.

Which brings me back to two final thoughts from Gloria Anzaldúa, the most important mentor I have had, and whom I never had the honor of meeting.

> If we do not create these institutions, we certainly perpetuate them through our inadvertent support...I see Third World peoples and women not as oppressors but as accomplices to oppression by our unwittingly passing on to our children and our friends the oppressor's ideologies. I cannot discount the role I play as accomplice, that we all place as accomplices, for we are not screaming loud enough in protest. (*This Bridge Called My Back* 207)

These words written almost thirty years ago are still true and I urge you to scream with me louder in protest. And finally remember that as *las Nepantleras* we must continue to "envision a time when the bridge will no longer be needed—we'll have shifted to a seamless nosotras. This move requires a different way of thinking and relating to others; it requires that we act on our interconnectivity, a mode of connecting similar to hypertexts' multiple links—it includes diverse others and does not depend on traditional categories or sameness" (*This Bridge We Call Home* 507). While presenting a version of this paper at the First International Conference on the Life and Works of Gloria Anzaldúa this past May, I was both impressed by the range of discussion and mix of genres and yet dismayed at the absence of these voices in English departments. Yet until we value Anzaldúa's struggle to be both of and outside the academy and take it as our own, her vision of a world without bridges will never exist.

**Works Cited**


Aigner-Varoz, Erika. "Metaphors of a Mestiza Consciousness: Anzaldúa's Borderlands/la Frontera." *MELUS* 25 (Summer 2000): 47-64. Print.

Anzaldúa, Gloria. *Borderlands/La Frontera: The New Mestiza.* San Francisco: Aunt Lute Books, 1987. Print.

Anzaldúa, Gloria and Cherríe Moraga, eds. *This Bridge Called My Back: Writings by Radical Women of Color.* 2nd ed. New York: Kitchen Table: Women of Color, 1983. Print.

Anzaldúa, Gloria and AnaLouise Keating, eds. *This Bridge We Call Home: Radical Visions for Transformation.* New York: Routledge, 2002. Print.

Anzaldúa, Gloria, ed. *Making Face, Making Soul/Haciendo Caras: Creative and Critical Perspectives by Feminists of Color.* San Francisco: Aunt Lute, 1990. Print.

Baca, Damian. *Mestiz@ Scripts, Digital Migrations, and the Territories of Writing.* New York: Palgrave Macmillan, 2008. Print.

Castillo, Debra. "Chicana Feminist Criticism." *Latino and Latina Writers.* Ed. Alan West-Durán. Vol. 1. New York: Charles Scribner's Sons, 2004. 1-19. Print.

Foss, Karen A., Sonja K. Foss, and Cindy L. Griffin. *Feminist Rhetorical Theories.* Thousand Oaks: Sage Publications, 1999. Print.

Keating, AnaLouise. *Women Reading Women Writing: Self-Invention in Paula Gunn Allen, Gloria Anzaldúa and Audre Lorde.* Philadelphia: Temple University Press, 1996. Print.

Keating, AnaLouise, ed. *EntreMundos/AmongWorlds: New Perspectives on Gloria Anzaldúa.* New York: Palgrave MacMillan, 2005. Print.

Lunsford, Andrea A. "Toward a Mestiza Rhetoric: Gloria Anzaldúa on Composition and Postcoloniality." *Crossing Borderlands: Composition and Postcolonial Studies.* Eds. Andrea A. Lunsford and Lahoucine Ouzgane. Pittsburgh: University of Pittsburgh Press, 2004. Print.

Reuman, Ann E. "Coming into play: An interview with Gloria Anzaldúa." *MELUS 25* (Summer 2000): 3-47. Print.

Sandoval, Chela. *Methodology of the Oppressed.* Minneapolis: University of Minnesota Press, 2000. Print.

Varese, Stephano. "Indigenous Epistemologies in the Age of Globalization." *Critical Latin American and Latino Studies.* Ed. Juan Poblete. Minneapolis: University of Minneapolis Press, 2003. 138-153. Print.

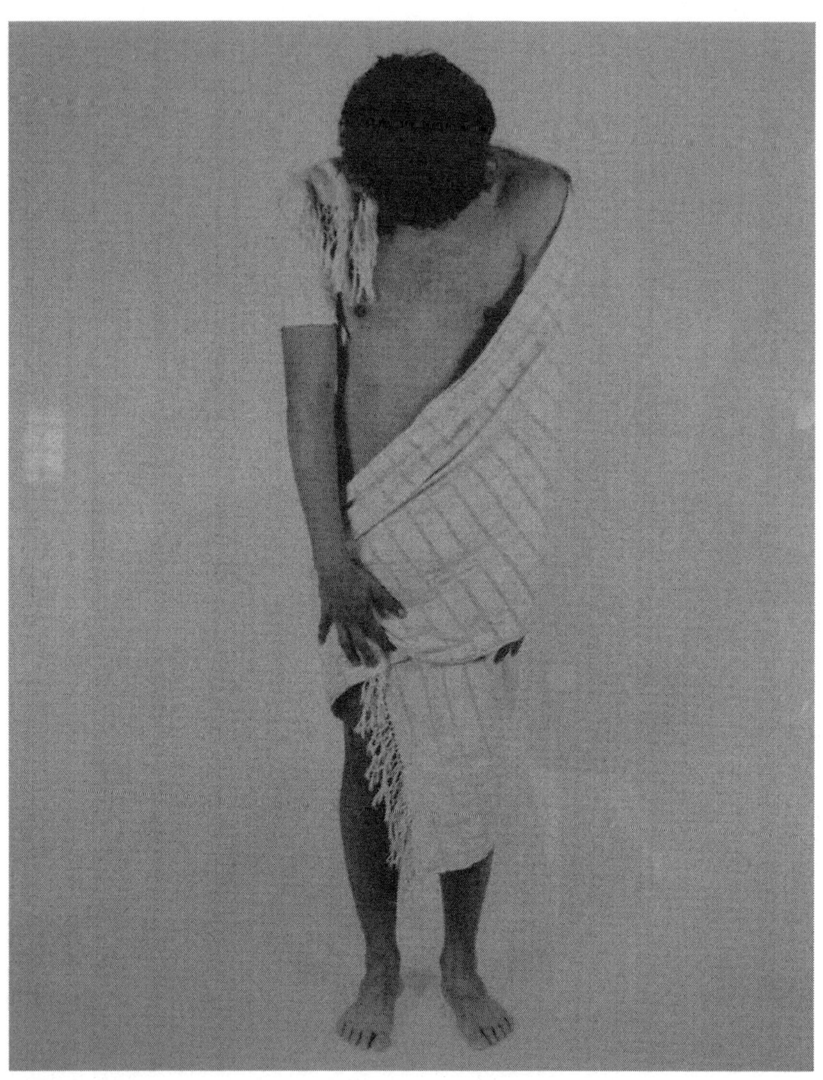

*Rebozo Man 4*
By JOSH T. FRANCO and ELYSE HARARY

# 8

# RUPTURING SILENCE, RUPTURING FORECLOSURE

*MICHAELA WALSH*

I was two years old when my mother drove me in our sky blue Corvaire down to Chino where my Mama Nina lay in a coma. The car, which would be used in a bank robbery the following year, barely made it there and back. It had to be started with a screwdriver, which my mother carried like a key in her purse, and because we couldn't afford a car seat, my mother had to hold me for the duration of the seven-hour drive. These things—the shifting morning light gathering momentum as we drove, the salt-air rising off the coast as she drove home to where her grandmother lay dying—I do not remember. These things—the winding coastal roads, how my mother held me, the sound of gravel popping under the car wheels when we arrived in Chino, this vast countryside that my great grandparents claimed as their home after fleeing the violence of the Mexican revolution—I could not have remembered.

The idea of foreclosure put forth by Jacques Lacan and later taken up by Judith Butler explores how the subject comes into being under the condition that she can never fully know herself. For Lacan, foreclosures are psychic—thus they become fixed. The subject can do nothing to fully know her origins and any attempt to understand the condition of her being will result in mental collapse. In contrast, Butler sees foreclosures as possibilities. Rather than psychic, they are social. The subject is not powerless in relation to foreclosure, but can assume an agency that's capable of reconfiguring the meaning of the foreclosure, thus allowing the subject to remake herself, in turn influencing the configuration of the social. As Butler argues, for Lacan "foreclosure" represented the "lack of self understanding for any subject" (Salih 332). This makes it impossible for the individual to recover her origins, to fully understand her history, and in turn herself. The affliction of unknowing constitutes the backdrop against which the individual comes into being. To attempt to "undo" this unknowing—to probe, explore, and unmask one's origins—is to run the risk of losing oneself as a subject, to become "undone." Against a bifurcated view of foreclosure as either psychic or social, I see foreclosure as psychic, social, spiritual and corporeal—as involving a process of "conocimiento," or what Gloria Anzaldúa describes as the opening of our senses at the innermost core of our being. This process involves a circling in, out, through, and across body, landscape, language, and emotion. More than encompassing "multi-leveled attention" to the visceral, to the land, to inner intuitive reactions of self to self, of me to you, of you to me, concocimiento also involves the force of the imaginary. "My soul makes itself through the creative act," writes Anzaldúa. She describes the process as the feeling of carving bone, of creating her own face, her own heart. "It is constantly remaking and giving birth to itself though my own body," she states (*Borderlands* 95). This embodied knowledge isn't isolated within the individual, but spirals outward in an inspired force in order to bridge, in order to connect.

The fractured structure of the braided essay parallels the fissures and faultiness of our individual and collective memory. The physical gap on the page signals transition. It signals a movement across space, place, and time. This empty space on the page is figured in a silence so tactile that the writer/poet begins to apprehend—to literally hold with her hands and her mind—this birthmark of identity that seeps like ink into skin. The particular composition of the braided form is premised on exchange—the gift of one thing in return for another understanding, be it of a voice previously unheard or unfelt, a sense of self previously unknown, or... It is at this juncture that foreclosure becomes "subject to renewal." Just as we cannot distinguish movement without a background, speech without silence, it is before and beside you that I find my voice, and my identity. As Butler explains the work of Andriana Cavarero, "I exist in an important sense for you, and by virtue of you" (Butler 32). Together, we infuse one another with a sense of belonging, "Without the 'you,' my own story becomes impossible" (Butler 32). Together, we inspire—literally breathing into one another through the intimate contact of breath against breath.

I can't remember my mother's reaction to her aunts, to her grandmother who lay like a shriveled potato in between crisp white sheets, her hair, now as thin and translucent as a spider web's thread, loose across the pillowcase. What did my mother remember of Mama Nina, the curandera who married the most handsome man in Guadalajara—Papa Nino? What did my mother remember of Mama Nina who fled with her mother, husband, and her firstborn on a mule across the border, hiding under the long tablecloths in people's homes as Pancho Villa's men searched for people fleeing the country? What came over my mother that after everyone had eaten, after we had settled in and I had fallen asleep on the plastic covered furniture, that she decided to place me in bed with Mama Nina where she lay supine and silent?

The erotic, that which Audre Lorde describes as a spiritual, political, emotional, and physical force, as "self connection shared," forms a bridge between the sharers. This bridge, she states, can be an opening for understanding that which isn't shared, thus diminishing the threat of difference. We are not immobilized by difference, she states. We are throttled by silence. Accordingly, transforming silence into language and action, grappling and giving voice to psychic and social foreclosure "is an act of self-revelation," that requires a risk taking (Lorde 42). What then, is revealed when the skin of silence is pierced? Whose voices are released, whose memories, experiences, and histories surface and resound when we pound our fists against the thick doors that for too long have been the dominion of body and breath? If, as the philosopher Jose Ortega y Gassett states, "silence has its identity as a stretch of time being perforated by sound" then rupturing silence can result in a reconfiguration of the personal and the political (Glenn 7).

What process allows me to name that which has been foreclosed to me? What is it that allows me to write this story? If my origins are in some way foreclosed to me, how do I approach... how do I begin to apprehend the shadow of my history? In *Loving in the War Years*, Cherríe Moraga writes, "On some level you have to be willing to lose it all to write—to risk telling what no one may want to hear, including you," (Moraga xii). Maybe it's the case that if we were to press on our sites of foreclosure that they would yield everything to us, whatever that everything might be...love, brutality, identity, sadness, satedness...producing a sensory overload that would result in the blowing of an emotional fuse. While Lacanian thought sees foreclosures as fixed and final, as releasing the subject from responsibility to itself and to its history, for women of color, our encounters with foreclosure are not confined only to the psychic realm, nor are they merely social. Rather, negotiating foreclosure is a commitment that involves psychic, social, and spiritual agency. "Daily, I battle the silence...," Anzaldúa writes. "Daily I take my throat in my hands and squeeze until the cries pour out, my larynx and soul are sore from the constant struggle" (*Borderlands* 94). Our silences, as Lorde so powerfully states, will not protect us. In her piece, "The Transformation of Silence into Language and Action," Lorde describes silence as that which prevents the individual from becoming whole. Unspoken, silence festers. Foreclosure becomes more formidable. We remain fractured in relation to ourselves. We remain fractured in relation to others. Reckoning with silence—rupturing foreclosure—requires an exorcism of self that Anzaldúa captures in her depiction of the physical extraction of voice. "....(B)eing punched in the mouth from the inside," until silence—now bruised—reveals its skin, until the disclosure of foreclosure gives way to a re-membering of self, requires a recognition of our vulnerability, transience, humanity (Lorde 42).

We are driving down the highway when my grandmother tells me that before murdering her cousin they skinned his feet, shaved them until the blue bone poked through the thin layer of skin. Then they made him walk to the cemetery, she tells me. They gave him a shovel and told him to dig.

The e/motion of deepening perception, Anzaldúa argues, engenders a joining of inner reflection to vision, a braiding together of "the mental, emotional, instinctive, imagined, spiritual and subtle bodily awareness with social, political action and lived experiences to generate subversive knowledge's" ("now let us shift" 345). Through this process an ethical imperative is forged. This question of ethics surfaces at the moment when we find ourselves at the threshold of connection and collapse, where pressed to grapple with the implications of participating in a dialogue where common ground can't be assumed, we are confronted with the limits of what we know in the face of the urgent need to recognize and to be recognized. As Butler argues, the "I" emerges via an address and against a backdrop of social relations and structures that for the most part are not part of its making (132). It's when the air, electrified with the forewarning of earthquake shocks the soil with a heartbeat of movement that the unraveling begins. It's when trembling against and in between the folds of earth, air and sky in the sweet aftershock of rupture, that we subject the normative to revision, that we contest hegemony, that we break the silences that impede connection. Ethics, according to Butler, requires that we "risk ourselves precisely at moments of unknowingness, when what forms us diverges from what lies before us, when our willingness to become undone in relation to others constitutes our chance of becoming human" (136). This is a necessary anguish. In the moment of our own arrest when we haven't yet found sound to vocalize what we are struggling not to succumb to, Lorde reminds us through her own account of battling cancer that by translating the unspoken, our silences undergo a transformation that works from the inside out to shift our awareness of self. Arrest, pushed to release, gives way to movement. In and through movement, the stalemate of silence—the chokehold of atrophy—is resisted. Within this moment, understanding becomes possible.

I see foreclosure as the shadow that follows us. It haunts us. We are aware of its presence, but it's nothing that we can see into. It's nothing that we can apprehend with our ordinary senses—smell, taste, hear or hold. The experience we undergo in our attempt to waken our senses to this force, to discern its color and features generates an unbearable vertigo. The only way that we can read dimension into our shadows is via experience and imagination, and the imagination of experience. But these processes are gradual. They require an archaeology that sends us to our knees as we endeavor to sift through artifacts, travel the physical and figurative landscape of memory, feel the breath of conversation wet against our skin as we absorb sound and imagery like the desert sand absorbs the rain.

I kneel beside my grandmother, our hands folded in prayer. On the highway she tells me about how during the 1920's the government in Mexico persecuted anyone who supported the church. Her cousin was wrenched from hiding. "His brother was, too," she tells me. "Isekial y Salvador, nuestros primos." When they wouldn't tell the government officials where the priests were hiding they were made to undress. Beside my grandmother I stare at the hair of the woman who kneels in front of me. I imagine my ancient cousins, naked and emasculated, digging their own grave. The point of this deconstruction is not to narrate, but to show the limits of the narrative. As Butler maintains, the "I" can have no recourse to the story of its own surfacing, nor can it relate the conditions of its own possibility without bearing witness to events prior to its own emergence as a subject (37). How then, can I bear witness to an event at which I was not present, and yet which informs who I am? It's at this juncture that the clean, linear line traditional to western forms of narrating becomes frayed, unraveling in disparate strands of thought, experience, voice, history, and power, resisting closure and explication. It's at this moment when imagination and fiction, not tethered to any referent, bleed together, giving way to a possibility for multiple accountings, cuentos y cantos. What is lost, borne, bared, laid bear in this attempt to conocer quién o qué yo soy.

We both woke one another at the same time. The last of the afternoon light poured orange into the room when her cold fingers found my head and began slowly to stroke my hair, my cheeks. Mistaking Mama Nina for my mother, I snuggled closer to her, reached for her small, brown, ear, which I rubbed like the ribbon on the white cotton blanket my mother tucked me in with at night. It was when she found her voice, mumbled throaty words in Spanish, and called me Rosa—my dead grandmother's name—that I realized that it wasn't my mother who had been holding me. Pulling away from her sour breath, from her awful face that looked like one of the drip castles that I would build on the beach, I cried for my mother, who ran across the room and pulled me from the bed where Mama Nina lay weeping, reaching for me, calling in a sandy voice that reverberated through my body, "Mija, mija, mi niña, mi Rosita, mi niña..."

According to Butler, the foreclosure of the referent represents a potential opening, the condition of possibility through which self-accounting takes narrative form. Thus, the stories of one's origin can be told over and again, and in multiple ways. However for Butler, who seems surprised to realize that "it may be that to have an origin means precisely to have several possible versions of the origin," these multiple stories the individual tells—because they are not always consistent—abdicates her from accountability to any one narrative in particular (37). All are plausible. Not one alone is true. For me, the question involves holding these various stories in productive tension, of being present to each telling, held accountable for each telling we offer. Butler's abdication of accountability on the basis of there being no singular truth, while anti-essentialist, baits a relativism that potentially deflates the capacity for what Anzaldúa sees as a "conscious rupture" that takes place when the individual "puts history through a sieve" (*Borderlands* 104). It's through this process that the individual comes into contact with her vulnerability and singularity. Navigating this exposure of self to self, of one to another, is part and parcel to a politics of location, love, and relation. That is, our accountability to who we are is shaped in part by this mining and husking of histories. We are, as Butler suggests, "authored by what comes before us and by what exceeds us" (37). Nonetheless, I argue that we are not released from the risk involved in endeavoring to give an account of ourselves. Gesturing to Aimee Carrillo Rowe, this self-accounting is a process shaped by who we are and who we are becoming as a function of be-longing. As the very term "be-longing" conveys, this is a movement infused with nostalgia and ache. Only it's an experience not figured solely in relation to the past. It is infused with la añura. Be-longing involves a seeking, a back-bending back and through and across history, a corporeal creation of bridge, connection, and crossing that links past to present to future to past to...me...to you...It is in and through this experience that agency and consciousness unfurl.

It is at this point that the braid begins.

My confrontation with foreclosure is an extraction. I am peeling back the layers of my skin, mining the foreclosures of my history—the furies and sufferings that course through the bloodlines of my family, the shame and the pride, the triumphs and the losses, the secrets and the brutality that have been swallowed, buried, and burned since Mexico was born. I am dwelling in the liminal moment between exhalation and inhalation, the pause at the peak of breath that marks the presence of the finite within the infinite. I am on my knees digging into the marrow of my body, searching for my placenta—ephemeral organ—intricate lifeline to my self.

This is an invocation for the weaving together of the theoretical with the poetic, for the recognition of what a body of literature means—that which is alive, that which cannot be fully evoked or contained to the bleached pages of tightly bound books. This tapestry allows readers to listen to the intonation of stories, to absorb the silences figured in the physical whiteout on the page, to question whose voices have been muted, whose words devalued, whose experiences covered over. The chords of braid and voice invite the reader to bear witness to the physical expression of emotion that the body betrays in gesture, through the eyes, in the way our sounds waver and resound. The braided essay unearths the presence of sequential readings, exposing us to the partiality of each constitutive reading. If, as Butler maintains, "truth becomes more clear in moments of interruption, stoppage, open-endedness, in enigmatic articulations that can't easily be translated into narrative form,"—in the silences—than the disjunctive rendering of language and memory constitutes an incitement and a seduction, an individual and collective opening to encounters that western forms of theorizing have foreclosed to us (66).

These stories, however disfigured, whatever their wounds, whatever their beauty—I see these stories that converge and diverge as the organs through which to socially remake sites of foreclosure, however fragmented, however imperfect. Against a Lacanian understanding of foreclosure as a vault-like structure that silences from the individual possibilities of self-knowledge, of origin, of history, by following the crisscrossing of lifelines that comprise me (even as they threaten to undo me) I resist the fixity Lacan assigns to foreclosure. At the same time,

I don't capitulate to the kind of coherence that produces a whole new set of foreclosures. Within this process of digging, sifting, and exposure, history is reinterpreted, silence finds dimension through sound. Symbols and myths are refigured, fingered, sculpted. Struggle is documented. And in and through this process, I unhinge foreclosure, thus allowing for the deconstruction and construction of myself, for the transformation "of the small 'I' into the total Self" (*Borderlands* 105). This story—these stories—of the "I" are necessarily stories of relation. My voice. My mother's voice. The voice of her mother. The movement of our voices—and disparate, estranged, foreign, connected, our breath rising and falling, our voices reverberating along the switchbacks, the over and under of our histories, our braids, the pulling, the release, the unraveling of the thread that undoes the foreclosure in a seizure of death and rebirth.

What would it look like to reconfigure the discourses that women of color have so often been disqualified and excluded from, to dwell in those zones of theorizing that have been reserved to preserve the homogeneity of voice? What warrior-scholar-poets like Moraga, Lorde, and Anzaldúa are calling for is an insurrection of ways of knowing, for the re-opening of memory and for new approaches and methodologies that transform how theorizing has traditionally been done. Implicit in this is Anzaldúa's claim that "ethnic identity is twin skin to linguistic identity" (*Borderlands* 59). If as Anzaldúa claims, she is her language, then to mute it, deny it, shame it, annihilate it, is to cut through the tongue and the heart of the speaker. "I will have my voice," she declares. "Indian, Spanish, white. I will have my serpent's tongue—my woman's voice, my sexual voice, my poet's voice. I will overcome the tradition of silence" (*Borderlands* 59). The gathering of breath, the transformation of silence into voice, and voice into poetry, is the organ through which thought and feeling are conceptualized, expressed, and actualized. Poetry, as Lorde states, involves a process of naming the unnamed, the un-thought, it is how we bear sound to the wild, ancient, creative, and powerful places of possibility within us. Our silences, she argues, are borne from fear. Poetry, "the skeleton architecture of our lives," is (vocal) chords echoing across space and time in contractions and expansions of life pushed to the threshold of ache and longing, until chaos gives way to eros. This reclamation of the physical, emotional, sensual, and psychic expressions of our blood, our buried bloodlines, the veins that form webs of intricate connection, gives way to a merging of the spiritual and the political.

We're traveling across Mexico on a bus. The sun strikes through the tinted windows, and my grandmother and I stare at the landscape, the slope and curve of the hills like breasts, like hips, like shoulders bowing under the weight of so much sky. We sip Cokes. The shadow of clouds look like birthmarks against the skin of the mountains. "I didn't learn to read until I was thirteen," she will tell me. "I couldn't speak English." I look at my grandmother through the reflection in the window. She has the same fair complexion of my mother. I make the connection between my grandmother and my mother, who as a child, was sent to live in Mexico. When she returned to Chino, the teachers didn't understand why someone so white and freckled could not speak English. And so my mother and grandmother lived with swollen tongues until they learned the language, until they learned how to pass.

The process of recording, this act of "making meaning" is inherently intimate. To sever theory from the body, to continue to render different ways of theorizing illegitimate registers as a collective loss. In the introduction of *Loving in the War Years*, Moraga writes,

> Some days I feel my writing wants to break itself open. Speak in a language that maybe no "readership" can follow. What does it mean that the Chicana writer, if she truly follows her own voice, may depict a world so specific, so privately ours, so full of "foreign" language to the anglo-reader, there will be no publisher for it. The people who can understand it, don't/won't/can't read it. I have been translating my experience out of fear of an aloneness too great to bear. (xii)

Here Moraga gestures to that liminal but charged space that exists at the threshold of silence and voice. Our estrangement, our yearning to share with others this feeling of estrangement, to mark its particular contours, requires a risk taking. If foreclosure is the condition under which the author becomes intelligible, then by bleeding together multiple languages, histories, and identities through which consciousness is configured, foreclosure begins to unravel.

Trenzas. The word to me always sounded like trenches. I imagined my mother's braids sucking her into the earth, strangling her, drowning her in the wet soil. My mother has skin the color of a flour tortilla. Her eyes are cornflower blue. It is only her hair that betrays her. "Tienes el pelo de una negrita sucia," Mama Nina would say to my mother as she yanked at her hair with the brush. "Una negrita sucia," she would repeat, "Que pena que tienes ese pelo." The hair, my mother's shame, was thick and black, untamed and untamable.

In the way she slides deliciously across languages, defining some terms, leaving others suspended in their unintelligibility on the page, Anzaldúa resistively enacts for the reader her own experience navigating the terrain of a country that continues to shun, punish, and patronize its non-English speakers. At the same time, unraveling foreclosure does not necessarily result in the concomittant rupture of silence because once again, the author is unintelligible. And yet this "living contradiction," as Alexander calls it, is nevertheless crucial to generating sanctuaries of identification and alliance. "We cannot afford to cease yearning for each other's company," Alexander states (91). This requires "becoming fluent" in our own histories, of putting our feet in the door of foreclosure in order to excavate the rubble and roots of our becoming. This process of becoming fluent in our own histories in order that we can incline our hearts to listen to the history of others requires an "undoing" of sorts, or what Moraga calls a "heart felt grappling" (52).

When I was 16, my mother, who had not cut her hair since I was a small child, took the cleaver that my father's mother had given him, and holding the end of her braid in one hand and the square knife in the other, silently sawed and pulled through her hair, until emasculated, empowered, unrecognizable, she held the thick root of her hair in one hand, the cleaver in the other.

This stirring of the heart, this movement of the gut, clenching of the jaw, this moment of interpellation, functions as an invocation. The strength of the braid is premised on a touching of strand to strand. It's premised on an exchange of movement. The multiplicity of threads is what informs and forms the braid, contributing texture, the twist of story, a chorus of chords that links me to you, to her, to them, to me, to us in an extension and deepening of conocimiento. This process of self-accounting is an act of kneading, of formation, and transformation. It is, as Lorde describes, a bestowing of name on the "nameless and formless, about to be birthed, but already felt" (36). By unraveling the sites of our foreclosure, silence is ruptured and identity reconfigured in the recovery of history and voice. This is a process infused with the ache and hope that comes with inhabiting the interstices, with digging into earth and self until flesh is raw, until we no longer know up from down, left from right, truth from false. Rupturing foreclosure requires the exhuming of self, of digging through our burials to unearth who we were, are/becoming. It requires a strangling of silence, until dead, it speaks. The awful ache of longing, be-longing, la añura, is mitigated in and through connection. "The space between two individuals shrinks with intimacy," Anzaldúa writes (*Borderlands* 20). The naturalization of a new set of foreclosures is resisted when the lines and threads of the story, the trail of our words, is not tied neatly together. This is an invocation for the continual unraveling, the continual attempt to re-braid, to remake, to reform...It's at this point that the braid begins.

**Works Cited**

Alexander, Jacqui. "Remembering This Bridge, Remembering Ourselves: Yearning Memory, and Desire." *This Bridge We Call Home: Radical Visions for Transformation*. Eds. Gloria E. Anzaldúa and AnaLouise Keating. New York: Routledge, 2002. 81-103. Print.

Anzaldúa, Gloria. "now let us shift...the path of conocimento...inner work, public acts." *This Bridge We Call Home: Radical Visions for Transformation*. Eds. Gloria E. Anzaldúa and AnaLouise Keating. New York: Routledge, 2002. 540-578. Print.

Anzaldúa, Gloria. *Borderlands/La Frontera: The New Mestiza*. San Francisco: Aunt Lute Books, 1987. Print.

Butler, Judith. *Giving an Account of Oneself.* New York: Fordham University Press, 2005. Print.

Glenn, Cheryl. *Unspoken: A Rhetoric of Silence*. Carbondale: Southern Illinois University Press, 2004. Print.

Lorde, Audre. *Sister Outsider: Essays and Speeches.* Freedom, CA: The Crossing Press, 1984. Print.

Moraga, Cherríe. *Loving in the War Years: lo que nunca pasó por sus labios.* Cambridge, Mass: South End Press, 2000. Print.

Rowe, Aimee Carrillo. *Powerline: On the Subject of Feminist Alliances.* Duke University Press, 2008. Print.

Salih, Sarah, Ed. "Changing the Subject, Judith Butler's Politics of Radical Resignification." *The Judith Butler Reader.* Australia: Blackwell Press, 2004. Print.

*Ahogante Mar*
By ANEL I. FLORES

# 9

# EMBRACING GLORIA ANZALDÚA'S *BORDERLANDS/LA FRONTERA* AS MULTICULTURAL PEDAGOGY

*MARGARET E. CANTÚ*

I did not study Gloria Anzaldúa's *Borderlands/La Frontera* in a class until my first semester as a doctoral student. I had read the text the summer just before I began my doctoral studies because a friend mentioned that it had been used in his Chicano History Graduate course. What I found disturbing was my own lack of exposure to Anzaldua's book especially since it is such a foundational text of Chicana literature. My dismay however, did not stop there. In my first semester as a doctoral student I also came across the corridos of Gregorio Cortez and the "true story" of Juan Seguín. What is of concern to me is that had I declined to continue with my Ph.D. studies I may never have discovered these texts, histories, and literature. It also made me wonder: if I only encountered such texts because of my decision to enter a Ph.D. program, then what about the thousands of other Chicano students who, for many reasons don't attend graduate school? The fact is that high school, undergraduate, and perhaps even graduate students do not study texts like *Borderlands*, suggesting that school curriculums are in dire need of multicultural pedagogies. I argue that it is necessary to make students and educators aware of Gloria Anzaldúa's work, while also encouraging the use of it in graduate level classrooms, and eventually bringing her work on multicultural issues to the undergraduate and even secondary levels of education. In this paper I will assert that Gloria Anzaldúa's work is a critical ingredient to any multicultural pedagogy, in particular at the undergraduate and graduate levels, because without it, many students of color remain ignorant of significant elements of their identity.

Identity has always played a significant role in my life, both as an educator and as a student. In high school, I barely noticed the lack of multicultural texts in our school curriculum. I do remember quite clearly that there was an effort to incorporate multicultural literature at some point in my high school English career, but those texts deemed "multicultural" still did not include many women or writers of color. Despite these facts, I was not aware of the problem of multicultural pedagogies until I began my undergraduate studies, where I sought out literature that I could identify with. However, the necessary components of a liberal education did not include multicultural pedagogies or literature; instead, the canon was predominantly focused upon British and American works with an occasional International literature course that was used to seemingly lump all the other "stuff" that couldn't be easily classified among traditional canons.

My understanding of this canon problem became more pronounced as my role changed from student to educator. As a sophomore English teacher, my lessons were supposed to focus upon multicultural literature. The pre-selected anthology for the course only provided a cursory selection of stories, poems, and novels written by either women or authors of color. The same problem existed both in the International and Freshman Composition courses that I later taught at local universities and colleges.

I did not realize how much of a problem this lack of multicultural pedagogy really was until I learned that students of diverse backgrounds could not fully identify with any of the texts read in class. Anzaldúa also discusses how her identity is entwined with the literature that she read. She writes, "When I first saw poetry written in Tex-Mex for the first time, a feeling of pure joy flashed through me.

I felt like we really existed as a people" (82). Anzaldúa is so overjoyed with her literary discovery that she attempts to teach her own students some of the literature as well, but she is reprimanded and forbidden to do so by her school principal. Though Anzaldua is discussing the seventies, her feelings can easily be applied to the lack of multicultural literature and pedagogies nearly thirty years later. The lack of success of minority students still lays in the same pedagogies that Anzaldúa critiques, which begs the question: how are students of color expected to succeed in courses, especially English classes, when their cultures, ethnicities, and sexes are not represented? Teachers find themselves wondering why students are disinterested in the classes they teach, while never understanding that perhaps it is the lack of multicultural texts that may be the problem. This pedagogical disregard for the diversity of its subjects leads to problems in school where some students stray from their culture because it is assumed that perhaps their lives are not represented or unimportant. Thus, it is necessary to develop multicultural pedagogies that provide identification and support for minority students. Gilda L. Ochoa asserts that multicultural pedagogies

> help students see themselves and their families in what they learn; [while affirming] their families' histories and knowledge; [and] encourages students to understand how all of our lives are interrelated and influenced by similar historical, political, and economic factors, though experienced differently; and allows students to envision possibilities of change. (197)

Without these pedagogies, dire consequences exist for a student when he or she reaches this feeling of insignificance. They are faced with a decision to either abandon their culture in order to learn the "canon" or fail in school because they dare to challenge the established curriculums. Even Anzaldúa describes her difficulties in trying to establish the study of Chicano literature as a legitimate dissertation topic. She writes, "in graduate school, while working toward a PhD, I had to 'argue' with one advisor after the other, semester after semester, before I was allowed to make Chicano literature an area of focus..." (82). Anzaldúa's revelation offers an alternative for teachers and students alike. Through the experience of Anzaldúa's text, students are better equipped to learn about their own positions in the education system as well as in the larger society. Beth Berila states that the examination of texts like *Borderlands* encourages a

> re-reading of constructs of nation and race...However, in confronting issues of nation and national identity, experimental multiethnic literatures offer an aesthetic and pedagogical experience that reduces the likelihood of violence by developing alternative modes of engagement. A valuable re-reading process of constructs of nation and borders becomes possible through experimental multiethnic literatures precisely in that moment when comfortable ideologies are unsettled and counter-narratives performed so that dialogue and critical inquiry can begin. (36)

Students learn that their culture, ethnicity, and sex should be represented and celebrated instead of repressed and shunned. For students of color, and of Chicano background in particular, the concepts and history of Mexican identity contemplated with the vigor of Gloria Anzaldúa in *Borderlands* allows these students to break free of the hegemonic constraints that school systems have placed on them since the beginning of their education. These re-readings provide students with a space where they can safely contest hegemonic literatures, histories, and society. At the same time, Ramírez insists that texts "push for students...to read texts that are about them so we can work 'toward composing ourselves lest we be composed by others'" (69).

In the introduction to Anzaldúa's second edition of *Borderlands,* Sonia Saldívar-Hull explains that her text is a "*testimonio*-like pedagogy" (2). "It is a pedagogy that offers knowledge that Anglo-centric schools tend to erase, interjecting a counter-narrative that tells of the appropriation of land by Anglo-Americans who did more than take territory" (Saldívar-Hull 2).

The inclusion of a text that offers a counter-narrative to the one often taught in schools allows a student to acknowledge a different history while encouraging them to challenge previous lessons. More importantly, texts like *Borderlands* discuss cultures and histories that students of color may finally identify with. In addition, Berila claims that

> multiethnic literary works [like Anzaldúa's] present perspectives on

> the experiences of those shifts in meaning that are often excluded from hegemonic discourse about the US nation and often aesthetically invite readers to identify with those counter-narratives. Pedagogically, this identification can prove immensely useful in helping students to reconceptualize narratives of national identity as both relational and contestatory. (39)

The identification with counter-narratives encourages students to question what they have been taught in hegemonic classrooms perhaps even leading to a questioning of society as well. It is this questioning that then encourages a desire to challenge hegemonic institutions like schools or even society, while allowing students to finally be able to identify with a narrative familiar to them.

In addition, students who cannot fully identify with the counter-culture or narratives being presented also benefit from such multiethnic texts. The reading and examination of such texts places students in positions of new understanding. María Lugones suggests that multiethnic literature allows readers to "trave[l] to someone's 'world' [and] identify with them because [it is] by traveling to their 'world' [that] we can understand *what it is to be them and what it is to be ourselves in their eyes.* Only when we have traveled to each other's 'worlds' are we fully subjects to each other" (17). Thus, texts like Anzaldúa's allow students of color to identify with the cultures and counter-narratives being presented. At the same time, they encourage critical discussion of the problems that minorities face, making both them and students that are part of the hegemony aware of issues that must be challenged and reformed.

The issue of multicultural pedagogies is especially prevalent for undergraduate and graduate students because they are often the people who will enter society ready to change the world for the better. When students become aware of the issues that texts like Anzaldúa's deals with they are better equipped to actively and intellectually challenge hegemonic institutions, while also making other people aware of what they learned as undergraduates and graduates. Especially significant is the fact that many of the students at these levels will more than likely move into educational institutions, whether formal or informal. Once in these positions, it is possible for these former students to challenge hegemonic institutions and teachings actively through their own lessons. However, the move from discussing challenging hegemonic institutions to actually implementing these challenges in one's own classroom, especially at the secondary level, is more complex than it seems. Deborah Lustig suggests that "successful multicultural education requires an analysis of the dynamics of student relations across all ethnic groups—"minority" and "majority"—and must begin with the particular culture of each school, as well as encompass broader societal patterns of access to power and privileges" (576). As teachers, we must be aware of the relationships between minority and majority students as well as the intergroup tensions present. We must also recognize the complexity in teaching multicultural literatures and histories, focusing not only on one particular ethnicity but on every representation, while fostering a safe place of understanding. In addition, Henry A. Giroux writes that critical educators must address

> important social, political, and cultural issues from a deep sense of the politics of their own location; they must also see the necessity of engaging and often unlearning the habits of institutional (as well as racial, gender, and class-specific) privilege that buttress their own power while sometimes preventing others from becoming questioning subjects. (3)

Thus, what educators learn at the undergraduate and graduate levels about challenging hegemonic institutions should continue with their new positions. Keeping in mind their positions as authorities of power, agents capable of passing on the same hegemonic teachings or challenging them, they help their students achieve the same agency and critical thinking skills they developed as students of higher education. With these issues at the forefront, educators are fully capable of passing along awareness and encouraging their students to challenge hegemonic institutions that oppress them.

Especially significant are people who occupy both the role of educator and student. Such a position gives me and others a unique advantage because we continue to work on our own awareness through the courses we take as students, while also imparting that same knowledge to our own students. My newly acquired knowledge has made me more aware than ever of the lack of multicultural pedagogies throughout education systems from graduate to secondary levels. The first step toward reforming such institutions is by understanding that change is needed. The second and hopefully final step involves transforming traditional pedagogies of exclusion into new pedagogies that address the diversity of our students. This can be accomplished by instituting a curriculum where works by men and women of color, such as Anzaldúa's text, which I discovered nearly by accident, are taught with emphasis throughout the various levels of education.

Ultimately, the incorporation of Anzaldúa's text or any other multicultural literature or pedagogy allows students to embrace their own identities and better understand their peers while becoming aware of the cultural conflicts that exist. Simply put, it is necessary to acknowledge the different histories, literatures, and cultures of our students. Ignoring our diversity only encourages students and colleagues to remain in the dark. Anzaldúa addresses the dilemma quite simply, when she states that "ignorance splits people, creates prejudices. A misinformed people is a subjugated people" (108). The eradication of such ignorance must begin with those students preparing to enter the work force, ready to impart their knowledge and awareness into their surroundings, and willing to challenge traditional institutions. Anzaldúa stresses that such awareness of our situation "must come before inner changes, which in turn come before changes in society. Nothing happens in the 'real' world unless it first happens in the images in our head" (109).

**Works Cited**

Anzaldúa, Gloria. *Borderlands/La Frontera: The New Mestiza.* 2nd ed. San Francisco: Aunt Lute Books, 1999. Print.

Berila, Beth. "Unsettling Calls for National Unity: The Pedagogy of Experimental Multiethnic Literatures." *MELUS* 30.2 (Summer 2005): 31-47. Print.

Giroux, Henry A. "Literacy, Pedagogy, and the Politics of Difference." *College Literature* 19.1

(Feb. 1992): 1-11. Print.

Lugones, María. "Playfulness, 'World'-Travelling, and Loving Perception." *Hypatia* 2.2 (Summer 1987): 3-19. Print.

Lustig, Deborah Freedman. "Of Kwanza, Cinco de Mayo, and Whispering: The Need for Intercultural Education." *Anthropology & Education Quarterly* 28.4 (Dec. 1997): 574-592. Print.

Ochoa, Gilda L. *Learning from Latino Teachers.* New York: John Wiley and Sons, 2007. Print.

Ramírez-Dhoore, Dora and Rebecca Jones. "Discovering a 'Proper Pedagogy:' The Geography of Writing at the University of Texas-Pan American." *Teaching Writing with Latino/a Students: Lessons Learned at Hispanic-serving Institutions* Albany: Suny Press, 2007. Print.

Saldívar-Hull, Sonia. Introduction. *Borderlands/La Frontera: The New Mestiza.* By Gloria Anzaldúa. 2nd ed. San Francisco: Aunt Lute Books, 1999. 1-18. Print.

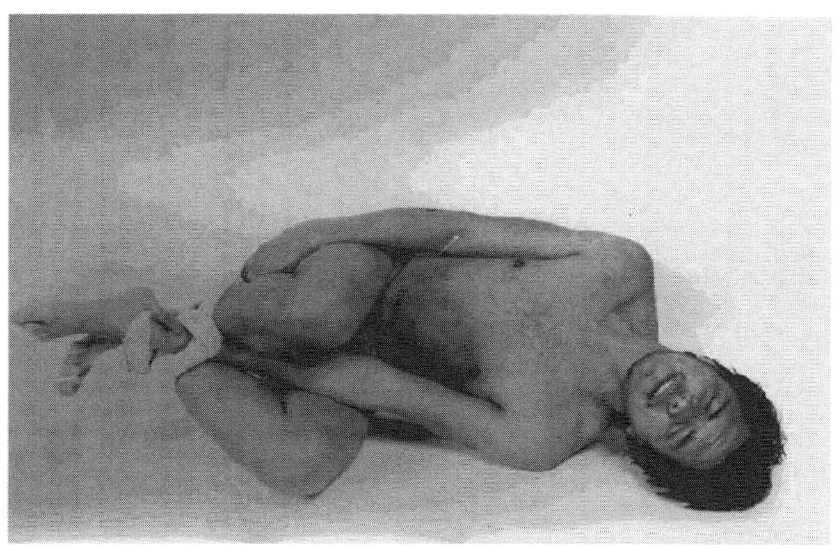

*Rebozo Man 2*
By JOSH T. FRANCO and ELYSE HARARY

# 10

# HISTORIES BURIED IN FLESH: SKIN COLOR AND THE CHICANA EXPERIENCE IN THE UNITED STATES

*SANDRA D. GARZA*

Merging Mexican American history, Chicana feminisms, and qualitative research methods, this essay discusses skin color as a salient factor for women of Mexican descent living in Texas. Studying skin color is important because it points to a complicated history of racialization, thus contributing to our knowledge of the Mexican American experience. Women experience skin color in unique and telling ways that point to a history of colonization. I begin the essay with an overview of the existing literature in the field. Next, in order to contextualize my approach to skin color, I situate the reader within the cultural terrains of Texas. To connect sociocultural history of racialization in Texas to personal experience, I introduce some of the personal narrative of one participant from my larger research. Born in Victoria, Texas, Ellie, now fifty-eight years old, was raised in a predominately-white suburb in Houston, Texas. Identifying as both Mexican American and Texan, Ellie's personal narrative is simultaneously unique and social as it is connected to a larger history of racialization. As I look to personal narrative to explore what is meaningful to Ellie as well as uncover a history of racialization, I call upon Gloria Anzaldúa's concept of *facultad* as a method of analysis. According to Anzaldúa, facultad is the "capacity to see in surface phenomena the meaning of deeper realities, to see the deep structure below the surface" (*Borderlands* 60). As an interpretive tool, facultad locates deeper meaning in personal narratives by recognizing embodied legacies of oppression as they are tied to histories of racialization.

I do not wish to promote the idea that skin color affects the lives of women more so than it does the lives of men. Rather, I argue, men and women, because of deep-rooted systems of raced, classed, and gendered patriarchy, experience skin color differently. In this same vein, I do not seek to argue that skin color affects the lives of those with darker skin more so than it does those with lighter skin. The existing literature evidences a measurable socioeconomic advantage tied to having lighter skin and disadvantage to darker skin. At the same time, Mexican descent people living in the United States as a whole remain among the lower rungs of the socioeconomic ladder. Under these terms, my concern is not so much with continuing to rank[1] the experiences of Mexican descent women based on skin color. I argue that women of Mexican descent experience and make meaning of skin color in different ways and it is within this difference that a discussion about embodied racialization can take place. Thus, I offer a discussion of skin color as a way to consider how we have learned to carry and respond to messages about skin color in our everyday lives.

## REVIEW OF THE LITERATURE

Skin is often the first physical attribute used to identify group membership. We carry out dialogues about skin color in our private spaces such as our homes and in our communities, adhering to codes that express acute perceptions of difference: güera/o, blanca/o, prieta/o, and morena/o. Despite this awareness of skin color in everyday life, few studies exist that examine skin color and the Mexican American experience.

Most of the existing research directly or indirectly draws its data from the Mexican Origin People in the United States study, better known as the 1979 National Chicano Survey (NCS). Conducted by the University of Michigan's

Survey Research Center, the NCS explored topics such as language, culture, social identity, political consciousness, mental health and personal well being, work and labor force histories, and family life. Though the NCS, and the literature that stems from it, lay the foundation for any research regarding skin color and the Chicana/o experience, my research design differs in several ways.

First, while the NCS is quantitative, I rely upon qualitative interview methods as a way to account for the depth and breadth of lived experience. Second, while conducting the surveys for the NCS, interviewers rated the respondents' phenotype recognizing two categories: skin color and physical features. The interviewers did this using a five-point scale, wherein '1' meant "very light/ güero" and '5' indicated that the respondent was "very dark/moreno." Physical features were labeled '1' for "European looking" and '5' for "Indian Looking." The study does not make clear how the interviewers went about measuring and ranking phenotype. To account for subjectivity and focus on lived experience, during the interview session, I instead asked Ellie to describe her skin color to me using personal narrative. Under these terms Ellie can speak about and elaborate on what is meaningful to her thereby expressing how she has learned to carry and respond to messages about skin color. For example, when asked to describe her own skin color, Ellie responded

> Well, I'm, I'm definitely not güera. So I consider myself olive, you know dark-skinned, but not dark, dark, dark, dark. And I've seen some people that are extremely dark, Latinas, and uh you know they can be quite beautiful especially if they have the green eyes-Dark skin and green eyes. But I definitely am not fair skinned so I consider myself morena.

Ellie calls upon several terms to talk about her skin color. She describes herself as olive, dark, and morena. Ellie goes on to discuss women with darker skin and green eyes, thereby disclosing some of the ways she has learned to carry and respond to ideas of beauty as it relates to skin color and phenotype. Following a set scale of one to five would not have allowed for this kind of discussion.

Third, considering the body of literature that exists, my decision to focus on women of Mexican descent speaks directly to an historical erasure of women's voices. During the early stages of inquiry, I sought to identify research that focused specifically on skin color in the lives of Mexican descent women. I found it difficult to locate literature that spoke to the experiences of this focal group. A handful of studies examine women's experiences with skin color, but they do so comparatively with a tendency to consider the experiences of Mexican descent women against those of African American women. This approach is useful because it highlights our shared experience as women of color in the United States. In some ways, however, a comparative approach overlooks the distinct experiences of Mexicans in the United States, particularly in Texas, a factor that emphasizes the need for research that is region-specific and takes into account the specific histories of racialization.

Much of the existent literature gives little thought to the complexities of racialization as it occurs by region. The earliest study making a correlation between class and phenotype took place in San Antonio, Texas. The researchers, however, did not set out to demonstrate a relationship between skin color and class as it occurs by region. Nevertheless, the study inadvertently found a correlation between skin color and socioeconomic status among men and women in San Antonio, thereby illustrating a racialization model that ranks skin color by assigning value to lighter skin and thereby devaluing darker skin. In addition, the researchers argued that Mexican Americans in San Antonio have experienced greater admixture with Anglo Americans than "traditional" mestizo populations in Mexico. They further concluded that in general males were found to be slightly darker than females.

Murguia and Telles further outline regional distinction by comparing rates of educational attainment in California and Texas. Using the data from the 1979 National Chicano Survey, Murguia and Telles determined that phenotype was a more significant factor in Texas. The authors explained these results by pointing to the history Texas has with Jim Crow policies and ideologies. As I situate this research in a specific geographic region, I do not aim to compare regions. Instead, I call upon socio-historical evidence to demonstrate the legacies of racialization as they occur in Texas in an effort to contextualize my discussion of skin color as a significant component of the "racial project"[2] in this region.

## MAPPING CULTURAL TERRAINS

In the United States, the history of racialization is also a history of skin color stratification wherein darker skin represents savagery, irrationality, ugliness, and inferiority, and idealized notions of whiteness represent civility, rationality, beauty, and superiority. In the historical process of racialization, physical appearance is a significant issue. Texas, however, emerges as a cultural borderland reflecting the tension between the sometimes-flexible Spanish colonial racial hierarchies and the rigid rules of hypodescent that characterizes the U.S black-white paradigm. That is to say, while some Texas Mexicans may have been able to *pass* as Spanish, after 1836 anyone who was not Anglo white was subject to the othering process of racialization.

After Mexico won its independence from Spain in 1821, settlement in the otherwise sparsely occupied region between the Nueces and the Rio Grande became a priority. The Mexican government passed Colonization Laws between 1824 and 1830 in an effort to encourage settlement. Though the law gave preference to Mexican citizens, Anglo Americans were enticed by the stipulation that, as foreigners, they would receive land, security, and tax exemptions. The law guaranteed one-third of a league of land to unmarried men, further promising an extra quarter of a league to those who married a native Mexican female. For this reason, Palomo Acosta and Winegarten argue, Anglo immigrants "sought to marry daughters of the landed elite in the region" (39).

By 1835, Anglo immigrants outnumbered Tejanos by six to one. Within a year, racial tensions manifested into armed insurrections against Mexican authority that culminated in 1836 with the bloody Battle of San Jacinto. Texas infrastructure since 1836 illustrates some of the ways skin color and phenotype informs physical and psychological formation in the region. According to Menchaca, "In Texas the racialization of the Mexican population began in 1836 immediately after the Texas War of Independence, and continued after the rest of the Southwest was annexed to the United States" (228). Anti-Mexican sentiments that fueled the Texas Revolution continued after Texas became a republic.

During the decade of the Texas Republic, the constitution held that only "Texas whites and 'Spanish' Mexicans who aided in the Texas revolt against Mexico were entitled to a first-class 'headright' for one league and a labor of land, provided they could persuade the court that they were white and not of Indian or African descent" (Foley 19). As evidence, Foley offers the example of José María de la Garza. In 1860, De la Garza, legally renounced any African or Indian blood in a court of law claiming solely Spanish heritage so that he could purchase land in Corpus Christi, Texas. Yet, as Neil Foley notes, only small numbers of "usually light-skinned middle-class Mexican Americans claimed to be Spanish and therefore white" (5). Although the reign of the Texas Republic ended in 1845, De la Garza's story illustrates how the anti-Mexican implications of the Republic's constitution continued after Texas became part of the union after 1848. I argue that Foley's examination of land politics is one of body politic, wherein the lighter skin, more "Spanish"[3] looking people of Mexican descent could and sometimes did attain "whiteness" in Texas. Not everyone had this option. Some did not or frankly could not, because of skin color or phenotype, access some of the power and privilege attributed to whiteness. Requiring Texas Mexicans to prove Spanish purity of blood in order to acquire land is contingent on a normalized standard of white supremacy and points to a larger social process of racialization wherein all Texas Mexicans negotiated a sense of skin color consciousness that placed value on whiteness. Furthermore, attaining Spanish whiteness by denying Indigenous, African, or Mexican heritage did not guarantee whiteness.

During the nineteenth century, as the racial makeup of the region shifted, so did the interactions between Texas Mexicans and Anglos. In her discussion of this shift that occurred towards the end of the nineteenth century, Oboler argues that many landed elite Tejanos relied heavily upon the "money whitens" concept as a coping strategy to negotiate the decline of their status. According to Montejano "The only problem for upper-class Mexicans was that this principle offered neither consistent nor permanent security in the border region" (84) . This tenuous and arbitrary access to social mobility reflects a cultural stress developing in nineteenth century Texas as the racialization of Mexicans in the region developed into something between a fluid racial hierarchy and a rigid black-white binary.

## BURDEN OF BETRAYAL AND CONQUEST

During the 19th century, attitudes about women of Mexican descent varied. Nevertheless, women of Mexican descent were generally viewed as "objects" sexually available to Anglo men. The following poem, made popular in the summer of 1846, further illustrates this:

> The Spanish maid, with eye of fire,
> At balmy evening turns her lyre
> And looking to the Eastern sky,
> Awaits our Yankee chivalry
> Whose purer blood and valiant arms,
> Are fit to clasp her budding charms.
> The man, her mate, is sunk and sloth-
> To love, his senseless heart is loth;
> The pipe and glass and tinkling lute,
> A sofa, and a dish of fruit;
> A nap, some dozen times a day;
> Somber and sad, and never gay (Quoted in Almaguer 61)

Almaguer argues that a dichotomous image of Mexican women emerged predicated on skin color. Even so, both the darker skin "lower class" and the lighter skin "landed elite" were viewed as sexually available. "Mexican women, it appears, were often seen as mere spoils of war awaiting the amorous embrace of the white man's valiant arms" (Almaguer 61). Although there is ample evidence of an Anglo male desire for "interracial" sex, the female brown body becomes central to the discussion of miscegenation.

Writing about Anglo attitudes towards Mexicans in nineteenth century Texas, De León points to sexed, raced, and classed bigotry of William H. Emory. In 1853, Emory traveled to the U.S. - Mexico border region to map out the newly agreed upon boundary. When writing his report, Emory noted buildings, bodies of water, land formations, and other general geographical markers of the region.

While mapping the United States-Mexico border, Emory also documented his ideas about the people that inhabited the region, sometimes referring to people of Mexican descent as a "mongrel race of Indians, Negroes, and Spaniards" (House Executive Doc 2). Speaking of inter-ethnic unions between Anglo men and women of Mexican descent, Emory asserted that

> The offspring have a constant tendency to go back to one or the other of the original stock; that in a large family of children, where the parents are of a mixed race but yet of the same color, the children will be of every color, from dusky cinnamon to chalky white. (Quoted in De León 18)

Emory's depiction of inter-ethnic unions and the resulting offspring brings into sharp relief the ways in which women often carry the weight of change on the body. As a warning to Anglo men, seeking to reproduce with women of Mexican descent, Emory reasons that *even* lighter skinned women of Mexican descent will produce "children of every color, from dusky cinnamon to chalky white." By pointing to the female body in his discussion of the "mongrel race," Emory's statement emphasizes the histories buried in our flesh beneath the variant colors of our skin.

Suzanne Bost writes "...debates about the nature of mixed-race identity are mapped out on the body of a woman because thinking about racial mixture inevitably leads to questions about sex and reproduction"(2). Because skin color variation is often understood in heteronormative terms of racial mixing, women of Mexican descent have had to carry the burden of betrayal and conquest on our flesh, an ideology that reaches far back to the stories of Eve in the Garden of Eden and *Malinche* during the Spanish conquest of what is now Mexico.[4] Under these terms, the body is understood as a text inscribed with social meaning and my aim is to read the histories that are written upon the body by recognizing that personal narratives are constructed as both a product of, and a response to a raced, classed, and gendered racial project.

## CULTURAL TYRANNIES AND CREATIVE SURVIVAL

Through her concept of *cultural tyranny*, Anzaldúa recognizes that within the dominant paradigm, women confront a system that is sustained through cultural expectations, tools, and consequences. According to Anzaldúa, these cultural norms, while claiming to "protect" women, actually, "keep women in rigidly defined roles" (*Borderlands* 39). As a raced, classed, and gendered process, racialization in Texas was often violent. Saldívar-Hull argues "While Chicano (male) historians have done much to expose the realities of violent acts against Tejanos, they have, to a great extent, been reluctant to voice the perhaps unspeakable violence against Tejanas particularly for women" (75). According to Castañeda, "Under conditions of war or conquest, rape is a form of national terrorism, subjugation, and humiliation, wherein the sexual violation of women represents both the physical domination of women and the symbolic castration of men of the conquered group" (25). Anzaldúa's poem "We Call Them Greasers," written from the perspective of an Anglo man, centers on the brown body and speaks to a history of sexual violence.

> ...She lay under me whimpering
> I plowed into her hard
> Kept thrusting and thrusting
> Felt him watching from the mesquite tree
> Heard him keening like a wild animal
> In that instant I felt such contempt for her
> Round face and beady black eyes like an Indian's.
> Afterwards I sat on her face until her arms stopped flailing,
> Didn't want to waste a bullet on her.
> The boys wouldn't look me in the eyes.
> I walked up to where I had tied her man to the tree
> And spat in his face. Lynch him, I told the boys (*Borderlands* 156-157)

Anzaldúa's poem offers an alternative story that speaks to the complex history of "otherness" and its relationship to skin color and somatic difference in the United States. In her discussion of Anzaldúa's poem, Saldívar-Hull points to the "hierarchy of powerlessness" wherein "the woman occupies a position below the already inferior Brown man" (76). With her depiction of the hatred felt towards people of Mexican descent, Anzaldúa offers us a glimpse into the history that places value on lighter skin while devaluing darker skin by emphasizing how difference was used to rationalize violence. Women are at the center of this history, often targeted with messages that encourage a desire for lighter skin.

In her examination of twentieth century advertising campaigns aimed at women in Spanish language newspapers, Vicki Ruiz discusses some of the messages women confronted through the media. According to Ruiz, "Advertisements aimed at women promised status and affection if the proper bleaching cream, hair coloring, and cosmetics were purchased" (51). One popular publication, selling a skin-bleaching product boasted: "Those with lighter, more healthy skin tones will become much more successful in business, love, and society" (Ruiz 57). By linking consumerist culture to notions of "whiteness" and beauty, Ruiz illustrates the obligation placed on women of Mexican descent to buy "whiteness" and therefore beauty by lightening their skin and altering their hair color. Ellie, one of the participants in my research spoke to the internalization of this obligation as she explained her reasons for lightening her hair,

> Some people say well why do you put the streaks in your hair? I say hey, why not. That's the style right now you now. I know I'm not a blonde and I think most people around me know I'm not a blonde, but I have a few highlights in my hair. You know it's obvious. You know, even blondes have highlights in their hair. So it's not that I want to be white, I want my hair a certain way.

Ellie's discussion of style as it relates to her desire for lighter hair glosses over a history of white supremacy that places idealized white beauty at the top. Saying "that's the style right now" effaces the cultural tyranny of beauty and treats it as a simple matter of taste that exists independent of race, class, and gender.

Within the constructs of cultural tyranny, Anzaldúa argues, "Males make the rules and laws; women transmit them" (*Borderlands* 38). This is evidenced in Anzaldúa's essay *La Prieta* where she recalls messages she received about skin color from the women in her family to memories of learning to negotiate and make meaning of her physical self in the world.

> "Don't go out in the sun," my mother would tell me when I wanted to play outside. "If you get any darker, they'll mistake you for an Indian. And don't get dirt on your clothes. You don't want people to say you're a dirty Mexican." It never dawned on her that, though sixth-generation American, we were still Mexican and that all Mexicans are part Indian. I passed my adolescence combating her incessant orders to bathe my body, scrub the floors and cupboards, clean the windows and walls. ("La Prieta" 198)

This narrative speaks directly to the legacies of racialization in Texas. According to Montejano, "Anglos commonly used the adjective 'dirty' as a synonym for dark skin color and inferiority" (227). Capturing what it means to be brown and live in Texas where the legacies of cultural tyranny are tied to skin color as a raced, classed, and gendered aspect of racialization, Anzaldúa writes,

> When I was born, Mamagrande Locha inspected my buttocks looking for the dark blotch, the sign of indio, or worse, of mulatto blood. My grandmother (Spanish, part German, the hint of royalty lying just beneath the surface if her fair skin, blue eyes and the coils of her once blond hair) would brag that her family was one of the first to settle in the range country of south Texas. ("La Prieta" 198)

During our discussion, Ellie often related her experiences with skin color to a particular kind of cultural stress that is felt and performed by women around childbirth.[5] She explains:

> I recall ever since I was a little girl, if anybody had a baby they'd always say: '¿Es güero?' or '¿Es güera?' '¿Salió güera?' ...Was she born fair skinned? And then if they ...[were born with dark skin]...I would hear: 'Ay, ¡pobrecito! ¡Ay, ¡pobrecita!' Like poor thing, she was born not fair, but dark skinned. So, it was like the lighter, the better.

Ellie adds that when her own children were born she looked for skin color stating that both her sons were "born sort of olive, but one never leaves the sun so he's dark because he is constantly in the sun." Explaining her own approach to raising her children Ellie adds:

> I always made it a point not to make a difference. It just doesn't matter. And I think my kids are pretty good about that. They have all sorts of friends and they have no trouble with different groups. You know they've had African American friends, they've had lots of Anglo friends, lots of Latino friends so it really doesn't matter...I think growing up parents nowadays...make it clear that color shouldn't matter. At least I think that. I know there is still prejudice out there but I'd like to think it's very isolated and that people are more open now.

While Ellie argues that difference "doesn't matter," her narrative continuously points to a relationship between personal experience and social processes of racialization. Turning to a discussion about her grandchild Ellie says, "My grandson...I consider him on the fair side because his mother is very fair, but you know my son is not." Ellie again feels the need to explain the difference between her son's skin tone and her own adding "He's more like me, although now he's not but because of being out in the sun he's about ten shades darker because of being out in the sun so much." Continuing with her discussion of her grandson's skin color, Ellie says

> I think he's got a beautiful complexion, even though he's more on the fair side, but he's just got a beautiful skin color that I think is unique because he's uh, because of the mixing of the two and uh you know I like the way he looks, I like that.

When Ellie says, "the mixing of the two" it is not clear whether she means the mixing of the two people (her son and his wife) or the mixing of the two ethnic groups (Mexican and Anglo). For this reason, I asked Ellie for clarification:

(Me) I wanted to get clarification on something. Your daughter in law, you have mentioned several times that she is very light; is she of Mexican descent?

(Ellie) No she's Anglo.

(Me) Okay I see.

(Ellie) Very, very light yeah. I'm not prejudiced.

Despite her best intentions, Ellie's "colorblind" approach to teaching her children about race and ethnicity, minimizes difference and ignores the vestiges of racialization that her children carry and confront daily.[6] Ellie explains that her children have always had multi-ethnic friends, but tries to brush over the fact that her son married an Anglo woman. She also becomes clearly uncomfortable with this realization expressing defensively that she is not prejudiced. Anzaldúa's concept of la facultad encourages a recognition of the "survival tactic[s] that people, caught between the worlds, unknowingly cultivate" (*Borderlands* 61). For example, Ellie discusses her sister's tendency to refer to herself as Spanish rather than Mexican heritage. Ellie states: "…she says 'I not Mexican, I am Spaniard.'" Ellie explains that she is baffled by her sister's desire to pass as Spanish. She assures me that nobody in the family has ever claimed Spanish heritage before her sister.

On the one hand, Ellie describes her family's preoccupation with skin color whenever a child is born. Yet, when her adult sister attempts to "pass" thereby denying her Mexican heritage for a more highly regarded Spanish one, Ellie brushes off this behavior as irrelevant explaining, "She's deceived," and "We ignore her." Considering the family's emphasis on skin color that begins at childbirth, it is doubtful that this behavior is irrelevant; instead, it is likely tied to a social practice of placing great emphasis on skin color. These actions are expressions of internal conflict that reveal trauma tied to skin color and the history of racialization. According to Ruiz, middle-class Mexican Americans, with hopes of "melting into the American landscape," attempted to "pass" as "Spanish" (45). Claiming Spanish heritage over Mexican, in this way acted as a form of "whitening." Under these terms, physical appearance greatly influenced identity formation among Mexican American women in ways that reached into their private spaces urging them to question their place in the world as it was determined by their flesh.

By exploring the relationships between personal narrative and historical systems of racialization, this essay advances a discussion about how we have learned to carry and respond to ongoing oppression and inequality. I rely on the scant literature about skin color and the Mexican American experience, historical data, and personal narrative to tease out messages regarding skin color in a way that privileges the complexities of lived experience. Using la facultad as an interpretive tool, personal narrative serves to produce a critique of the racial project in an effort to discuss how systems of racialization are embodied and expressed thereby uncovering the stories of cultural tyranny and creative survival that are buried in our flesh beneath the colors of our skin.

**Notes**

1 Moraga, "The danger lies in ranking the oppressions. The danger lies in failing to acknowledge the specificity of the oppression. The danger lies in attempting to deal with oppression purely from a theoretical base. Without an emotional, heartfelt grappling with the source of our own oppression, without naming the enemy within ourselves and outside of us, no authentic, non-hierarchical connection among oppressed groups can take place" (52).

2 Omi and Winant (1994) introduced the concept of "racial project" as a way to discuss how racialization occurs as a political and social maneuver rather than a natural phenomenon.

3 I place quotation marks around "Spanish" to acknowledge another narrative of racialization that relies on the assumption that people of Spanish descent are white.

4 For more on Malinche as a symbol of betrayal similar to "patriarchy's Eve" see Alarcón, N.(1989). "Traddutora, Traditora: A Paradigmatic Figure of Chicana Feminism." *Cultural Critique*, 13, 57-67.

5 Montalvo (2004) discusses the concept of "Bicultural Stress" as it is experienced by women with regards to childbirth and the skin color of the offspring.

6 Sonia Nieto (2004) discusses color blind teaching strategies stating that "...color blindness may result in refusing to accept differences and, therefore, accepting the dominant culture as the norm" (145).

**Works Cited**


Acosta, Teresa Palomo, and Ruth Winergarten. *Las Tejanas: 300 Years of History*. Austin: University of Texas Press, 2003. Print.

Alarcón, Norma. "Traddutora, Traditora: A Paradigmatic Figure of Chicana Feminism." *Cultural Critique* 13 (1989): 57-67. Print.

Allen, Walter, Edward E. Telles, and Margaret Hunter. "Skin Color, Income and Education: A comparison of African Americans and Mexican Americans." *National Journal of Sociology* 12.1 (2000): 130-180. Print.

Almaguer, Tomás. *Racial fault lines: The historical origins of White supremacy in California*. Berkeley: University of California Press, 1994. Print.

Anzaldúa, Gloria E. "La Prieta." *This Bridge Called My Back: Writings By Radical Women of Color*. Ed. Cherríe Moraga and Gloria Anzaldua. New York: Kitchen Table Press: Women of Color Press, 1983. Print.

-----. *Borderlands La Frontera: The New Mestiza*. 2nd ed. San Fransisco: Aunt Lute Books, 1999. Print.

Arce, Carlos H. *Mexican Origin People in the United States: The 1979 Chicano Survey*. Ann Arbor, MI: Inter-university Consortium for Political and Social Research, 1985. Print.

Arce, Carlos, Edward Murguia, and W. Parker Frisbie. "Phenotype and Life Chances Among Chicanos." *Hispanic Journal of Behavioral Sciences* 9 (1987):19-32. Print.

Arreola, Daniel D. *Tejano South Texas: A Mexican American Cultural Province*. Austin: University of Texas Press, 2002. Print.

Bonilla-Silva, Eduardo, and David R. Dietrich. "The Latin Americanization of Racial Stratification in the U.S." *Racism in the 21st Century: An Empirical Analysis of Skin Color*. Ed. R. E. Hall. New York: Springer, 2008. 151-170. Print.

Bordo, Susan. *Unbearable Weight: Feminism, Western Culture, and the Body*. Berkeley: University of California Press, 1993. Print.

Bost, Suzanne. *Mulattas and Mestizas: Representing Mixed Identities in the Americas 1850-2000*. Athens and London: University of Georgia Press, 2003. Print.

Castañeda, Antonia I. "Sexual Violence in the Politics of Conquest." *Building with Our Hands: New Directions in Chicana Studies*. Eds. A. D. L. Torre and B. M. Pesquera. Berkeley: University of California Press, 1993. Print.

De León, Arnoldo. *They Called Them Greasers: Anglo Attitudes Toward Mexicans in Texas, 1821-1900*. Austin: University of Texas Press, 1983. Print.

United States. House Executive. *United States and Mexican Boundary Survey, 1857*. 34th Cong., 1st sess., ser. 861. 2 vols. Doc.135. Washington: GPO, 1857. Print.

Foley, Neil. *The White Scourge: Mexicans, Blacks, and Poor Whites in Texas Cotton Culture*. Berkeley: University of California Press, 1997. Print.

Glesne, Corrine. *Becoming Qualitative Researchers: An Introduction*. 3rd ed. Boston: Pearson, 2006. Print.

Hunter, Margaret. "The Lighter the Berry? Race, Gender, and Color in the Lives of African American and Mexican American Women." Diss. U of California, Los Angeles, 1999. Print.

-----. "If You're Light You're Alright:' Light Skin Color as Social Capital for Women of Color." *Gender and Society* 16.2 (2002):175-93. Print.

-----, *Race, Gender, and the Politics of Skin Tone*. New York: Routledge, 2005. Print.

Maynes, Mary Jo, Jennifer L. Pierce, and Barbara Laslett. *Telling Stories: The Use of Personal Narratives in the Social Sciences and History*. Ithaca, NY: Cornell University Press, 2008. Print.

Menchaca, Martha. *Recovering History, Constructing Race: The Indian, Black, and White Roots of Mexican Americans*. Austin: University of Texas Press, 2001. Print.

Montalvo, Frank F. "Surviving Race: Skin Color and the Socialization and Acculturation of Latinas." *Journal of Ethnic & Cultural Diversity in Social Work* 13.3 (2004.): 25-43. Print.

Montejano, David. *Anglos and Mexicans in the Making of Texas, 1836-1986*. Austin: University of Texas Press, 1987. Print.

Moraga, Cherríe. *Loving in the War Years: Lo que nunca paso por sus labios*. Boston: South End Press, 1983. Print.

Murguia, Edward, and Edward E. Telles. "Phenotype and Schooling among Mexican Americans." *Sociology and Education* 69.4 (1996): 276-89. Print.

Nieto, Sonia. *Affirming Diversity: The Sociopolicital Context of Multicultural Education*. 4th ed. Boston: Pearson Education Inc., 2004. Print.

Oboler, Suzanne. *Ethnic Labels, Latino Lives: Identity and the Politics of (Re)Presentation in the United States*. Minneapolis: University of Minnesota Press, 1995. Print.

Omi, Michael, and Howard Winant. *Racial Formation in the United States: From the 1960s to the 1990s (Critical Social Thought)*. 2nd ed. New York: Routlege, 1994. Print.

Relethford, John H., et. al. "Social Class, Admixture, and Skin Color Variation in Mexican-Americans and Anglo-Americans Living in San Antonio, Texas." *American Journal of Physical Anthropology* 61.97 (1983): 97-102. Print.

Rondilla, Joanne L., and Paul Spickard. *Is Lighter Better? Skin-Tone Discrimination among Asian Americans*. New York: Rowman & Littlefield Publishers, Inc., 2007. Print.

Ruiz, Vicki L. *From Out of the Shadows: Mexican Women in Twentieth-Century America*. Oxford: Oxford University Press, 1998. Print.

Saldívar-Hull, Sonia. *Feminism on the Border: Chicana Gender Politics and Literature*. Berkeley and Los Angeles: University of California Press, 2000. Print.

Telles, Edward E., and Edward Murguia. "Pheotypic Discrimination and Income Differences among Mexican Americans." *Social Science Quarterly* 71.4 (1990): 682-96. Print.

Weber, David J. "The Mexican Frontier 1821-1846: The American Southwest Under Mexico." *Histories of the American Frontier*. Ed. R. A. Billington and H. R. Lamar. Albuquerque: University of New Mexico Press, 1982. Print.

Wolf, Naomi. *The Beauty Myth: How Images of Beauty Are Used Against Women*. New York: Perennial-Harper Collins, 2002. Print.

Zavella, Patricia. "Reflections of Diversity Among Chicanas." *Challenging Fronteras: Structuring Latina and Latino Lives in the U.S.* Eds. M. Romero, P. Hondagneu-Sotelo and V. Ortiz. New York: Routledge, 1997. Print.

## CONTRIBUTORS

**Grisel Acosta** is a doctoral student at the University of Texas at San Antonio. Her studies focus on Caribbean Latino literature, poetry, oral tradition/songwriting, language and identity, intersecting cultures and identities, and education reform. Grisel's poetry has appeared in numerous publications, including *¡Tex! Literary Magazine* in 2008.

**Norma Alarcón** is a noted Chicana theorist and scholar. She is Professor Emeritus of Ethnic Studies, University of California, Berkeley. She received her doctorate in Latin American Literature and Culture from Indiana University. Her path breaking essays shaped Chicana Studies and paved the way for contemporary theories of Chicana subjectivity. For over 25 years she owned and ran Third Woman Press, publishing key writers and texts in Chicana and Latina Studies. Writers such as Sandra Cisneros and Ana Castillo were first published in Third Woman Press. She resides in San Antonio and is currently working on a collection of her essays.

**Paola Bacchetta** is Associate Professor of Gender and Women's Studies at the University of California at Berkeley. She is also Director of the Beatrice Bain Research Group (BBRG), Berkeley's research center on gender and women. Her Ph.D. is in sociology from The Sorbonne, Paris. Her geopolitical areas of specialization outside the U.S. are India and France. She is author of *Gender in the Hindu Nation: RSS Women as Ideologists* (New Delhi: Women Unlimited, 2003), co-editor of *Right-Wing Women: From Conservatives to Extremists around the World* (New York: Routledge, 2002), and author of numerous articles and book chapters (in the U.S., France, India, and Britain) on gender, sexuality, "race"-racism, postcoloniality, political conflict, space, social movements, and social movement subjects (feminist, lesbian, queer, right-wing). Her current research has a two-fold, focusing on sexuality in Hindu nationalism and on sexuated "race"-racism and lesbians "of color" in France. She is translating work by Gloria Anzaldúa for publication in France.

**Rusty Barceló** is a Chicana and Vice Provost and Vice President for Equity and Diversity at the University of Minnesota. From her birthplace in California's San Joaquin Valley, Dr. Barceló began her career as an educator, administrator, and diversity advocate at the University of Iowa, where she received her Ph.D. in higher education administration. Before assuming her current position in 2006, she was Vice President and Vice Provost for Minority Affairs and Diversity at the University of Washington. Today, she is one of the nation's most highly respected authorities on equity and diversity in higher education. She is also an avid bicyclist and accomplished storyteller, songwriter/lyricist, and guitarist.

**Grace Barraza-Vega** was born in Gómez Palacio, Durango, México. She is currently pursuing a Master of Arts degree at Texas A&M University in Corpus Christi, where she also received her BFA degree. In addition, she attended Northwestern State University in Natchitoches, Louisiana and the University of Texas at Brownsville. Barraza-Vega has participated in numerous group and solo exhibits through the U.S. Her painting entitled "Cantinera, que triste estás" was selected to be on the front cover of the *Latino LA Magazine* issue for the month of February, 2010, and for the invitation card of the 5th Anniversary Celebration for ChimMaya Gallery of Los Angeles, California. Her work has been published in numerous collections across the U.S., Mexico, Saudi Arabia, and England. She describes her work as "depict[ing] the struggles, accomplishments and daily life activities of my people of Mexican heritage."

**Marisa Belausteguigoitia** is the director of the Program in Gender Studies at Universidad Nacional Autónoma de México. Her work focuses on the generation of social movements near Mexico's borders, and uses a transdisciplinary approach to questions of race, gender, identity, and cultural relations. She is co-editor of the books *Fronteras y cruces: cartografías de escenarios culturales latinoamericanos* (2005), and *Géneros prófugos: feminismo y educación* (1999). She is also the author of numerous book chapters and articles on cultural studies, feminism, border studies, subjectivity, and information technologies.

**Suzanne Bost** is an Associate Professor of English at Loyola University Chicago. She is the author of two books. *Mulattas and Mestizas: Representing Mixed Identities in the Americas, 1850-2000* (University of Georgia Press, 2003) compares representations of sex and racial mixture in texts by African American, Latina, Chicana, and Caribbean writers. *Encarnación: Illness and Body Politics in Chicana Feminist Literature* (Fordham University Press, 2009) examines the political and theoretical implications of pain, illness, and disability in the works of Gloria Anzaldúa, Cherríe Moraga, and Ana Castillo. She has also published articles on Latina/o and Chicana/o Literature, Cultural Studies, and Feminist Theory in a number of journals, including *Aztlán*, *Nepantla*, *Postmodern Culture*, and *MELUS*, and two essay collections, Stacy Alaimo and Susan Hekman's *Material Feminisms* and Cynthia Lewiecki-Wilson and Jan Cellio's *Disability and Mothering*.

**Margaret E. Cantú** is currently a Ph.D. student in the English Department at The University of Texas at San Antonio. She received her B.A. and M.A. in English at St. Mary's University in San Antonio, Texas. After attaining her graduate degree, she taught high school English, where she discovered a need to incorporate cultural education in schools and vice versa. Her primary research interests include exploring identity in relation to cultural education and formal schooling among Latinos. Specifically, she is interested in understanding how Latinos cope with the identity conflicts that emerge when their cultural education contrasts with formal schooling. Her research has included an exploration of her own family's attempt to balance both types of education through *cuentos*. She hopes that her research will eventually help students realize that a balance between both their culture and formal education is needed.

**Melissa Castillo-Garsow** is a first year student at Fordham University pursuing a master's degree in English with a concentration in Creative Writing. She completed her Bachelor of Arts at New York University in Journalism and Latin American Studies in 2007, where she spent a semester abroad at the Universidade Federale de Minas Gerais in Belo Horizonte, Brazil. Her work has been published in *Latin Beat Magazine*, *The Ithaca Journal*, *Gay City News*, *Washington Square News*, *University Wire*, *El Diario/La Prensa*, *Underrated Magazine*, *The Journal of Mathematical Biosciences and Engineering*, and *The Journal of Theoretical Biology*, and others. Her research interests include Latino literature, Street literature, and popular culture. Her short story, "Start Anywhere," was awarded the Sonoran Prize for Creative Writing at Arizona State University, and was a finalist for Crab Orchard Review's 2009 Charles Johnson Student Fiction Award. She is currently at work on her first novel.

**Randy P. Conner**, Ph.D. Humanities (Religion & Philosophy), was a close friend of Gloria Anzaldúa for thirty years and assisted in editing her work. He recently taught a course in Feminist Thought at UC Berkeley in which he discussed Spiritual Mestizaje in her work. Anzaldúa wrote the Foreword to his *Encyclopedia of Queer Myth, Symbol, & Spirit*, written with his partner David Hatfield Sparks and their daughter Mariah. Anzaldúa was a key inspiration for his recent book, *Queering Creole Spiritual Traditions*, which focuses on LGBT practice of African-Caribbean religions. A native of Texas, he has taught at UT Austin, Austin Community College, Florida Atlantic University, Los Medanos College, UC Berkeley, and the California Institute of Integral Studies.

**Guadalupe Cortina** is Associate Professor of Spanish in the Department of Modern Languages and Literatures at the University of Texas-Pan American. Cortina teaches courses on contemporary Mexican Literature, Latin American Literature, Latina and Chicana Literature, and Latin American women writers and activists. Cortina's publications include *Invenciones multitudinarias: Escritoras judíomexicanas contemporáneas*, and the book edition of *Mujeres y literaturas, políticas y compromisos en el nuevo milenio: Diálogos trasatlánticos*. She has collaborated with critical articles in numerous academic journals and anthologies in the U.S. and Mexico. Cortina edited the critical volume of 2008 on border women writers of *Río Bravo: Journal of the Borderlands*. Since 2006, she has been the editor of the electronic publication of *Grafemas*, of the Asociación Internacional de Literatura y Cultura Femenina Hispánica. Her recent research interests deal with women writers of la frontera and their excursions in the science fiction genre, as well as the border women's grassroots activism against violence on both sides of the border.

**Anel I. Flores** holds her B.A. in English and MFA in Creative Writing. She is a *Tejana* border-born *lesbiana*, writer, educator and multidisciplinary *artista.* She believes access to *arte* and expression creates a channel towards healing, understanding and empowerment for all people, and thus a vehicle for social justice. She is the author of the novel, *Sweet Bread: Una Cuenta Lesbiana en Probaditas* (fothcoming) and the play, *Empanada*, produced nationally. Her work has been published in *Sinister Wisdom*, ALLGO's anthology: *ROOTED*, the *Lodestar Quarterly, iungo Arts Magazine, The Pitkin Literary Review, La Voz de Esperanza, Revolution: The Reclaiming of Tradition and Voice, Scarcely Scholarly, The Quirk,* and *Mother Tongues.* She has served as a Board Member of the Esperanza Peace and Justice Center. Other memberships include: the Macondo Writers Workshop, *Mujeres Activas en Letras y Cambio Social,* the Society for the Study of Gloria Anzaldúa, and the National Association of Chicana and Chicano Scholars.

**Josh T. Franco and Elyse Harary** are a collaborative team residing in Binghamton, New York. Together, they engage their respective fields of study praxically, through photography and performance. Franco is a native Tejano and a graduate student in the Philosophy, Interpretation, and Culture program at Binghamton University. He studies and teaches Chican@ art with an eye towards its decolonial and coalitional possibilities. Harary calls New York City home and studies theories of photography in the Art History department at Binghamton. Her focus is 'vernacular photography,' the photographic detritus of times past and present. Conceiving and executing *Rebozo [Man] in Nepantla* was and continues to be a fertile ground for transformative conversation between the two, and hopefully for those who encounter it. They are currently conceiving *Rebozo [Man]'s* next phase as they continue to contribute to the perversion of the lines between theory and practice, intellect and creativity, art, identity, and politics.

**Sandra D. Garza** is a high school dropout turned Tejana/Chicana-scholar-activist. The daughter of Mexican immigrants, Garza was born and raised in Harlingen, Texas. A graduate student in the department of Bicultural-Bilingual Studies at the University of Texas at San Antonio, she is completing a thesis that explores the ways women of Mexican descent living in Texas experience and make meaning of skin color as a raced, classed, and gendered aspect of racialization. Currently, Garza serves as the Manager/Review Coordinator for *Chicana/Latina Studies: The Journal of Mujeres Activas en Letras y Cambio Social.*

**Alma Gómez** is a visual artist and adjunct professor in the art department at Boise State University. Her work has been selected by jurors, including distinguished art critics Lucy Lippard and Judy Chicago, for regional/national exhibitions. Her work is published in *Contemporary Chicana and Chicano Art: Artist, Works, Culture and Education* and in *Chicano Art in our Millennium*. She has painted murals for the Idaho Migrant Council, Hispanic Cultural Center of Idaho, Boise State, and Terry Reilly Health Services. She earned an MFA in 2001 from Boise State. Her work looks into parallels between Mesoamerican and Catholic religious syncretism and how the concept of "nepantla" informs her Chicana identity. Currently she is working on a body of work consisting of drawings/paintings done in the Mexican retablo style. In addition to her role as artist and professor, Alma works for the College Assistance Migrant Program, advising Latino/a students as they pursue degrees at Boise State.

**Ellie Hernández** is an Associate Professor in the Department of Feminist Studies at UC Santa Barbara where she teaches feminist theory, transnational studies, and LGBTQ studies. Among recent publications, *Postnationalism in Chicana/o Literature and Culture*, UT Press 2009), examines the dynamics of gender in the 21st century.

**Lahib Jaddo** is a Middle Eastern woman born in Bagdad. She spent her childhood in Iraq. Her parents were the first generation liberals in a country struggling to find its voice. In 1965, they found themselves, along with their five children, in exile because of politics. Lahib's formative years were spent in Beirut, Lebanon, a country beautiful, open and on the ground of the Middle East. At the age of twenty-two she moved to the United States and continued her education in architecture and art. She settled in Texas to raise her children and become an artist. She currently is an Associate Professor at the college of Architecture at Texas Tech University in Lubbock. Her work continues to be about the dilemma of being a woman on the fence between the Wild West and the conservative Middle East.

**Claire Joysmith** is a scholar and translator who works at the Centro de Investigaciones Sobre América del Norte (CISAN) at the Universidad Nacional Autónoma de México (UNAM). Her main research focus is on Chican@ and Latin@ Literature, Mexico-U.S. transborder cultural and identity issues, and cultural/linguistic translation. She organized the Chicana Colloqium and the Mexicana and Chicana Writer's Meeting at the UNAM in 1993, the first to take place in Mexico City and at the UNAM. She is editor of *Las formas de nuestras voces: Chicana and Mexicana Writers in Mexico,* co-published by CISAN, UNAM and Third Woman Press, Berkeley, co-editor, with Clara Lomas, of *One Wound for Another/Una herida por otra. Testimonios de Latino@s in the U.S. through Cyberspace (11 de septiembre de 2001-11 de marzo de 2002),* and editor of *Speaking desde las heridas. Testimonios transfronterizos/Transborder Testimonios (11 de septiembre de 2001-11 de marzo de 2007).*

**Deborah Kuetzpalin Vásquez** grew up in San Antonio, Texas's East Side, where she learned to embrace Black and Chicana/o cultures. She received her B.A. in Painting and Clay from Texas Woman's University and her M.F.A. from the University of Wisconsin-Madison, where she studied 2-dimensional and 3-dimensional art with an emphasis in Painting and Installation. She has also earned a scholarship at the Chicago Art Institute, and a certificate in traditional culture from Universidad Náhuatl in Ocotepec, Mexico. Vázquez's work has appeared in over thirty-five exhibitions in the U.S. and abroad, many of which included several solo shows, such as her 2005 one-woman exhibition, Tlasohtla: El Amor Tiene Muchas Caras, funded by Andy Warhol Foundation for Arts. She has received awards from the Astraea Foundation and the National Association of Latino Arts and Culture, and her work on the Mexican-U.S. border wall was exhibited at Movimiento de Arte y Cultura Latino Americana in San Jose, California. She is also the creator of "Citlali-La Chicana Super Hero," a cartoon character who has become a focus of Vázquez's artistic career. Today, Vázquez is an art instructor at Our Lady of the Lake University, where she founded the art group "Barro en el Barrio," whose mission is to provide a safe space and workshops where victims learn to use indigenous and other symbols to explain and negotiate their encounters with domestic and sexual violence. She has also recently opened "Café Citlali," an art and green food establishment inside Gallista Gallery, a Chican@ Art Space in San Antonio.

**Smadar Lavie** was born in Jaffa, Israel to a Yemenite mother and a Lithuanian father. She regards herself as a Mizrahi (Hebrew: "Easterner"), an Arab-Jew. Lavie received her doctorate in Anthropology from the University of California at Berkeley. She specializes in the anthropology of Egypt, Israel and Palestine, with emphasis on issues of race, gender, and religion. She published her book, *The Poetics of Military Occupation* (UC Press, 1990), on resistance theatre of the Mzeina Bedouin of South Sinai in Egypt. She is also the co-editor of two texts: *Displacement, Diaspora and Geographies of Identity* (Duke Univ. Press, 1996), and *Creativity/Anthropology* (Cornell Univ. Press, 1993). She received the Hubert H. Humphrey Distinguished Visiting Professorship of Islam and the Middle East at Macalester College, St. Paul, Minnesota. Currently, she is an Associate Professor at the Department for Studies in Women and Gender at the University of Virginia, Charlottesville. Lavie has served in several international NGO and women's organizations.

**Amelia María de la Luz Montes** is a Chicana lesbiana, manflora, tortillera born and raised in Los Angeles, Califas. She is an Associate Professor of English and the Director of The Institute for Ethnic Studies at The University of Nebraska-Lincoln. Professor Montes is editor of the nineteenth-century novel *Who Would Have Thought It?* by Maria Amparo Ruiz de Burton (2009, Penguin Classics) and is finishing a fictional memoir, and a critical work on Midwest Latinas.

**Lara Medina** holds a doctorate in American History from the Claremont Graduate University. Her research and publications focus on Chicana/o religious history, public ritual, and Chicana feminist spirituality. Her book is titled *Las Hermanas: Chicana/Latina Religious-Political Activism in the U.S. Catholic*

*Church* (Temple University, 2004). Recent published works include "Nepantla Spirituality: Negotiating Multiple Identities and Faiths Among U.S. Latinas" in *Rethinking Latino(a) Religion and Identity,* Miguel De La Torre and Gaston Espinoza, ed. (Cleveland: Pilgrim Press, 2007) and "Communing with the Dead: Spiritual and Cultural Healing in Chicano/a Communities" in *Religion and Healing In America,* Linda L. Barnes and Susan S. Sered, ed. (New York: Oxford University Press, 2005). Lara is a Professor in Chicana and Chicano Studies at California University, Northridge.

**Edna Ochoa** is assistant professor in the department of Modern Languages and Literature at The University of Texas Pan-American. She is the author of four books: *Respiración de raíces, Sombra para espejos, Ruinas,* and *La cerca circular.* Ochoa has written numerous plays, including *La Boda de la Mujer Maravilla, El método más efectivo,* and *Nocturnos.* Her writing has appeared in numerous publications, including *Archipiélago, Lucero, La ventana, BorderSenses, Grafemas,* and the anthologies *Nueva poesía y narrativa hispanoamericana, La mujer rota, Líneas desde el Golfo, Escena con otra mirada, A través de la piel, Teatro para estudiantes de teatro,* and *Teatro Joven de México.* Her translations to Spanish include *Zoot Suit* by Luis Valdez, and *How the Frog and His Friend Saved Humanity* by Víctor Villaseñor (Arte Público Press). Her plays have been produced and read in numerous places. She is also an artist performer and member of the Colectivo Voz de Tierra.

**Patricia Pedroza** was born in Morelia, Michoacán, Mexico. She has crossed the borders of education between the academic world and the world of the artist through the creation of her own performance pieces with focus on feminism, spirituality, sexuality, citizenship language, and cultural issues. Currently, as faculty member at Keene State College, New Hampshire, she has crossed the geographical borders, teaching feminism as philosophy and integrating her acting background in classroom activities. She has a Ph.D. in Chicana Studies and Feminist Pedagogy from Union Institute & University in Cincinnati, Ohio. Her research interests are Chicana epistemologies, theories, and spiritualities of women of color.

**Romana Radlwimmer** was born in Austria. She studied at the University of Vienna, Austria, and at Universidad Autónoma de Madrid, Spain (2000-2007). She obtained her Master's Degree in German and Latin American Philology at the University of Vienna. She is currently a doctoral student at the University of Vienna and writing a dissertation on Latina Feminist Theorists. In 2008/09, she was a language teacher at North Atlanta High School, Atlanta, Georgia, and is now Lecturing Professor (Profesora Lectora) at the University of Salamanca, Spain. Her publications include: "Die Nestbeschmutzerin. Jelinek & Österreich" (Ed. Pia Janke) Vienna 2002, "Mittler zwischen Welten." University of Vienna 2007, and "Fremdes Eigenes, Eigenes Fremdes." in Universidad de Sevilla (Ed.): Revista del grupo de investigación Filología Alemana. Vol.16. Editora Fénix 2010.

**Irma Carolina Rubio** is a San Antonio-based artist and art educator, born in Lubbock, Texas to Mexican immigrant parents. She holds a BFA from Texas Tech University and a Master of Arts in Art Education from The School of the Art Institute of Chicago. Her cultural work has centered around social justice via art education and administrative praxis at public schools, museums, galleries, and grassroots organizations throughout San Antonio, Texas and Chicago. At present, her work seeks to explore and record family memory of the U.S.-Mexico frontera, per the perspective of women and reflections of their place within the sacred. She will soon begin a Ph.D. in Art Education and Women's Studies at Pennsylvania State University.

**María Socorro Tabuenca Córdoba**, Ph.D., is currently a professor at the University of Texas, El Paso. Her areas of specialization include Chicana/o literature and border studies. Dr. Tabuenca is a Cultural Theorist and served as Dean for the North West Region, Colegio de la Frontera Norte, Ciudad Juárez, Mexico. With Debra Castillo, she has authored the book *Border Shots: From Theory to Practice.*

**Fabiola Torralba** was born in Acapulco, Mexico and raised in the Westside of San Antonio, Texas. She has participated in various community-based projects as a Buena Gente of the Esperanza Peace and Justice Center. Her interests include learning about world struggles, dance, and community-based research. She hopes to continue exploring ways to facilitate grassroots efforts.

**Edén Torres** is an Associate Professor at the University of Minnesota in the Department of Gender, Women and Sexuality Studies, and is currently the Chair of the Department of Chicano Studies. A specialist in Chicana feminist and cultural studies, Torres tries to inspire students to analyze and think critically about their own social locations so that they will be ready to function ethically and with purpose in a transnational context. Of all the honors she has received, she is most appreciative and proud of winning the Arthur "Red" Motley Award for Exemplary Teaching 2003-2004, because she was nominated by her students. Torres is the author of *Chicana Without Apology/Chicana sin vergüenza: The New Chicana Cultural Studies* (Routledge, 2003).

**Analiese Ellis Trujillo** is a seventh grader at Jefferson Middle School in Albuquerque, New Mexico. Along with writing poetry, Analiese dances baile folklórico, chairs the Women's Caucus of her school's Model United Nations, and recently won several prizes for her science project on new innovations in cleaning oil spills with mushrooms and human hair. Her future goals include a combination of all her current interests.

**Rita E. Urquijo-Ruiz** is a Mexicana/Chicana who was born in Hermosillo, Sonora, México and grew up in Southern California. She received her doctoral degree from the Department of Literature at UC San Diego. Currently, she is an Associate Professor of Spanish in the Department of Modern Languages at Trinity University in San Antonio, Texas. In addition to her academic work, she writes poetry and performs. She has presented her theatrical skits as "La Chata," her *peladita* character based on tejana artist La Chata Noloesca, at national and local venues. Her areas of interest are Mexican and Chicana/o literatures and cultures, gender and sexuality, as well as theater and performance studies. Her work has been published in *La Voz de Esperanza, Ollantay Theatre Magazine, Nerter* and *Chicana/Latina Studies*: *The Journal of MALCS*. Her book entitled *Wild Tongues/Lenguas Necias: Chicana/o and Mexican Popular Culture 1929-2004*, is forthcoming in the Chicana Matters Series at the University of Texas Press.

**Raquel Valle-Sentíes**, artist, poet, and playwright, was born and raised in Laredo, Texas. She was an Art major at Texas Women's University. She has five sons, eight grandchildren, and three great-grand children. Primarily a portrait artist, Sentíes has exhibited her oil paintings in galleries in Laredo, Nuevo Laredo, San Antonio, and Las Cruces, New Mexico and was inducted into the Laredo Women's Hall of Fame for her contribution to the arts. Sentíes's first collection of poetry, "Soy Como Soy y Qué," was awarded the prestigious international José Fuentes Mares Literary Prize by the Universidad Autónoma de Ciudad Juárez in 1997. She was the first woman to receive this award. Her poetry has been published in numerous literary magazines and anthologies in the United States, Mexico, and India. She's the author of two award winning plays "Alcanzando Un Sueño" in Spanish, and "La Mala Onda de Johnny Rivera" in Spanglish. In 2007, her play "Path of Marigolds" premiered in Laredo and was also presented in San Antonio at the Jump Start Theater and in McAllen at the Teatro de Nuestra Cultura. In 2009, two fifteen minute plays were presented in the Chicano Theater Festival in Laredo. Sentíes is presently working on her fourth full length play, "Two Chicanas in Paris," and her second collection of poetry, "The Ones Santa Anna Sold."

**Minerva Margarita Villarreal** es poeta y profesora universitaria. De su obra poética destacan los libros *Dama infiel al sueño* (1991), *Pérdida* (Premio Nacional de Poesía Alfonso Reyes 1990), *Epigramísticos* (1995), *El Corazón más secreto* (Premio Internacional de Poesía Jaime Sabines 1994) y *Adamar* (1998). Es autora de *Brújula solar: Nuevo León 1876-1992* (antología de la poesía de Nuevo León).

**Michaela Walsh** completed her MFA in Creative Nonfiction Writing and her MA in Religious Studies from the University of Iowa. She is currently pursuing a Ph.D. in Communication Studies at the University of California, San Diego. Walsh's work explores the physical space of the U.S./Mexico border as a biopolitical zone of classification, a site of inclusion and exclusion, entrance and exit, as a prolonged threshold that marks a place of entering or beginning, but also a point where physiological and psychological effect begins to be produced. Her work has been published in the Iowa Journal of Cultural Studies and the

Human Communication Review.

**Liliana Wilson** is a Chilean artist who immigrated to the United States in 1977. She was part of major exodus of artists and scholars who left Chile through forced and voluntary exile during the military regime headed by the Chilean dictator Augusto Pinochet. Through her drawings and paintings, she invests her work with a life history based in her transnational experiences. Her work reflects narratives of exile, migration and immigration, and memory with a surrealist dream-inspired vocabulary of images. Her works have been exhibited in many museums and galleries: Austin Museum of Art, El Paso Museum of Art, San Antonio Museum of Art, San Francisco State University, San Francisco Mission Cultural Center for Latino Art, San José Center for Latino Arts, Galería de la Raza, Esperanza Peace and Justice Center, La Peña Latino Arts Organization, Centro Cultural Universitario, Saltillo, Coahuila and at Benito Juárez University, in Oaxaca, Mexico.

Aunt Lute Books is a multicultural women's press that has been committed to publishing high quality, culturally diverse literature since 1982. In 1990, the Aunt Lute Foundation was formed as a nonprofit corporation to publish and distribute books that reflect the complex truths of women's lives and to present voices that are underrepresented in mainstream publishing. We seek work that explores the specificities of the very different histories from which we come, and the possibilities for personal and social change.

Please contact us if you would like a free catalog of our books or if you wish to be on our mailing list for news of future titles. You may buy books from our website, by phoning in a credit card order, or by mailing a check with the catalog order form.

Aunt Lute Books
P.O. Box 410687
San Francisco, CA 94141
415.826.1300
www.auntlute.com
books@auntlute.com

This book would not have been possible without the kind contributions of the Aunt Lute Founding Friends:

Anonymous Donor
Anonymous Donor
Rusty Barcelo
Marian Bremer
Marta Drury
Diane Goldstein
Diana Harris
Phoebe Robins Hunter
Diane Mosbacher, M.D., Ph.D.
Sara Paretsky
William Preston, Jr.
Elise Rymer Turner